THE PHANTOM TRAIN

THE PHANTOM TRAIN

DEPORTING PRISONERS FROM OCCUPIED FRANCE

THE ACCOUNT OF
FRANCESCO FAUSTO NITTI, 1944

LUDIVINE BROCH & MARTIN SORRELL

Pen & Sword
MILITARY
AN IMPRINT OF PEN & SWORD BOOKS LTD.
YORKSHIRE – PHILADELPHIA

First published in Great Britain in 2025 by
Pen & Sword Military
An imprint of
Pen & Sword Books Ltd
Yorkshire - Philadelphia

ISBN 978 1 39904 371 7

A CIP catalogue record for this book is available from the British Library.

Typeset in INDIA by IMPEC eSolutions
Printed and bound in England by CPI Group (UK) Ltd, Croydon, CRO 4YY

The Publisher's authorised representative in the EU for product safety is Authorised Rep Compliance Ltd., Ground Floor, 71 Lower Baggot Street, Dublin D02 P593, Ireland.
www.arccompliance.com

For a complete list of Pen & Sword titles please contact

PEN & SWORD BOOKS LIMITED
47 Church Street, Barnsley, South Yorkshire, S70 2AS, England
E-mail: enquiries@pen-and-sword.co.uk
Website: www.pen-and-sword.co.uk

or

PEN AND SWORD BOOKS
1950 Lawrence Rd, Havertown, PA 19083, USA
E-mail: uspen-and-sword@casematepublishers.com
Website: www.penandswordbooks.com

Contents

Acknowledgements

Ludivine Broch

My thanks go first and foremost to Professor Martin Sorrell, for his wonderful translation of the original text and for his thoughtful comments on drafts of the introduction. I feel very privileged that he came to me with this project and trusted me to put it into historical context. I would like to thank Pen & Sword, and especially Heather Williams, for taking it on. Thanks to the School of Humanities at the University of Westminster who awarded me a sabbatical which allowed me to research and write this. Several institutions and individuals have been very gracious in giving me access to their archives and letting me publish some unique images. Thanks to Chris Sparks for the stunning map. I am deeply grateful for the generosity and guidance of Guillaume Piketty as I started to explore the sensory history of war. My heartfelt thanks also to those who read over the manuscript, Hanna Diamond, Julian Jackson, Chris Millington, and Andrew Smith. It is much improved thanks to their comments. All errors remain entirely my own.

This book would not have been possible without the warm welcome of Rosemarie Oster-Grellety and her family who shared invaluable photographs and stories with me; and of Corinne Brillié, Norbert Nardone, Hugues de Roquemaurel, and Jean-Daniel Simonet from the *Amicale du Train Fantôme* who shared stories, memories, and even meals with me. A special thanks, too, to Edith Silve, Jeannine Teissier, and Henri-Georges Mauri who I had the chance to meet in Sorgues in August 2024. The knowledge of *Amicale* members and their willingness to share their personal accounts and archives has not only been very touching but also absolutely necessary to uncover the life of Francesco Fausto Nitti and his experience on that deportation train. Thanks also to Elérika Leroy from the Musée de la Résistance et de la Déportation in Toulouse, whose deep knowledge of Toulouse and this period more generally were so helpful.

My final thanks go to my husband, Phil, and my three children, Elliott, Camille, and Raphaëlle. The text was written while tiny hands tapped at my door asking when I was finished working; I hope they enjoy it when they are old enough to read it.

Ludivine Broch,
September 2025

Martin Sorrell

Some years ago, when I was putting together an undergraduate course on the literature of travel, a colleague introduced me to *8 Chevaux 70 Hommes*, a slim book written in French by an Italian journalist and antifascist fighter called Francesco Fausto Nitti. I should have known this book long before, for at least two reasons. First, because it bears unparalleled witness to the horror of existence inside a Second World War cattle-wagon train, this one taking – or rather, trying to take – eventually over 700 deportees including Nitti himself from Toulouse to Germany in the summer of 1944.

My second reason was more personal. That year, 1944, and all through the war, my French grandparents and aunt were living in Toulouse, where they ran a *pension de famille*, a long-stay boarding house, near the Place du Capitole. My aunt, then in her early 20s, and as far as I know never a member of the Resistance, played her part, nonetheless, in helping various 'undesirables', including a few of her Jewish friends, evade capture by the German authorities.

She didn't speak that often of her wartime activities. But she did tell me that the family *pension* became, if not quite a safe house, certainly an occasional shelter for people on the run, among whom were a Polish agent, a British airman, and a sex worker who apparently was feeding the Resistance whatever bits of information her German officer clients – she refused to entertain the lower ranks – let slip. And someone altogether different was also lodging in the *pension*: a very young French operatic soprano whose father, a Nazi sympathiser, had defected to the enemy and was serving in the German army with the LVF, the infamous *Légion des Volontaires Français Contre le Bolchevisme*. She was being sought by certain Resistance members intent on revenge; if they couldn't get the father, the daughter would have to do.

At some point my aunt decided to volunteer her services to the city's Quaker group, and from time to time she was sent on its behalf with provisions to the trains of deportees preparing to leave for Germany from the Raynal goods yard outside Matabiau station. I'd like to think that one of those trains was Nitti's. Maybe it was, maybe it wasn't, maybe it was the very one my aunt tried but failed to get access to in the final twelve months of the war, as she told me one autumn day in the late 1990s over lunch in her tiny fifth-floor bedsit within sight of the Eiffel Tower. Despite her protestations, despite her Quaker credentials, she was sent packing by the German sentry guarding the entrance to the yard. Try as she might, she simply could not get past him. In fact, eventually he got a bit rough with her, thrusting his rifle across her chest and pushing her backwards with a degree of force, and shouting at her to *scram or else* … Still she tried to hold her ground. But then something in the eyes of that battle-weary soldier told her that his *scram or else* was not so much a threat as urgent advice to save herself, get away from the area as fast as possible. He surely knew, as in her naivety my young aunt did not, that with her dark ringlets and her distinctly un-Arian features, she was at risk of arrest and possibly much worse.

***

There has been no published English translation until now of Nitti's account of the Phantom Train, as he himself refers to it. I wanted to put that right, in part to honour its remarkable author, who not only survived the ordeal but amazingly managed to record it in a daily log; to pay homage to the deportees aboard the train, most of whom did finish up in Dachau, Mauthausen or Ravensbrück; partly in memory of my late aunt; and, of course, because it's such a valuable historical document.

My thanks go to Dr Ludivine Broch for so fully and expertly setting the story of Francesco Nitti and the Phantom Train in the wider context of the Second World War. Particularly striking is her section on the effects of a deportation journey on the five senses. My thanks also go to Pen & Sword, in particular its commissioning editor, Heather Williams, for agreeing that Nitti's book needed to be made available to an English-speaking readership, and for her help and guidance in its preparation.

Martin Sorrell,
September 2025

Maps

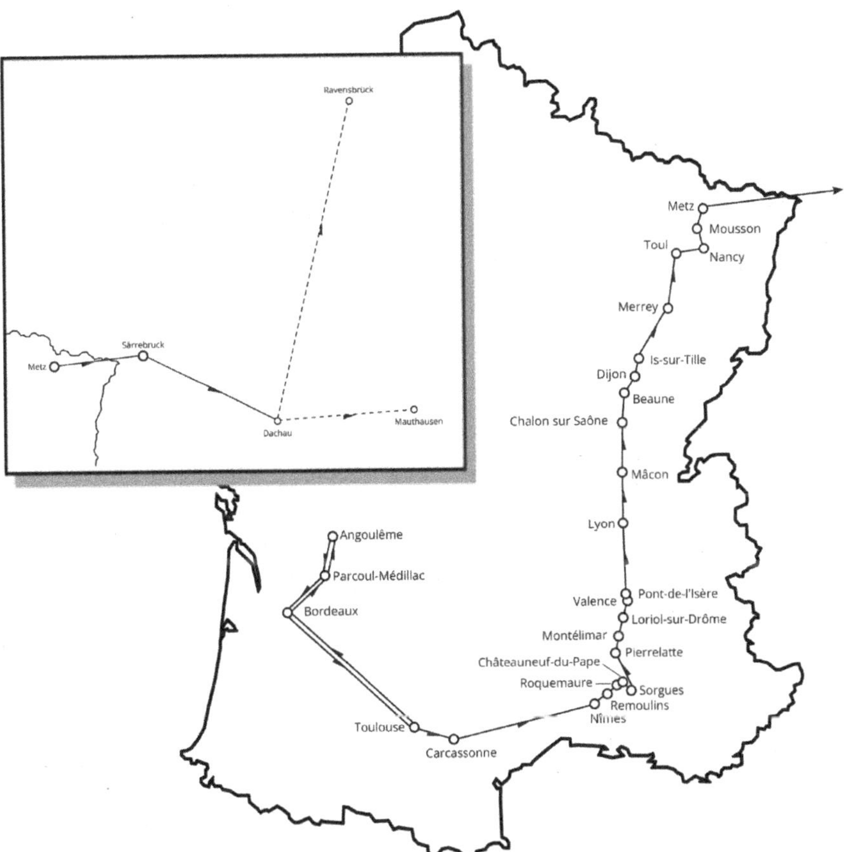

Map 1: Map of the Phantom Train trajectory from Toulouse to Dachau. Departing from Toulouse, the train initially went north-west towards Bordeaux, but relentless aerial bombing meant that the train had to turn back on itself at Angoulême. It headed back to Bordeaux, then Toulouse, and finally crawled north through eastern France before arriving in Dachau. The women in the convoy were then deported to Ravensbrück, while many of the men would eventually be deported to Mauthausen. (Copyright author's own)

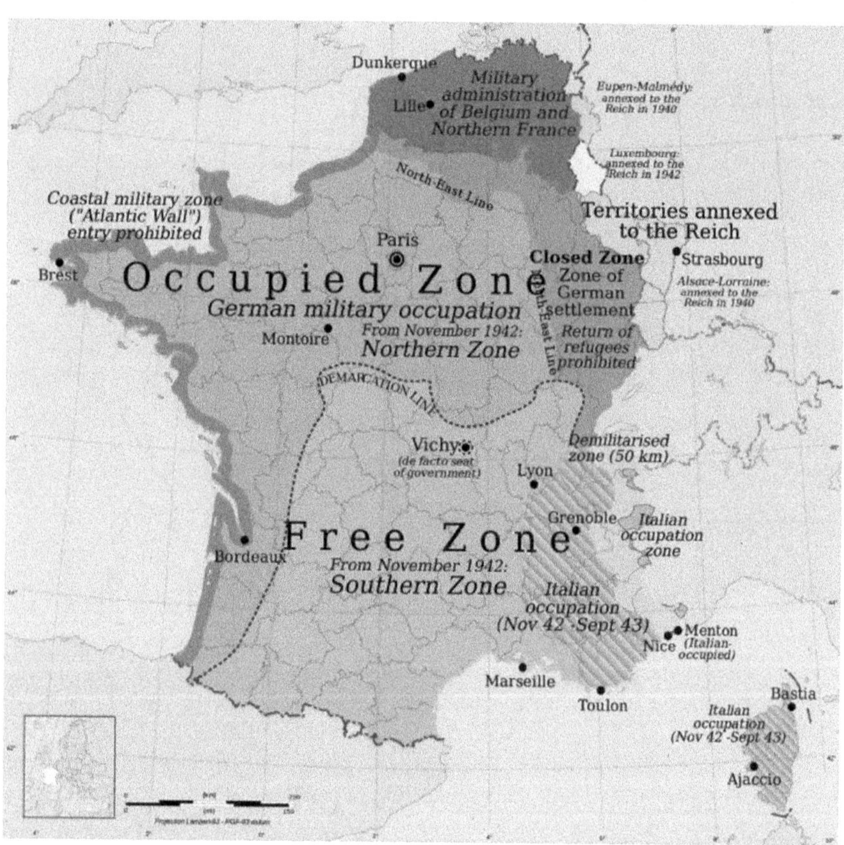

Map 2: This map of France between June 1940 and August 1944 shows the different zones of occupation as well as French regions and departments. (Public domain, via Wikimedia Commons)

Map 3: Many camps were set up for refugees after the Spanish Civil War in 1939 and became major internment and transit camps during the Occupation. Nitti was in several of these, notably Argelès-sur-mer, Mauzac, and Le Vernet. (Public domain, via Wikimedia Commons)

Graph 1: Escapes from the Phantom Train before crossing the German border. Based on data from the Amicale du Train Fantôme and the Fondation pour la Mémoire de la Déportation.

Abbreviations

ADIR	*Association Nationale des Anciennes Déportées et Internées de la Résistance*; National Association of [Female] Resistance Deportees and Internees
Amicale	*Amicale du Train Fantôme*; Phantom Train Association
APR	*L'Amicale des Prisonnières de la Résistance*; Association of [Female] Resistance Prisoners
AS	*Armée Secrète*; Secret Army
BCRA	*Bureau Central des Renseignements et d'Action*; Central Bureau of Intelligence and Operations
BEF	British Expeditionary Force
BS1	*Brigade Spéciale 1*; Special Brigade 1, Paris Police
BS2	*Brigade Spéciale 2*; Special Brigade 2, Paris Police
CFLN	*Comité Français de Libération Nationale*; French National Liberation Committee
CPL	*Comité Parisien de Libération*, Paris Liberation Committee
CNR	*Conseil National de la Résistance*; National Resistance Council
FEA	French Equatorial Africa
FK	*Feldkommandantur*; Field Command
FNDIP	*Fédération Nationale des Déportés et Internés Patriotes*; National Federation of Deported and Imprisoned Patriots
FNDIRP	*Fédération Nationale des Déportés et Internés Résistants Patriotes*; National Federation of Deported and Imprisoned Resistance Fighters and Patriots
FTP	*Francs-Tireurs-Partisans*; Francs-Tireurs Partisans

FTP-MOI	*Francs-Tireurs-Partisans Main d'Oeuvre Immigrée*; Francs-Tireurs Partisans Immigrant Workers
GPRF	*Gouvernement Provisoire de la République Française*; Provisional Government of the French Republic
LVF	*Légion des Volontaires Français Contre le Bolchevisme*; Legion of French Volunteers Against Bolshevism
MBF	*Militärbefehlshaber*; Military Command
MLN	*Mouvement de la Libération Nationale*; National Liberation Movement
MUR	*Mouvements Unis de la Résistance*; United Movements of the Resistance
ORA	*Organisation de Résistance de l'Armée*; Army Resistance Organisation
OSS	Office of Strategic Services
PCF	*Parti Communiste Français*; French Communist Party
PSI	*Partito Socialista Italiano*, Italian Socialist Party
RSHA	*Reichssicherheitshauptamt*, Reich Security Main Office
SNCF	*Société Nationale des Chemins de Fer Français*; French National Railways
SIS	Secret Intelligence Service
SOE	Special Operations Executive

Foreword

Francesco Fausto Nitti (1899–1974) was an Italian antifascist journalist living in exile in France in the thirties before being arrested, interned, and deported during the Second World War. At the end of 1944, before the war had even ended, he wrote and published a slim volume of wartime memories.[1] Rather than being an overview of the war, it was an account which focussed exclusively on the last weeks of occupation in France, from June to August 1944, when he escaped from a deportation train from Toulouse to Dachau, otherwise known as the *Train Fantôme*, or Phantom Train (see Map 1).

On 2 July 1944, 653 prisoners were forced aboard a train at the Raynal goods yard in Toulouse. Four hundred and three of them, including Nitti, had come from the Le Vernet camp south of Toulouse, and 150 (including twenty-four women) had been taken from the Saint-Michel prison in the city itself. Initially the train headed towards Bordeaux, and they assumed that they were being transferred to Paris, but the attacks on the railways by aerial bombing and resistance sabotage meant that the railway network was barely usable, and the train was soon stuck. After spending over a week in these mostly immobile rail wagons, the men were interned in the Grand Synagogue of Bordeaux for four weeks, from 12 July to 8 August. When they left Bordeaux, an additional seventy-one prisoners from the Fort du Hâ prison joined them. The train went back through Toulouse before twisting, halting, and crawling across southern France and going up towards Lyon, Dijon, and Metz. Heading to the German border, it eventually arrived in Dachau on 28 August. By that point, however, Nitti was no longer aboard the train: he had managed to escape on 25 August.

While deportation journeys from France to Germany generally took about three days, the Phantom Train took fifty-seven, Nitti himself enduring all but the last three. The deportees spent half of July and August trapped in rail wagons made to transport a maximum of eight horses or forty men. In Nitti's convoy, however, almost twice that number of people were jam-packed in every wagon, which is reflected in the French title Nitti gave to his book: *8 Chevaux 70 Hommes*. The train's progress was interrupted by an incarceration of almost four weeks in the Grand Synagogue of Bordeaux, and there were to be other briefer occasions when the train was emptied as it could no longer advance and the deportees were forced to march considerable distances to board another set of wagons. A long march through Sorgues – a small village in South-East France near Avignon – on 18 August was particularly harrowing. As the convoy zig-zagged interminably through France, their journey was shaped by claustrophobia, bombings, and deaths, and occasionally punctuated by humanitarian aid and escapes. By the time the train arrived in Dachau – fifty-seven days after they had left Toulouse – 161 deportees had managed to escape, including Nitti; the others entered the Nazi concentrationary universe. Half of them would never return.

The translation of Nitti's account into English for the first time introduces new audiences to the story of the Phantom Train, but this edition is also an opportunity to set this story within a wider context. Through an overview of the history of occupation in France, a biography of Nitti's life, and a critical reflection on Nitti's account itself, this edition tells a broader and deeper story of deportation, war, and resistance in the early twentieth century. The story of the Phantom Train ultimately shows the importance of foreigners in the resistance in France, and of the link between interwar antifascism and the fight against the Nazis; it highlights the presence of Republican fighters from the Spanish Civil War in the French resistance and in the network of incarceration, deportation, and camps across Europe in 1939–45; it is a story of men and camaraderie, of feelings and of senses, of survival and of loss. Few accounts published in the immediate post-war years have been translated into English, those of Primo Levi being more of an exception rather than the rule.[2] And yet in France this was the period with the highest level of publication of personal accounts relating to the Second World War. It was a fertile time, and the books in those first few years are recognisable through their rawness, their accusations, and their urgency. To have such a source now available in English is a privilege which will only further enrich our understanding of the twentieth century.

Nitti's account – a testimony of the immediate post-liberation – is short, and he will be unknown to most readers, even specialists.[3] His narrative style does not have the poetry of Jorge Semprún or Charlotte Delbo, the revelations and insider-knowledge of Charles Rist or Raymond-Raoul Lambert, or the immediacy of the diaries of Léon Werth or Hélène Berr.[4] But therein lies its strength: this is raw material, stories of a past which has been barely digested and which is still traumatic. The decision to write his experience of this journey seems as much a rational one as it was a physical impulse: in the original French version, he remarks that the memory of the train '*est encore en moi*' – is still inside me – as if it was physically within him.[5] The book opens with Nitti sitting on a different train in newly liberated France, but its jolts and sounds throw him back into the wagons of the Phantom Train:

> A few days ago I was returning home from Paris by train. Comfortably settled in a second-class compartment between an old man with a white moustache and a generously-proportioned woman reading a romantic novel … At some point, I was overwhelmed by a sudden and strange vision … I closed my eyes and as I listened to the rhythmic clickety-clack of the wheels on the rails, I said to myself, 'Open your eyes again and you'll find yourself squatting on your haunches in a different vehicle on a different train, the Phantom Train, which wandered about for more than two months before finally disappearing over the

> German border. You'll be back on the floor of that putrid wagon among seventy near-naked comrades, your body squeezed tight against theirs, curses and groans filling the contaminated air.'[6]

Nitti was a master of long accounts of war and internment, and wrote two books about his time first in Mussolini's convict colonies (1930) and then in the Spanish Civil War (1953). However, here he does not dwell on his experience of the Second World War. He does not talk about his time in the Réseau Bertaux, the resistance network he joined in Toulouse and which led to his arrest in 1941; he does not recount his time in the *maquis* after his escape from the train; he barely mentions Le Vernet, the infamous internment camp where he spent a whole year before his deportation. It is the experience of the wagon – this sensorial overload of asphyxiation, stench, filth, noise, thirst – and of his comrades within that convoy which he chooses to describe.

When reading Nitti's account we get a different view of resistance and repression in German-occupied France, and we are able to reassess the idea of an 'odourless past', which is how most historical narratives gloss over the sensorial experience of captivity. We can almost feel the plague of lice on the bodies of these men interned in the synagogue; are deafened by the sounds of the inescapable bombing campaigns; are nauseated by the smells of human fluids which cover the floors of the wagons; shudder at the idea of the bare flesh of strangers pressed against each other against their will. Deportation in wagons during the Second World War erased all conventional codes and conducts, stripping deportees of their civility. As historian Simone Gigliotti has underlined, the sensorial world of wagons dehumanised those within them: 'Pestilent and fermenting odours of excrement, urine and vomit in transit worked to unmake the body in transit captivity,' she explains, and this was 'the symbolic undoing of civilization's order'.[7] It created previously unimaginable, and ultimately traumatic, sensory experiences, which were all made worse by the duration of the journey, the intensity of its conditions, and the technology which allowed it in the first place. Railway transportation, so central to this most modern form of mass murder, was an attack on all of the senses: smell, taste, touch, sound, sight, but also the sense of movement, the vestibular sense. Nitti brings to life this sensorial world of war.

In order to fully understand Nitti's account, this edition includes an extended introduction in three parts. The first is a condensed history of France under German occupation, for the story of Nitti's deportation and escape cannot be fully understood without understanding the context in which they happened. From the fall of France and the Vichy government's collaboration with Germany, to the rise of resistance and the brutality of its repression, we explore the major themes of France under German occupation and guide the reader in their reading of the memoir. This section will be especially useful to students and non-specialists learning about the Second World War, and readers can deepen their interests by exploring the endnotes and bibliography. At times Nitti's own life is woven into this section, as are the lives of some of his fellow deportees from the Phantom Train.

The second section focusses exclusively on Nitti's life and his unique trajectory as an Italian antifascist living in exile in France. We see more clearly how his intellectual pursuits, political affiliations, and participation in the Spanish Civil War paved the way to his integration in the first resistance movements in Toulouse and, ultimately, to his arrest, internment, and deportation. Nitti's story offers a unique perspective on the history of resistance and deportation, where the importance of transnational networks, of traditions of transgression and defiance, and of the role of foreigners in the fight against Vichy and the occupier come to the surface. Not only this, but his account ultimately lies at the origin of the post-war memory of the Phantom Train. As we will see, the story of the train, its deportees, and its ongoing commemorative association, the *Amicale du Train Fantôme*, or Phantom Train Association, are entwined with Nitti's account.

The final section is a short essay on sensory history, a way to highlight one of the critical contributions of Nitti's account. Reading Nitti invites us into the sensorial world of deportees, a world which we rarely see. The poet and critic Jean Cassou wrote a personal and touching preface to the first edition, describing Nitti as a specialist in escape stories; while that is certainly true, his account is much more than this.

Part I

Vichy – A Short History of France Under German Occupation, 1940-44

Few moments in French history remain as controversial as those four years when France was occupied by Germany, from June 1940 to August 1944. The shock of defeat in May–June 1940 was followed by the humiliation of occupation and the tragedy of collaboration, matched by daily struggles for food and materials, pains of separation, and tragedies of persecution. Many of these agonising conditions were caused by the terms of the Franco-German armistice and the ever-tightening demands of German authorities, but many were also the result of tensions within France itself, and of diverging visions of its future. Ideas of national revolution and anti-republicanism not only challenged but attempted to crush existing republican norms.

Nitti lived within this web of political, social, and moral tensions, sometimes as a civilian, but more often as a prisoner. As a foreigner and an antifascist his trajectory reveals the passions and inner workings of resistance networks in the Unoccupied Zone before showing the dark underbelly of Vichy's xenophobia and repression and of the Nazis' deportation policies. The journey he describes in his account took place in the summer of 1944, when violence peaked across France as a result of Allied bombing, resistance activity in the *maquis*, and German brutality. But to understand the last months of the occupation, we must start at the beginning.

The Road to War

It is almost impossible to overestimate the trauma of the Great War of 1914-18 on French society. The interwar years unfolded under the shadow of mourning and commemoration, mixed in with resentment and fear. The French army had suffered over 4 million wounded and 1.4 million deaths, almost three quarters of its forces. The physical and emotional devastation caused to families, homes, and towns weighed heavily on the entire country. Life went on, of course, and daily life was punctuated with its usual mixture of joys, humour, anxieties, boredom, and more. Yet the fear of another war was real, and the price of peace could never be too high. At Versailles in 1919 the French had insisted on punitive measures against Germany in the hope of preventing any military revival there. After all, before 1914 the French had suffered the Prussian invasion in 1870-71, which had led to the loss of Alsace. In addition to imposing a strict political and economic agenda on Germany, the French began to build fortifications along their borders in the late 1920s to ensure their own security. Known as the Maginot Line, its aim was to protect the French from future invasion. The fortifications ran through all of France's northern and eastern borders. Dense and heavily armed fortifications appeared along the German side, although these were sparser in territories which strategists believed had natural protections of mountains and forests. A combination of smaller fortifications had initially been established in the late twenties and early thirties in the Alps to protect the French from the Italian fascist threat.

Yet the peace that had been so desperately sought after the First World War was not to be. The rise of communism in Russia, of fascism in Italy, of Nazism in Germany, and the outbreak of the Spanish Civil War in 1936 were signs of deep ideological tensions bubbling within Europe. France itself had seen intense political divisions across the 1930s, although the rise of far-right groups seemed to have been dampened – at least temporarily – with the election of the left-wing

Popular Front government led by socialist Léon Blum between June 1936 and April 1938.

The life of all ordinary citizens came to be shaped by these interwar ideological battles, not least that of Francesco Fausto Nitti. Committed to socialism and antifascism, he was imprisoned by Mussolini in the twenties and sent to a convict colony from which he managed to escape. He fled to France and lived there from 1929. In Paris and later in southern France, he became part of a vibrant antifascist community in exile. When war broke out in Spain in 1936, he decided to join the International Brigades to fight fascism alongside the Spanish republicans. The fighting in Spain was a precursor to a much bigger conflict, but the possibility of another world war became particularly likely after the Munich Agreement. This agreement was signed in September 1938 when France, Britain, and Italy allowed Hitler to annexe the Sudetenland territory in Czechoslovakia. Some believed that this compromise would keep Hitler satisfied and ensure peace in Europe, but others saw it as a concession for a land-hungry dictator to build an empire within Europe. Soon after, Franco's victories in Spain in late 1938 and 1939 meant that France was suddenly surrounded by authoritarian regimes.

Following the defeat of the Republican armies in Spain, Nitti had returned to France in early 1939 in a wave of half a million refugees escaping Franco. He was interned for several months in the make-shift refugee camps of South-West France before returning to the town of Périgueux, where he had lived with his family since the early 1930s. Although we know little of his whereabouts during 1939 and 1940, the French police authorities had him listed as a potentially dangerous foreigner, an 'individual suspected of terrorist activity'.[8] In fact, he had been identified by the French authorities as a capable journalist and notorious antifascist since arriving in France in exile in the late twenties.

During that summer of 1939, as Nitti was reuniting with his wife and two sons, tensions with Germany were growing fast. French plans for military mobilisation and civilian evacuation were under way, and on 23 August 1939 Germany signed a non-aggression pact with the Soviet Union. This completely unexpected agreement between Nazis and communists threw the French Communist Party into disarray.[9] Also known as the Nazi-Soviet Pact or the Molotov–Ribbentrop Pact, the accord essentially ensured that Stalin would not attack if Hitler were to invade Poland, and divided Eastern Europe into Soviet and Nazi spheres of influence. On 1 September 1939 Hitler's armies invaded Poland, and on 3 September Britain and France declared war against Germany. The plan was now to mobilise the French army on the German and Belgian borders, where the British Expeditionary Forces (BEF) would join them.

War raged across Eastern Europe in those first few months, but all was still relatively quiet on the Western Front. In this period known as the 'Phoney War' in France, most soldiers sat waiting for battle for months, wavering between anticipation and boredom. There is no official trace that Nitti joined the war effort, although it is likely that as a foreigner under surveillance, he would not have been allowed to join the fight against the Nazis. He would have seen the tightening of measures, the intensification of an anti-communist campaign, and heard the growing antisemitic and xenophobic cries of the Far Right. Of course, if Hitler was initially consumed with the war on the Eastern Front, he eventually turned his attention to Northern Europe, successfully invading Denmark and Norway before looking to Western Europe in the spring of 1940. It is at this point that everything changed.

The Fall of France, 10 May to 25 June 1940

On Friday, 10 May 1940, Germany launched its offensive on Western Europe both on the ground and in the air. Belgian and Dutch civilians began to evacuate their homes immediately, but the French were not truly worried at this stage: it was inconceivable, in those early spring days, that German soldiers would be marching in the streets of Paris in a matter of weeks. Still, the Allies had been taken by surprise: they had expected the German military command to head for Belgium's North Sea coast before sweeping down into France, but its forces instead took a short cut through the Ardennes Forest. This stretch of borderland between France and Belgium was a natural fortification which the French had dismissed as a possible entry point. Yet by the end of that first day, it was clear that the French town of Sedan, in the Ardennes department and close to the Belgian border, was the target. Over the following hours and days, panic would spread across the entire country. The BEF – who had been told to go into Belgium, west of the Ardennes, in anticipation of German invasion – were too far away to help the French army. On 13 May, when the Germans started to attack the French position on the Meuse in Sedan and established bridgeheads to cross the river, panic truly set in. Evacuation from Belgium and northern France became improvised and chaotic, with carts piled with foods and belongings. The French had not managed to counter-attack, and the Germans were creating a gap in the Ardennes, and a gateway into France (see Figure 1).

The French military and government were beginning to panic. On 15 May, Paul Reynaud, who had replaced Edouard Daladier as head of the French government just a few weeks before, had woken up Winston Churchill, himself appointed Britain's prime minister only five days prior: the Germans had broken through, he said, the French were beaten, it was the end.[10] This statement was not so much defeatist as it was realistic, for the French army had failed to counter-attack, and the Germans were crossing the Meuse. The worst was still to come, and the following day, on Thursday, 16 May, the German army built a giant bridge 95 km wide along the Meuse. For days very concentrated lines of highly manoeuvrable German tanks poured into France, advancing swiftly and easily across fields, villages, and towns. When the British were ordered to fall back, officers were in tears. By Saturday, 18 May, it was clear that the Germans were not making straight to Paris but rather were heading for the Channel ports. The French, British, and Belgian armies were unable to join up, and the mass exodus of by now millions of people on the road was making any kind of swift military movement even more complicated.[11] In those late days of May, Boulogne-sur-Mer was under siege, with its civilians running for cellars to hide from the bombing. They were sleep-deprived, unable to find coffee or running water, deafened by the roar of planes and sirens, and surrounded by waves of refugees.

The situation in late May was looking disastrous, and on 19 May the commander in chief of the French army, General Maurice Gamelin, was replaced by General Maxime Weygand, an energetic general considered the heir of the revered Marshal Foch. Yet by bringing in Weygand as the leader of the French army, the possibility of an armistice became more and more likely. For Weygand, a prolonged, unpredictable, and most likely doomed fight against the Germans was out of the question. He first mooted an armistice in late May, but on 12 June he formally proposed this as the only real option. By this point the last British had been evacuated from the beaches around Dunkirk on 2 June, and the French government had fled Paris to settle briefly in Tours. By early June, Denmark (9 April), Luxembourg (10 May), the Netherlands (15 May), Belgium (28 May), and Norway (10 June) had all surrendered to the Nazis. As for French soldiers, over 1.8 million were taken prisoner in those weeks of invasion.

Heated discussions about the future of France were now at the heart of French political life: should France continue to fight the German army, or should it sign an armistice? Should the French government remain in France, or should it flee into exile in order to continue the fight? On 26 May, Reynaud declared to Churchill that France would fight till the end. In early June he appointed Charles de Gaulle, recently promoted to general but largely unknown, to discuss the option of transporting troops to North Africa.[12] The option of continuing the fight in North Africa would become a very serious suggestion for many; however, in those dizzying and devastating days in the middle of June, and with Weygand at the head of the French army, the idea of requesting an armistice with Germany was spreading fast.

On 10 June, the French government left Paris for the châteaux in the Loire valley. Three days later, on 13 June, Churchill flew to Tours to meet with Reynaud and was presented with a highly sensitive and controversial question: what would Britain do if France requested an armistice with Germany? Churchill knew too well at this point that the French army was unable to continue fighting, but the French and the British had signed a pledge that 'no separate peace would be entered into by either ally'.[13] For Churchill and for several leading French politicians – Georges Mandel, Édouard Herriot, Jules Jeanneney – there was a real possibility of getting American support while the French government retreated to Brittany or North Africa and mobilised its great empire. Yet nothing would come of these alternative plans; after showing an initial sign of support, Roosevelt quickly withdrew any ideas of American assistance and the dream of a government in exile began to seem more and more impossible. Those in the French government supporting the idea of an armistice with Germany would soon win out. That evening, Marshal Philippe Pétain announced that he would not consider continuing the fight abroad, but would remain on French soil, staying loyal to France and refusing to betray French people by leaving their side. As the revered hero of the First World War, Pétain had an exceptional reputation among the French population, and his views carried extraordinary weight. At Verdun his military strategies but also his direct contact with the soldiers had relieved the soldiers, raised morale at the very lowest and darkest points, and had prevented mutinies within the French army. His foresight and humanity had cut across political lines and won him the eternal gratitude and trust of the population.

On the following morning of 14 June, Parisians woke up to the sound of German being spoken in the streets: Paris was lost. That night the French government headed from Tours to Bordeaux. For a few more days, the question of an armistice seemed unresolved: Reynaud was maintaining discussions with Churchill through the liaison of de Gaulle, and a possible Franco-British union was even outlined in the heat of the moment. But the pro-armistice wing of the French government in Bordeaux was gaining momentum, with Pétain and Weygand at its head. On the night of 16 June Reynaud stepped down as prime minister and was replaced by Pétain, the only man who could ask Hitler for armistice conditions. The decision had been made: France would lay down arms and request an armistice. On Monday, 17 June, at 12:30pm, Pétain's voice resounded over French radio: 'It is with a heavy heart that I tell you today that the fighting must stop. I approached the enemy in the night to ask him if he was ready, between soldiers, following the struggle and with honour, to discuss terms to end the hostilities.'[14] (See Figure 2)

The level of chaos and uncertainty of those late June days between Pétain's broadcast (17 June) and the signing of the armistice (25 June) is difficult to imagine. A few hopeful politicians, including Georges Mandel and Jean Zay, sailed on the *Massilia* to Casablanca on 21 June in case the fight could continue from North Africa. But by the time they landed, they found out that the armistice had been signed. The French armistice delegation, headed by General Huntzinger, was presented with the conditions of the armistice on 21 June in the same rail car, and in the same Compiègne forest, where in 1918 the Germans had signed their own surrender. At the last minute, Hitler – who walked at the head of the German delegation as it arrived – had had the original 1918 railway carriage placed at the centre of the Rethondes clearing. A giant Nazi flag flapped in the wind above. It was a moment loaded with symbolism, revenge, and humiliation.

The French had hoped to negotiate the terms of the armistice, but any such illusions quickly vanished. The conditions offered by the German delegation, headed by General Keitel, were tough, and they were final. France was largely split into an Occupied Zone in the north – the industrial territories and the entire Atlantic coast – and an Unoccupied or Free Zone in the south – where it would retain autonomy. France would have to carry the financial burden of the occupying forces, reduce its army to 100,000 men, decommission its fleet, and ensure that civilians in the Occupied Zone abided by German rules. Yet the fact that the French retained control of this Free Zone was hugely important as it offered the illusion that the French still had a nation to govern.

The release of the 1.8 million French prisoners of war was also something the government hoped it could negotiate. On 22 June, following an order from the government in Bordeaux, the armistice was signed. Three days later, on 25 June, it officially came into force: France was now under German occupation.

The Germans were not the only ones at the negotiating table: Italy, under its fascist ruler Benito Mussolini, had declared war on France on 10 June 1940. With the French on the brink of collapse, Mussolini sent in Italian troops ten days later. The war with Italy was short-lived and the Italian army was notably weaker than the Germans, but the French understood that they needed to send an armistice request to the Italians as well as the Germans. On 24 June, a Franco-Italian armistice was signed. It was less onerous than the German one, not least because Italy did not have the same negotiating power as the Germans.[15] Still, a section of south-east France came under Italian occupation.

Not everyone agreed with Pétain, however. After hearing his words on the radio on 17 June, the future resister Daniel Cordier, not even 20 years old, felt completely distraught: 'Whilst my mother sank into the arms of my stepfather, I hurried towards the stairs and went up to my room to hide my tears. Throwing myself on the bed, I sobbed in silence.' If his mother chose to trust Pétain and follow his guidance, Cordier was certain of one thing: 'God had not abandoned France; it was Pétain who had betrayed her.'[16] On that same morning, as Pétain was speaking over the airwaves to end the fighting and Cordier was crying in his room, Charles de Gaulle was arriving in London with Churchill's Major General Spears. For him, the fight had to go on.

On the evening of 18 June, de Gaulle delivered a speech on BBC radio which would come to be known as the *Appel du 18 juin.* In his speech, the then-unknown general announced with great solemnity and seriousness that although France had lost a battle, this was an international war, and it could still fight on with the help of the Allies and the resources of the French empire. He called upon all of those outside of France to join him to continue the fight against the Nazis from North Africa. It is useful here to comment on the legacy of this speech: the *Appel* is often considered to be the start of de Gaulle's rise to power and the root of his later legitimacy. However, at the time not many people actually heard the *Appel*, and fewer still answered de Gaulle's call in the coming days and weeks. One therefore often talks about the 'myth' of 18 June, warning us not to overestimate its immediate impact nor oversimplify the birth of the resistance and the Free French. But as historian Julian Jackson has pointed out, 'the speech was no myth', and perhaps 'what matters is that it was made'.[17]

From 18 June the future of France seemed like a choice between accepting the armistice and following the guidance of Pétain, or refusing it. The latter meant continuing the fight against the Nazis, whether from within or outside of France. At this point the British themselves were still undecided about whether to pursue relations with the new French government – in the hope that it would hand them over its fleet – or to listen to this peculiar general whom no one knew. For Daniel Cordier, based in France, rumours of a French general's speech led him to believe that the fight could continue alongside Churchill and the North African army: he and a group of friends boarded a ship heading to North Africa on 21 June 1940. Yet at the last minute the captain changed direction, heading to England instead; arriving days later in London, Cordier would be one of the first to rally to the general. By 28 June de Gaulle would be recognised by the British as the commander of the political and military organisations which constituted 'Free France' (see Figure 3).

National Revolution

Many words have been used to describe the state of the French in late June 1940: shock, anger, relief, humiliation, devastation. When the voice of Marshal Pétain spread across radio channels on 17 June, the disbelief was so great in some quarters that another message had to be issued that same day.[18] But amidst this disbelief was also a certain level of reassurance. This old man, with his noble bearing and his bright blue eyes, held the hearts of the French. As devastating as it was, Pétain's message would have simultaneously reassured many French people: if the fighting ended now, then the horrors of the First World War – still so fresh in the minds and souls of every family across the country – could be avoided. The cult of Pétainism, and the myth which had developed around him since Verdun, helped smooth over the difficult transition after the defeat.

Even those outraged by the armistice, like the resistance hero Henri Frenay, who we will mention again later, could not help but believe in Pétain's leadership in the summer of 1940. As long as Pétain was in charge, the flame of French honour was still there – flickering perhaps, but there nonetheless. In fact, a new France might even emerge. After all, France was not crushed under the Nazi boot like Poland: the armistice had carved France out into different zones, and the existence of a large Free Zone suggested a very different kind of relationship with the Nazis. Perhaps France could find her place in the new Nazi vision of Europe.

The new government was set up not in Paris but in a small yet elegant town in central France. Far away from the politics of the great capital, Vichy sits, tranquil, along the Allier, framed by charming and luxurious buildings, with archways and promenades welcoming visitors from all over. The historic spa town had many hotels and a casino, making it a convenient place to quickly relocate an entire government on the move. The Germans had offered the government to return to Paris, but there would have been too much proximity with the Germans. Better to settle in the Free, Unoccupied Zone, where French administration was not under the constant gaze of the Nazis. The healing waters of Vichy were perhaps an optimistic metaphor for France's current situation: under the careful guidance of Pétain, the men at Vichy believed that France could start healing from the wounds of the defeat.

While Pétain was being settled into the rooms of the Hôtel du Parc in Vichy, the Third Republic was being unravelled once and for all. Weygand in particular had been quick (and keen) to blame the Third Republic politicians for the defeat of the French army. By 10 July, the full force of the defeat, the exodus, and the armistice were being felt as the National Assembly, in the Casino of Vichy, voted full powers to Marshal Pétain. It is important to understand that Pétain never seized power but rather was legally given power. On 9 July, 624 parliamentarians voted for a bill proposing a new constitution, only four voted against. The next day, on 10 July, 569 parliamentarians voted to grant Pétain full powers, and only eighty voted 'no'. This symbolic gesture would matter after the war, but its immediate effect was insignificant, and Pétain was granted full powers by an overwhelming majority. The French historian who commented that 'in the National Assembly, in July 1940, you found only Pétainists' was not too far off the mark.[19] On 11 July, Pétain formally declared himself head of state and prime minister, and the republican parliament was dismissed. Decades of republican order had suddenly been reversed, and an authoritarian government had been put in its place.

There would be many Vichy governments during the dark years between 11 July 1940 and 20 August 1944, but a glance at the first government gives a taste of the personalities involved. After Marshal Pétain, the most important person in government was Pierre Laval, the son of a shopkeeper who had begun his political career on the left before leaning more and more towards the right. He was appointed Deputy Prime Minister, and although he was dismissed in December 1940 – and replaced by Pierre Flandin and later Admiral Darlan – he would return to the corridors of power in April 1942 under request from the Germans. Laval was a hugely important figure during those years of occupation, always close to the Germans and regarded as the mastermind behind French collaboration. Meanwhile, the majority of Pétain's first – and later – cabinet(s) were traditionalists, military men, and experts: from General Weygand as Minister of Defence, to the royalist Raphaël Alibert as Minister of Justice, to the anti-German agriculture expert Pierre Caziot as Minister of Agriculture. Technocrats such as Jean Bichelonne and Pierre Pucheu were also among those important figures in Vichy in the early years. Interestingly, fascists and pro-German sympathisers were not included in the new government, and figures such as Marcel Déat – who would soon create the collaborationist party National Popular Rally – and Gaston Bergery soon left for Paris when they realised that there were no opportunities for them in Vichy.

For the ideologues of Vichy, France had collapsed because of the decadence that was rife under the Popular Front and what followed, and a new ideology was needed in order that France be reborn to take its rightful place. The founding principles of this new France were work, family, country – or '*travail, famille, patrie*' – and the new slogan which replaced the well-known republican motto '*liberté, égalité, fraternité*'. The rebirth of France was intended to be political but also social, economic, and above all cultural. Pétain's project of national renovation, or National Revolution as it is better known, was a moral crusade which would ensure the moral and intellectual recovery of France. This crusade emphasised Catholic values, the love of the land, motherhood, procreation, hard work, family, outdoor sports, and discipline. Laws in autumn 1940 saw the rapprochement between the Catholic Church and the state system as religious orders were given the right to teach and religion was brought back into the primary school syllabus. Family was seen as a central building block of renovated France. Some believed that the weakness of the Third Republic had been due in part to women abandoning their natural roles as mothers, so now large families were given special subsidies and Mother's Day became a propaganda coup to honour women as mothers; meanwhile, an anti-abortion law in 1942 threatened the safety of thousands of women. Young men were recruited into youth camps, the *Chantiers de la Jeunesse*, where they were taught important moral lessons, the value of a return to the soil, and the aspirations towards a new social order.

An emphasis on small farms aimed to transform French agriculture and celebrate the peasantry, while craft, folklore, and regionalism were celebrated.[20]

The National Revolution never really revolutionised anything. It was implemented in 1940–42, but the rhetoric became impossible to uphold after 1942, when everyday conditions were worsening and, from November 1942, the Germans occupied the whole French territory. The slogan 'Work, Family, Country' soon became dubbed 'Worry, Famine, Patrol'.[21] Laws looking to expand the Church's influence were reversed and the *Compagnons de France* scouting groups which had been created to promote a new, Pétainist version of the French male only recruited a few thousand youths. The French writer Jean Guéhenno described it as '[t]he same soppy nonsense on the family, the crafts, religion, folklore ... flowing interminably on like a dribble of dirty water'.[22] Pétain used the term 'National Revolution' for the last time in January 1943.

Another important failure of the Vichy government was its inability to gain the release of its prisoners of war held in Germany. Around 92,000 soldiers died in the Battle of France, and 1.8 million soldiers were taken prisoner. From the very beginning their fate was a central preoccupation for the new government, and General Huntziger, who signed the armistice on 22 June 1940 as the head of the French Armistice Commission, had asked for their immediate release. The Germans ignored this and in August 1940, the ink barely dry on the armistice, 1.5 million French prisoners were sent to German stalags. If it was a relief that France was no longer at war, anxieties continued in those families who did not know the fate of their sons, husbands, brothers, or fathers or where they had gone. Vichy would manage to obtain the return of some soldiers, while others like Jacques Silberfeld – who was deported on the Phantom Train in 1944 – managed to escape on their own and lived clandestinely.[23] Yet the fact that over half of them were still in Germany by late 1942 was a festering wound for the French government. In total, 900,000 French prisoners of war were still in Germany at the end of the war, and 37,000 would die in captivity, some of them in Rawa Ruska, the disciplinary camp in Ukraine for those who were punished for escape attempts, sabotage, and general insubordination. As for the 70,000 colonial prisoners of war, they suffered crueller fates at the hands of the Germans in the summer of 1940: in May–June 1940, between 1,500 and 3,000 black French soldiers were murdered in summary killings and massacres as a result of Nazi racist ideology. In Chasselay, fifty non-white soldiers were taken away and murdered before being buried by local civilians. Non-white prisoners of war were then sent to Frontstalags in France rather than their equivalent on German soil.[24]

However, Vichy was efficient in other ways, and some aspects of the National Revolution rhetoric rooted themselves firmly in France, not least the discourse on the 'enemies' of France. These discourses were not new to France as such, but they gathered a different and tragic momentum in the early 1940s. First, there were the politicians of the Third Republic, whose 'loose' morals and politicians were blamed for the defeat. In 1942, the Vichy government brought six political leaders including Edouard Daladier and Léon Blum to trial in Riom for their responsibility for the defeat of 1940, although the trial ended in a fiasco for the regime: the defence ultimately shifted the accusation onto Pétain, and the Germans were frustrated by this excessive fixation on the defeat. Second, there were the British. Tensions with the British were already visible during the defeat and the evacuation from Dunkirk, but it was after the armistice that Anglophobia intensified. On 3 July 1940, the British bombed the French fleet in the port of Mers-el-Kébir in North Africa, killing almost 1,300 French sailors. The French fleet had always been a concern for Churchill and while the terms of the armistice had not required the French navy to be handed over to the Nazis, the risk that it might slip into German hands seemed too high. The decision to bomb the fleet had not been taken lightly, but the British saw no other realistic option. The French media seized the moment to denounce the unnecessary death of its young sailors. A few weeks later, the alliance between Churchill and de Gaulle became a very real threat to Vichy's legitimacy as they tried to bring the French empire back into the war: a British–Gaullist raid on Dakar in September 1940, and later the fighting in Syria in 1941, fuelled resentment towards the British and became visible in Vichy's propaganda campaign. Third, there were the communists. The initial Nazi–Soviet Pact made France's relationship to communists unclear, but after the Nazi invasion of the Soviet Union in June 1941, the full force of Vichy's anti-communism was unleashed. The *Légion des Volontaires Français Contre le Bolchevisme* (LVF) was launched in August 1941, and a detachment of French volunteers in German uniform was sent off to the approval of Marshal Pétain. Pétain later denied having read the document fully, but the damage was done. An intense anti-communist propaganda campaign – exhibitions, press, radio broadcasts – was matched by police repression and brutality, with special police units created specifically to hunt down communists and resisters.

Among Vichy's 'enemies' were foreigners and Jews, many suffering a tragic fate. If the National Revolution had aimed to give a clear idea of what France *should* be, it had also given a clear idea of what it *should not* be, and foreigners, freemasons, and Jews were actively excluded from Vichy's new vision of France. Over a decade earlier, in August 1927, a law had been created to facilitate obtaining French nationality, a consequence of the waves of interwar migration and the historic French fear of falling birth rates aggravated since the First World War, known as '*dénatalité*'. Since then, over half a million people had been naturalised. However, on 22 July 1940, barely two weeks after the birth of the Vichy state, a law was passed to review all naturalisations since 1927. Suddenly, all files were under review, and 15,000 people would see their French citizenship revoked.[25] Just a few months later, in October 1940, and then again in June 1941, more laws were imposed to strip Jews of their rights to work. Combined with the Aryanisation of the French economy – whereby Jews were expropriated, had their goods confiscated, and were excluded from economic activity in both zones after the summer of 1941 – and with the internment of those who in the eyes of the Vichy regime threatened national security – communists were explicitly targeted after June 1941 – the xenophobia and anti-Semitism of Vichy's legislation were starkly visible. The offer to assist Germans in the arrest and deportation of Jews in the summer of 1942 would eventually symbolise the epitome of collaboration, but it is important to understand that these accords were rooted in the French xenophobic and antisemitic legislation introduced under French initiative in those early weeks and months of occupation. In fact, these new regulations were an extension of the increasingly xenophobic atmosphere in 1930s France, and so they were not so much a sudden change in policy as they were the acceleration and intensification of a longer history of racism and antisemitism in France.

The government in Vichy was therefore not a mere blot on the history of France, a dark stain which could easily be covered: the government in Vichy was founded on moral and legal legitimacy. In fact, Americans maintained diplomatic relations with Vichy for a long time. The shock of defeat and the cult of Pétain helped enable a parliamentary vote which gave Pétain full powers to transform French politics, economy, and society. For many French people there was also the comfort of knowing that France still had its empire: after all, with their resources and manpower, the imperial colonies could still give the impression of France's ongoing power status in spite of the armistice.

The Desire for Collaboration

What had begun as an armistice and a national revolution soon slipped into full-on collaboration with the Germans. The French had assets – notably their empire and their fleet – and a politics of collaboration could offer benefits to both parties. The first key moment was more of a propaganda coup than an actual agreement between the two countries: on 24 October 1940, while Hitler was doing a tour of the Mediterranean powers to meet Franco and Mussolini, he stopped in the town of Montoire-sur-le-Loir, just north of Tours, to meet with

Marshal Pétain. For Pétain, this was his first time back in the Occupied Zone. When they met, Hitler held out his hand and the Marshal accepted it; photographers immortalised that handshake, and the image soon spread across France and Europe. Even for Pétainists, this was a huge blow: how could Pétain be shaking hands with the leader of Nazi Germany? It marked the end of those who believed Pétain might be playing a *double jeu*, a double game. A few days later, Pétain gave a radio broadcast to contextualise the handshake and make clear to the French that he was not under the Nazi thumb, but that he believed that collaboration with Germany was the way forward. 'It is honourably and in order to maintain French unity – unity that has lasted ten centuries – in the context of an activity helping to build the new European order, that I enter today upon the path of collaboration. … To all those who will be kept distant from our way of thinking by noble scruples, I am anxious to say that the first duty of every French citizen is to have trust.'[26] After the war, collaboration was often portrayed as the only way to 'shield' the French population from the worst of German excesses (this was a particularly popular rhetoric among pro-Pétainists); what is clear, however, is that the intensification of collaboration saw France lose, rather than gain, materially and morally.

An economic collaboration which went beyond the terms of the armistice was initially developed in 1941 in the Darlan government. But in 1942, when Laval returned to power, the full extent of collaboration became clear, with French material goods and human resources being sent en masse to the Reich: coal, furniture, food, and eventually workers too. By early 1942, the Germans were in a crisis and needed more men and resources for their difficult battle on the Eastern Front and to maintain (as much as possible) standards of living in Germany. As the historian Robert Paxton wrote, 'Like Darlan before him, Laval chose to regard increased German needs as an opportunity rather than a danger.'[27] A *Relève* system was put in place in spring 1942 to send three volunteer French workers to Germany for the return of one French prisoner of war. However, the scheme's lack of popularity meant that a law was created on 4 September whereby all French men between 18 and 50, or French unmarried women between 21 and 35, could be requisitioned to work for France, although Germany was not mentioned specifically. Protests began to erupt against these tightening measures.

By October 1942, tens of thousands of French workers had been sent to Germany but the German targets were still far from being met. A few months later, on 16 February 1943, the Forced Labour Service (STO) law broadened the September law and dictated that all young French people born between 1920 and 1922 could be summoned to leave to work for the Germans. Round-ups in cinemas and market squares underlined the violence of these requests, and created even more distrust among the civilian population. The forced labour service was not, however, limited to France: Germans relied heavily on foreign workers during this period and 7.6 million foreign workers from all over Europe were in the Reich working for the German economy in 1944.[28] Although there were many cases of exemption, the *Relève* and STO schemes sent between 600,000 and 650,000 French workers to Germany, affecting hundreds of thousands of young people as well as their families. This caused a wave of resentment across France and was only worsened by the fact that increasing quantities of materials and resources were being taken from the country. By 1943, the idea that France was being pillaged was widespread.

The folly of collaboration had become clear to some by November 1942. On 8 November, the Allies had landed in North Africa, and over the following days Laval sped to Munich to suggest to Hitler that France could take on an active role against the Allied forces, if in return the Germans granted it independence. He had been wanting to negotiate new terms on several points for a while, but this was, for Laval, a perfect opportunity. Hitler could not have been less interested: in reaction to the Allied invasion of Vichy North Africa, the Germans crossed the demarcation on 11 November 1942 and took occupation of the whole territory, with the exception of the Italian zone of occupation. As the months unfolded in 1943, it became evident that the Germans were the only ones benefitting from a Franco-German 'collaboration'; still, the government in Vichy would continue to work willingly with the Germans until the very end.

The Roads to Resistance

The exodus of 10 million people towards the south had been full of noise: trains pulling in and out of stations; carts being wheeled; people shouting; bombs falling from the skies; feet marching and running; children crying. But after Marshal Pétain's speech of 17 June, which announced the end of the fighting, there seemed to be almost an absence of sound. 'Cold, hunger for many people. Misery. And that awful silence,' wrote Guéhenno in his diary in December 1940.[29] He had noticed this silence immediately, when in early September he described a Paris which 'seemed dead': 'I am happy with Parisians. They cross paths with Germans as they cross paths with dogs and cats. They don't appear to see them, or to hear them.'[30] Could silence be a form of resistance?

Many things lay beneath this silence, not least a sense of relief. Pétain's guidance comforted millions in their angst and sorrow, and the knowledge that the military violence had stopped was in its own way deeply reassuring. This should not be confused with enthusiasm for the German occupation: the Germans were an old enemy whose invasion and occupation of French territory, in 1870–71 and then in 1914–18, were open wounds in recent French history. The re-annexation of Alsace-Lorraine in 1940 was a particularly painful affront. Therefore the pro-German, or even pro-Nazi, segments of French society were, if not completely absent, only a tiny minority of the population. A much larger section of the population was not happy about the German occupation as such but were content that the Third Republic had been overthrown, and that Pétain's rise signalled a new era of conservatism, Catholicism, and anti-communism in France.

Beneath this silence people also returned to their daily lives. They had to go back to work, put their houses in order, feed and raise their children, and all of those everyday concerns which dominate in peacetime. Yet things were not quite what they were before, not least for those in the Occupied Zone. Food soon became the first and foremost concern, often dominating the daily thoughts and rituals of every person in France. Food had already been an issue during the Phoney War, between September 1939 and the German invasion, but war and defeat brought additional strains. On 23 September 1940, mandatory ration cards were imposed on the entire French country. People were constantly looking for ways to supplement their food. Trips to the countryside were organised to collect provisions, or packages were sent from family members in rural areas, where they generally had more access to food.

Unsurprisingly, a vibrant black market emerged. Peasants in rural areas could now wield considerable power due to their access to food supplies, and rich peasants in particular were increasingly loathed by city dwellers.[31] The post-war novel *Au Bon Beurre* by Jean Dutour described how one family of grocers became more and more rich, as well as more and more gluttonous, over the course of the occupation.[32] Having said that, most French people suffered from absence of coal, electricity, and food. Market days, which were a cornerstone of daily life, were not quite the same, with authorities monitoring queues and the gradual disappearance of essential products like butter, fruit, and meat. People were forced to think of alternative ways to supplement their meagre rations. Every week for two years, the writer and resister Simone Martin-Chauffier made a long trip to the heart of the countryside: 'We went from farm to farm scraping a couple of eggs here and a few potatoes there,' she explained, until she found the farm of the Martin family. Simone remembered every detail of her first visit there, walking away with 'some duck, some white flour, two or three bottles of wine … a cheese and a small saucisson'.[33] The cold was almost harder to deal with: relentless, it never alleviated over the long months of winter.

But resistance as we know it today was not visible yet, not in those early days. The noises and rhythms of everyday life had, in fact, quickly returned to French life. Plays were staged and attended; films were produced and released; books were written and published. In fact, the years of the occupation were highly literary ones. For artists, this was a time to return to their craft, and Louis Martin-Chauffier, a writer and resister like his wife, Simone, returned to his biography of Chateaubriand, which he published in 1943. That same year philosophers Jean-Paul Sartre and Simone de Beauvoir published their acclaimed works *L'Être et le néant* (1943) and *L'Invitée* (1943). Sacha Guitry, a famous playwright among other things, wrote and directed the film *MCDXXIX–MCMXLII (De Jeanne d'Arc à Philippe Pétain)* in early 1944, which became deeply controversial after the war.

It was not only the social or intellectual elites who enjoyed life's creative energy and charms. Poetry contests, flower bed competitions, and art exhibitions were regularly organised in local communities. Although Guéhenno had derided Vichy's enthusiasm for folklore, local traditions of arts and crafts were deeply embedded in French society. The Festival of the *Santons* in Marseille, which celebrated those small ceramic figurines arranged at Christmas time around a menagerie scene, had been going on since the very early nineteenth century and formed part of people's daily lives and material culture. Clandestine dances were organised, too, for people to come together and enjoy themselves.[34] In the journal of Hélène Berr, a young Jewish woman studying at the Sorbonne in the early 1940s, one of the most shocking things is precisely this overlap between the darkest moments in history – when she describes the enforcement of the yellow star in June 1942 – with the humdrum and simple pleasures of her daily life – enjoying picnics and a budding romance.[35]

It was only if one listened closely that one could catch murmurings of resistance and defiance, not least from across the Channel, in London. There was, of course, de Gaulle's famous *Appel* aired on the BBC on 18 June 1940, although we must be careful not to overemphasise its impact at the time. De Gaulle had flown back to London on 17 June

1940 when he understood that the French government was going to ask for an armistice. For him, this was unacceptable, and the fight could – and should – continue from foreign shores with the support of the British and the French empire. However, as the youngest general in the French army, he was a nobody. The British had allowed him to speak on the radio on 18 June not because he offered the right alternative to Pétain but because they had no idea about how the situation was going to unfold; a speech from a relatively unknown general would do little harm considering the total chaos of the situation, and this way they kept their options open. De Gaulle hoped to stir support among the colonies and he appealed directly to General Noguès, the commander in chief of all French Forces in North Africa. But his appeal was met with silence: Noguès, who may have been briefly tempted to consider continuing the fight from North Africa, decided to follow the guidance of the marshal. Far from being an exception, the large majority of French colonial territories sided with Pétain. Administrative elites in Africa, Indochina, the Indian Ocean, the Caribbean, and the Pacific Islands tended to be conservative, traditionalist, military men for whom the cult of Pétain meant everything. Most of the French empire thus hitched its support to those in Vichy.[36]

But de Gaulle was not completely alone: Félix Éboué, the Guyanese Governor of Chad, declared in late June that he would not implement the terms of the armistice. In fact, signs of rallying to Britain and de Gaulle were visible across French Equatorial Africa (FEA). De Gaulle sent emissaries to see Éboué and from there they infiltrated neighbouring territories to seize power alongside local colonial officers. It was a resounding success, and by late August most of the region had rallied to de Gaulle. If there had been a rallying cry after de Gaulle's proposal to carry on the fight, the FEA – often considered a marginally important colony by comparison to North and West Africa – had risen to the occasion. As the historian Eric Jennings recently argued, the first Free French combatants were African.[37] Brazzaville, the capital of the Congo, became the capital of de Gaulle's Free France in 1940.

The impulse for resistance could also be witnessed within France.[38] From the very beginning, some were unable to accept the terms of the armistice. At first, it was met with disbelief. As mentioned earlier, the resister Daniel Cordier had felt he was living a 'nightmare'.[39] Agnès Humbert, who had fled Paris during the exodus, was similarly distraught: 'It was at Valençay that we learned that France was seeking an armistice. All around me, men were weeping silent tears. Jumping out of the car, I stamped and yelled: It's all lies, it's all lies, … It can't be true, it's not possible.'[40] For both of them, the only way forward was to organise French society and fight the invader: '[t]he Boches will be powerless if forty million Frenchmen rise up against them,' wrote Cordier.[41] If the young man decided to flee French territory and continue the fight abroad, Humbert would stay in France and build her fight from within. For Ginette Vincent Baudy, who was deported on the Phantom Train to Ravensbrück, resistance emerged instinctively but also slowly: 'Often we get asked "how did you join the Resistance", and I think very naturally, without barely even realising it. You had to struggle with the lack of freedom, with a joyless life without distractions and with the shame of the occupation to first slip into isolated acts, and then slowly regroup and commit.'[42]

Small signs of defiance and transgression began to bubble beneath the surface of the armistice. On 6 August 1940, Humbert found the French writer Jean Cassou in her office at the *Musée de l'Homme*: 'He too has aged,' she observed, 'In six weeks his hair has turned white and he appears to have shrunk into himself.' She took a leap of faith to confide her thoughts to her friend and colleague: 'I blurt out why I have come to see him, telling him that I feel I will go mad, literally, if I don't do something, if I don't react somehow.' Luckily, she had chosen the right audience:

> Cassou confides that he feels the same, that he shares my fears. The only remedy is for us to act together, to form a group of ten like-minded comrades, no more. To meet on agreed days to

> exchange news, to write and distribute pamphlets and tracts, and to share summaries of French radio broadcasts.[43]

Henri Frenay, a military officer who was 'fervently devoted to Marshal Pétain', also felt compelled to act: 'Those about me accepted defeat as irrevocable,' he commented, but for him '[a]s long as the war continued, as long as England held fast, there was still hope.'[44] There were countless small gestures, and some were punished by death: Etienne Achavanne was executed on 20 June 1940 for cutting the telephone wires at an airport used by the Wehrmacht.[45] The first public protest took place on 11 November 1940, the anniversary of the end of the First World War. Students gathered around the Tomb of the Unknown Soldier in Paris, under the Arc de Triomphe. The crowd was broken up initially by French police and their batons before being suppressed much more brutally by the German army; despite rumours of casualties, only a few were wounded and 100 arrested. Still, this was 'a break in the uneasy calm' which had settled throughout France since June.[46]

Resistance was thus a reality from the summer of 1940, a reality which swelled, intensified, and transformed over the course of the occupation. This does not mean, however, that resistance was a mass movement: only a minority of French people can be identified as active resisters who consciously and repeatedly put their lives on the line in order to disrupt the occupier and to make clear that they had not laid down arms. After careful consideration, historians have suggested that 2 per cent of the population actively resisted, with numbers of recognised resisters wavering between 250,000 and 300,000, or even 500,000. A generous estimation of people who had regular contact with active resistance movements or networks would be 1 million. Of these resisters, thousands were foreigners: communists, Jews, colonial subjects, antifascists, and more joined the fight on French territory. As historians have remarked, it was not the French resistance but resistance in France.[47]

Cordier, Humbert, and Frenay: one was in London; another in Occupied Paris; another in the Free Zone. None of them had ever met, none of them would speak to each other for at least several years, but in their own personal networks and environments they were building some of the first resistance movements in France. Resistance within the French metropole can roughly be divided into two types. First, resistance movements. These emerged from 1940 in both zones, and primarily focussed activities on clandestine publications such as tracts and newspapers. The most famous resistance movements in the Northern Zone included *Organisation civile et militaire* (OCM), *Libération-Nord*, *Ceux de la Libération*, *Ceux de la Résistance*, as well as *Défense de la France*, *Résistance*, and *Lorraine*. In the Southern Zone, mostly based around Lyon, three major movements dominated the scene: *Combat*, *Libération-Sud*, and *Franc-Tireur*. Others such as *Témoignage Chrétien* were also active from early on. One movement, the *Front National*, was created by the French Communist Party (PCF) and covered both zones.

Second, resistance networks. Some of these also emerged as early as 1940, but by contrast to movements, networks were primarily focussed on helping prisoners of war, creating escape routes, or gathering information. They were linked to Allied information networks such as the British Special Operations Executive (SOE), the Secret Intelligence Service (SIS), the Free French *Bureau Central des Renseignements et d'Action* (BCRA), or the American Office of Strategic Services (OSS). Resistance networks were far more numerous than movements, with 266 officially recognised (or *homologués*) at the end of the war, by contrast to forty-five recognised movements. Resistance movements and networks, however, cannot be so neatly separated. Some movements had their own networks, and people could belong to several at the same time. Moreover, although movements might have focussed on clandestine printing, false papers, or escape networks, they were often involved in a broader range of resistance activities and had different priorities at different moments.

Resistance in France evolved over the years, shaped and re-shaped by major developments in the war. The Nazi invasion of the Soviet Union in June 1941 – Operation Barbarossa – had caused a tidal wave in the war, shifting military, political, social, economic, and cultural currents at global level. For the French Communist Party (PCF), it meant that it could now enter into the armed resistance against the Germans. Until then the party line had been nothing if not complicated: with the Nazis and the Soviets on the same side since the Nazi–Soviet Pact, resistance from communists had been more complicated (although not completely absent). This changed from the summer of 1941. Backed by the PCF, the *Front National* and *Franc-Tireur* partisans emerged that year. There were many disputes about whether or not armed resistance and individual actions – placing bombs, shooting Germans – were the best way forward, and the communists were often criticised for their armed resistance. The Germans took armed attacks extremely seriously, and these had tragic consequences including arrests, hostage-takings, and executions. As a result of this, violent resistance remained highly controversial until the insurrection of Paris in 1944. These kinds of fundamental differences in resistance methods and beliefs meant that when resistance groups tried to unify in 1942 and 1943, relations with communist movements could be extremely complicated. Still, their contribution to escalating resistance in France against the Nazis and Vichy was undeniable. The post-war myth of the 'party of 75,000 martyrs' may have romanticised their sacrifice to an extent, but communist resistance played an important role in the wider protests against Vichy and the Nazis.

The year 1942 was another important turning point. Laval returned to power in April and immediately set up the highly controversial *Relève* policy before tightening these into September laws to send French workers to Germany. That summer, the tragic round-ups and mass deportations of Jews from both zones began, leading to some of the most heart-breaking scenes in French history. Then in November 1942 the Allies successfully landed in North Africa, a highly successful coup militarily; as a result of this the Germans crossed the demarcation line and occupied the full territory, leaving little doubt as to the weakness of the Pétain government. This series of events encouraged new forms of resistance in a darkening climate. On one hand, passive or cultural resistance – those small daily acts of defiance like dressing in tricolour colours or giving an SS officer incorrect directions on the metro – became more widespread. These small acts of defiance were never officially classified as acts of resistance, yet they added up to small waves of frustration and transgression which changed the mood in homes, towns, and cities across France. Civil disobedience should not be overly generalised, but as historian Rod Kedward has explained, it needs to be emphasised.[48] On the other hand, attempts to unify and coordinate resistance action occurred through the efforts of Jean Moulin acting on behalf of de Gaulle.

The landscape of resistance changed further still in 1943 with the emergence of guerilla movements across rural France, known as *maquis*. These had started when Vichy escalated the *Relève* policy to the full-blown STO in February 1943. The STO laws made it harder to be exempt from forced labour service, but still thousands of young people refused to go. Vichy originally called them '*défaillants*', although over the following months the term '*réfractaire*' became widely used. Small camps and groupings of these *réfractaires* began to emerge across the French countryside, and by April 1943 the terms '*maquis*' and '*maquisard*' had become commonplace. *Maquis*, the Corsican term for 'scrubland', thus slowly began to appear in the rural and mountainous regions of southern France, and some of them morphed into important clusters of resisters involved in armed resistance, forever changing the visual landscape of resistance in France. Until then, urban centres such as Lyon or Toulouse had been hotbeds of resistance movements and networks. Yet by the end of the war, the names Vercors, Les Glières, l'Ain, Saint-Marcel, or Mont-Mouchet would all become associated with the resistance. The *maquis* were 'a surge of independent action' and 'inventiveness' at local level, emerging 'just at a time when the earlier Resistance was beginning to be more centrally organised and led'.[49] Interestingly, if they were made up of French civilians, the *maquis* had many ties with the Allies, not least because they received logistical assistance.[50]

By this point there had been increasing attempts to connect the disparate movements and networks surfacing across France. It was initially difficult to get a sense of who did or did not want to continue the fight against the Nazis because resistance was inherently wrapped in secrecy and clandestinity: resisters had very limited connections since knowing identities, locations, and strategies put the lives of individuals or even entire groups at great risk. Resistance propaganda helped spread awareness of different groups, but still the Free French had no overarching view of what was happening in France for those first months and even years of occupation. This was changing by 1942 as the different movements, networks, groups, and resisters were becoming more aware of one another. For de Gaulle, there was an obvious need to unify – and control – these groups. He put Jean Moulin, a French prefect turned resister, in charge of unifying the disparate movements, initially in the Free Zone. This was an incredibly difficult task considering the strains and suspicions between them. Movements and networks were for the most part not strictly tied to a specific political party, but political affiliations as well as tensions existed between communists, socialists, Christian democrats and radicals. Moreover, personalities clashed, not least among major movement leaders. After countless secret meetings across France and London, and thanks to his skilful if often heated negotiations, Moulin succeeded in bringing the leaders of major resistance groups to the same table.

The merging of groups and coordination of resistance activity did not mean that there was a uniform vision, however. In May 1943, Moulin – who would go on to become the most revered resister of this period in the post-war decades – presided over the *Conseil National de la Résistance* (CNR), the council meant to coordinate all resistance activity in France, including the communists. He had already managed to unite the three largest resistance movements in the Free Zone – *Combat* (Henri Frenay), *Libération-Sud* (Emmanuel d'Astier de La Vigerie), and *Franc-Tireur* (Jean-Pierre Lévy) – into a single movement, the *Mouvements Unis de la Résistance* (MUR), in January 1943. After Moulin's arrest, torture, and tragic death in the hands of the Gestapo in Summer 1943, the MUR fused with three other medium-sized movements in the north – *Défense de la France* (Philippe Viannay), *Résistance* (Marcel Renet), and *Lorraine* (Marcel Leroy) – and become the *Mouvement de la Libération Nationale* (MLN). Yet differences of vision meant that other movements and networks refused to join it, and the MLN never became the single resistance network they had hoped it could be. According to one historian, 'the history of the MUR reflects all the main controversies, obstacles, and questions of the French Resistance: relations with the Free French; debates over waiting for orders or starting direct action; relations with communists; positions towards the political parties of the Third Republic; and finally, relations between central organisations and their local rank and file.' If the MUR showed anything it was that it was impossible to create a national resistance, and that 'all resistance is local'.[51]

The divisions within France were also visible in relation to the Free French who operated outside of France for the majority of the war, although this would become particularly glaring after the liberation of the territory in 1944. De Gaulle's Free French troops had swelled over the years and gained momentum as General Leclerc marched up through the Saharan desert. Leclerc had been one of the first to follow de Gaulle to London in 1940 and became one of the most acclaimed Free French generals, leading troops into Italian Libya and famously taking Kufra in 1941 and the Fezzan in 1942–43. General Koenig's victory at Bir Hakeim in May to June 1942 was another major moment marking the contribution of the Free French forces to the war effort against the Axis powers. At the Liberation it became clear that these men who had rallied to de Gaulle's Free French forces were considered by him to be the true resisters, and they were awarded the highest medal of the resistance, the *Ordre de la Libération*.[52] By contrast, de Gaulle's lack of recognition and gratitude to those who had resisted *within* French territory became a very sore point for those who had managed to survive the occupation but had lost so many comrades to executions, deportations, and torture.[53] Meanwhile, the colonial soldiers who had resisted were barely visible in the post-liberation accolades. It is worth noting that the troops of the Free French were mostly made up of colonial soldiers, but it was not them who received the *Ordre*. The many divisions within the resistance in France would continue for decades, sometimes erupting in public debates where resisters accused each other of lying or betrayal.[54] When the Armenian resister Missak Manouchian and his wife, Mélinée, were brought to the Panthéon mausoleum in Paris in February 2024 – where France's great men (and some women) lie – it seemed that the dust had still not fully settled on the divided memories of the resistance.

Any quick overview of historical events means that individual stories risk getting brushed over. We cannot go into these hundreds of thousands of lives right now, but we can, nonetheless, take a brief pause and think of the sociological make-up of this resistance. Political allegiances, geographical locations, professional skills, family situation, gender, all of these meant that people were more or less likely to join the resistance or would carry out specific roles within it. Young, white, French men were for a long time the typical picture of the resister, and joining the resistance was easier when you were unattached, had no familial responsibilities. But fathers, like Louis Martin-Chauffier, and mothers, like Agnès Humbert, also risked their lives for the resistance from the very outset. Women, in fact, were everywhere, in movements, networks, *maquis*, and Free France: the typists at the typewriters; the bearers and passers of messages; the concealers of weapons in their baskets; the cooks for those on the run. The 'woman at the doorway', as Kedward described them, was an anonymous pillar of resistance groups.[55] There were many more women who never seem to have a clear affiliation with any resistance group, such as Ginette Vincent Baudy's mother, but who hid Jews in their homes.[56] Communists, especially after June 1941, resisted, but so did royalists, Pétainists, far-rightists, military men, anarchists, socialists, Catholics, Protestants, Muslims, and Jews. Colonial soldiers and workers stuck in the French metropole resisted, and there were also foreigners – Italians, Spanish, Poles, Germans, Russians, Romanians, Austrians, Hungarians. Meanwhile, many of the first Free French combatants were from Central Africa.

The dividing line is unclear between resistance, rescue and care. Many of those working with support and aid services acted as important bridges between different worlds, and their roles of care became combined with aid for survival and resistance activity. Pierre Razafy-Andriamihaingo, who worked for *Amicale des Malgaches* before the war, saw himself become deeply involved in supporting colonial prisoners on the run; the colonial soldier Thiagam Dierra Collo supplied his French 'godmother', who looked after him in the prisoner of war camp, with information about sabotages, strikes, and ships he noticed in Cherbourg.[57] Feeding, clothing, housing those on the run were invisible yet crucial parts of resistance activity. Meanwhile, humanitarian associations providing aid in France often crossed over into resistance activity. The Quakers assured the government of their apolitical nature, yet a number of them were accused of associating with the resistance, including hiding weapons.[58] Indeed, as witnesses to some of the most tragic scenes in France in internment camps or deportation trains, some humanitarian aid workers could not help but break with their apolitical codes in order to help those in need, even those outside of Vichy's laws. Damien Nardone, one of the deportees of the Phantom Train, remembered them well when they approached the train near Toulouse to distribute some sugar, gingerbread and chocolate: 'the nurses had tears in their eyes, because they must have known where we were going but were not telling us. They were English women, we called them the Quakers. We must not have been the first convoy they helped.'[59] (See Figure 4)

A mosaic of people thus made up the resistance in France, but crucially this resistance was part of a wider web of Europe-wide resistance, a multinational, pan-European coalition.[60] Connections with the Free French, the SOE, the OSS, and other transnational networks of resistance which cut through the Netherlands, Belgium, Switzerland, and Spain, meant that French resistance did not stand on its own. It was not isolated from the waves of action and protest and planning which swept through Western Europe at that time and was part of a much bigger struggle against Nazism and fascism more broadly. In short, the French resistance did not exist in a vacuum; rather, it was shaped by transnational currents of transgression and protest, not least antifascist politics; by Allied interests; and by the movement of people across borders. This, in fact, is what Nitti's account shows: his own path as an Italian antifascist in exile, and the paths of his fellow deportees in the Phantom Train who also cut across political and national lines, embody the transnational currents sweeping through France during the Second World War. But this is to be explained in detail at a later point.

Repression, Internment, and Deportation

Resistance, however, came at a price, and the large majority of the Phantom Train deportees had been resisters. Damien Nardone – who was not even 20 years old when he boarded the convoy – had been affiliated to the resistance group *Combat* since 1941 and had managed to avoid capture until he was arrested by French policemen in February 1944.[61] (See Figure 5)

Whether active in French resistance groups or antifascists in exile in France, the deportees of the Phantom Train had been arrested, tried, interned, shoved, beaten, starved, shamed, and more; but it was only when the Allies were at the door of Western Europe, as they were landing on Normandy beaches and fighting through the hedgerows to liberate the first French towns, that these men and women would experience the most excruciating and terrible part of their persecution. For some it would be the end as they died on that infamous journey of fifty-seven days, while some 160 managed to escape from the grip of death. For most it was the tragic beginning of life – and death – in the Nazi death camps.

It is hard to comprehend why, exactly, the Nazis were interested in transporting hundreds to the camps just as the Allies were making their first inroads into Western Europe. Why not save themselves, when the end was in sight? The answer lies in part in the development of repressive measures in Occupied France. Processes and policies of repression were very different in 1944 from what they had been in 1940 (although this does not mean that there were no continuities). Repression by the German and French authorities got more intense, more brutal, and more relentless as the years of occupation and war wore on. It affected those actively resisting the German authorities as well as the French government but also communists, Jews, Freemasons, foreigners, people trying to escape France, or even civilians held as hostages. Some were tried and sentenced in France; others were deported to Germany; others still were murdered in their homes, on the streets, or in prison courtyards. To be clear, deportation to Germany was never meant as a solace from the French camp system, far from it; it was a way to better control, repress, and murder those who posed the greatest threat to the Reich on racial or political grounds.

An overview of the different policies of repression helps us to understand how, a month after the allied landings in Normandy, a train of 724 deportees – groaning, fighting for breath, begging for water – was wandering across the country, dipping in and out of sight, like a ghost on the broken railways of France. When the Germans initially settled in to occupy France, the main policing authority was the military, with its *Militärbefehlshaber* (MBF). The MBF was in charge primarily of maintaining order in the occupied territory; after all, Hitler could not fight a war on multiple fronts if he had to dispatch excessive manpower all over occupied territories.[62] The MBF thus had units for counter-espionage, military justice, and propaganda, and it centralised information and kept careful reports on the situation in France. However, the idea was to rely on French services as much as possible, and to keep those services under careful watch, not least by the *Feldkommandanturen* (FK) who supervised the territory at prefectural level.[63] Between 1941 and spring 1942 the number of MBF officers dropped by two-thirds – from 100,000 to 35,000 – because the mobilisation of manpower on the Eastern Front was the priority. Still, the Germans adopted a legal policing system with military tribunals set up within the FKs, and arrests more than doubled between 1940 and May 1941.[64] The Sipo-SD, who were linked to the Reich Main Security Offices (RSHA) and specialised in surveillance of Jews, communists, foreigners, Freemasons, and spies, deported French 'spies' or anti-Nazi Germans to Germany. German authorities were exceptionally efficient in infiltrating and dismantling the first resistance groups, not least *Musée de l'Homme* and *Combat* in the Northern Zone. Surveillance and repression were therefore rigorous from the start, and a multi-faceted incarceration system existed from 1940, with people sentenced to prisons or sent to camps in France or Germany (see Figure 6).

Vichy's own aims had overlapped well with those of the occupying forces. Starting in November 1939, a French law had recommended the incarceration of anyone suspected as dangerous for national security. The situation escalated after the Armistice. In 1941 special French police forces were developed to monitor freemasons, Jews, and communists. Special Brigades in Paris were also developed to target communists (BS1) and armed resisters (BS2). These services worked with the Germans, although the French justice, police, and *gendarmes* services would always remain under tight German scrutiny. Vichy was packing people into prisons, to the point that they were overflowing by 1942.[65] Within this, a constellation of internment camps developed across France (see Map 3).

Camps were still used less frequently than prisons, but the evolving incarceration system was an important steppingstone to later policies. In 1941, German camps opened in Compiègne-Royallieu, Drancy, and Romainville. These would later become known as antechambers to Auschwitz. A satellite of camps also emerged in the Free Zone, making clear the extent of French policies of surveillance, repression, persecution, and, of course, collaboration.

For a while, deportation to the Reich remained the exception rather than the rule, but MBF sentences for deportation became more systematic after the invasion of the Soviet Union in June 1941. Deportation was a way to lighten the load of executions being carried out in an otherwise slow judicial process, but also a way to dissuade others from resisting. Even as a preventative measure, though, deportation was not fully effective, and as sabotage and attacks against Germans grew, the authorities cracked down further still. A second wave of deportation policies officially began in March 1942 when the mass deportation of hostages became a common form of repression: the first Jewish convoy to leave France, in March 1942, was not part of the Final Solution, but part of the hostage policies of repression. These waves of deportation were accompanied by a rise in executions, not least in Fort Mont Valérien, located in a west-Paris suburb. Those began in August 1941, and by the end of the occupation over 1,000 executions had been carried out in this fortress.

The real shift took place in June 1942 when the MBF were replaced by the SS who took control of repression in France. Things did not change too much initially, but the Sipo-SD were the ones who would impose policies of arrest, internment, repression, and deportation in the last two years of occupation. The implementation of the Final Solution, of course, was a major component of this. A plan to deport and exterminate European Jews was formalised at the Wannsee Conference in January 1942 and within a few months Adolph Eichmann, the 'architect' of the Final Solution, had decided to begin deportations of Jews from Western Europe to Auschwitz, Sobibor, Treblinka, and other extermination camps. Theodor Dannecker, in charge of Jewish Affairs in France, enthusiastically promised Eichmann he could organise the deportation of 100,000 Jews from France immediately – that is, almost a third of the Jewish population in France at the time. This was a very ambitious figure, and so the offer of René Bousquet, the head of French Police, to help arrest Jews in France had been a welcome one.

The Bousquet-Oberg accord would eventually become one of the most sordid moments of French collaboration, pointing to the willingness of the French state to take part in the arrest, internment, and deportation of the Jewish men, women, and children who had either been born or taken refuge on its soil. It meant that the almost 13,000 Jews who were torn from their homes on the night of 16–17 July 1942 and brought to the Vélodrome d'Hiver had been arrested and interned by (mostly) French gendarmes. Some French policemen warned families about the arrests and told them to flee; others had tears rolling down their cheeks as they helped Jewish families carry their luggage down staircases and into the streets of Paris; others still revelled in their new-found power. But it ultimately meant that after spending days in the squalor of the Vél'd'Hiv, Jews were transferred to Drancy before being deported, for the most part, to Auschwitz.

Even with this French 'help', however, Dannecker's figures had been too ambitious, and they needed more Jews to fill the deportation trains; this is when Laval proposed to deport Jews interned in Vichy's Free Zone to the Occupied Zone where they would then be put in German camps. That whole summer, French police across all of France aided the arrest, internment, and/or transfer of Jews prior to their anticipated deportation to Germany. 'I have just lived through the most tragic hours of my life since the first war,' wrote Raymond-Raoul Lambert, a French Jew who witnessed the mass deportations from the internment camps in the Free Zone to the Occupied Zone. 'They are deporting foreign Jews.' He described the scene in the Les Milles camp, near Marseille, in early August:

> Monday, August 10 is a terrible day, a heartrending spectacle. Buses are taking away seventy children from parents who are to depart that evening. … what a scene, under a blazing sun! We have to hold the fathers and mothers back as the buses leave the

> courtyard. What wailing and tears, what gestures as each poor father, faced with the moment of deportation, caresses the face of a son or daughter as if to imprint it on his fingertips! Mothers are screaming in despair, and the rest of us cannot hold back our own tears. ...[66]

This was one of the darkest moments of France's dark years.

Mass Deportation by Rail

Deportations from France in mass convoys for Jews as well as non-Jews thus began within this time frame when the Sipo-SD came to power, and they would continue until the very end of the occupation. They also coincided with a shift from the German policy of hostages – whereby hostages were taken and executed as retaliation for attacks against Germans – to a policy of deportation – whereby people could be deported to Germany without trial. The hostage policy peaked between August 1941 and October 1942 but it stirred up public opinion too much, and the Germans at this stage were keen to attract workers to go to Germany.[67] So instead they introduced policies of deportation without trial, and between January 1943 and August 1944 almost 40,000 people were deported from the internment camps in Compiègne and Romainville to the Nazi camps. The departure of mass convoys of prisoners coincided with an intensification of targeted arrests and retaliations. In August 1943, Nitti's uncle, the ex-prime minister of Italy Francesco Saviero Nitti, was one of the prominent figures identified as anti-German and pro-resistance and was arrested and interned in Itter.

At this stage, it is important to clarify the involvement of the French state and society in the mass deportations from France, especially since this question was at the heart of public debate in the late-twentieth and early-twenty-first centuries.[68] The question of responsibility of the French National Railway Company (SNCF) and its workers (the *cheminots*) has been especially prominent in the literature on Jewish deportations but also in the case of the Phantom Train. Indeed, immediately after the war French *cheminots* were lionised as resisters, not least through René Clément's award-winning film *La Bataille du Rail* (1946). However, decades later a much darker picture of their role in the war came to light. On the (few) photographs of railway wagons carrying deportees, one can often detect the letters 'S.N.C.F.' carefully painted on the side, just above the infamous '*8 Chevaux – 40 Hommes*', meaning that they could fit in forty men or eight horses. And after all, it was French railway workers who were driving the locomotives: how could they have accepted to carry this out? (See Figure 7)

In total, the railways were mobilised to deport more than 162,000 people from France between 1941 and 1944. This included approximately seventy-eight mass convoys of Jews and thirty mass convoys of non-Jews. By 'mass' convoys we generally mean convoys of several hundred people at once, typically around 1,000 but going up to 2,000, where men and women were crammed aboard. Most mass convoys left from the Paris area and headed east to the German border. SNCF representatives were involved in timetabling deportations from France but were not consulted on anything else: orders always came from above. Railway workers prepared the rail wagons according to specific instructions, and trains were then generally loaded and guarded by German SS or in the Free Zone by French police. Reports make clear that the choice of rail wagons – as well as the straw, pails, or other items – were also ordered by German or French authorities.

While the Germans organised deportations from Occupied France to Germany, it was the French in Vichy who organised all rail transfers to the Free Zone. The French police bureau as well as local prefects planned the details of the operation: Henri Cado, Director of the French Police, issued specific orders to the local prefectures, for example.[69] 'The train will consist of two third-class passenger carriages, and freight wagons that will each contain thirty passengers and two guards. Put hay inside these freight wagons (...) Make sure that each wagon has pitchers, drinking water, toilet buckets.'[70] Only then were the technical services alerted, such as bus and rail companies, and the allocation of food stuffs was also organised for the deportees and their guards. At the border, French railway personnel stepped down and German railwaymen took over; indeed, as a professional rule based on ideas of national sovereignty and security, only French railwaymen could drive trains on the national rail system. The question of billing was heavily debated in the 1990s, for the SNCF were paid for these transports. Putting this into historical perspective, though, is important: the SNCF were paid for every transport requested by the French or German authorities. The only transports free of charge were for charitable causes like transporting Christmas packages to prisoners of war. So while the idea of being paid to deport over 160,000 people from France sounds ethically dubious, the option to offer these transports for free is far from morally acceptable.

What becomes clear from recreating this hierarchy of logistics is that the German and French states were the ones responsible for requesting and organising the trains. Arguing otherwise risks misunderstanding the extent of the state's role in the deportation and murder of millions during the Second World War. Not only that, but the numerous testimonies from within the convoys repeatedly point to the humanity, empathy, and even help of the few *cheminots* who could ever approach the rail wagons, which were always heavily guarded due to the fear of escape. *Cheminots* picked up the letters that deportees would push out from between the boards and sent them off to the written addresses. It goes without saying that these letters were invaluable to their recipients.

The Germans were, in fact, deeply concerned by *cheminots*' assistance in escape attempts. They loosened floorboards and slipped tools into the wagons, or slowed down the trains at specific curves or in wooded areas to facilitate escapes. In one case, a *cheminot* offered to smuggle a Jewish man out of Le Bourget station before he boarded the wagons. German mistrust of French railway workers increased significantly over the months, and more broadly a growing fear of the active resistance – and especially of *maquisards* – changed the nature of the Sipo-SD's repression. The *maquis* swelled over the course of 1943 and 1944, from approximately 25,000 *maquisards* to 100,000 at the Liberation. Although no part of the major resistance movements and networks, they became one of the most important threats to German order and Vichy's policing services. Born outside of the resistance structures which had been put in place since 1940, they developed a powerful mystique which swayed between the communist revolutionary, the romantic fighter, and the terrorist, depending on one's perspective. Today, the memory of the *maquis* is extremely strong in the areas where they had been operating, not least because of the brutal and bloody repressions which they endured, with sometimes entire *maquis* groups surrounded and murdered in the last months of the occupation. In his account Nitti comments on German anxieties about the *maquis*. These informal groups of resisters had an incredibly powerful and penetrative psychological impact on France during those years, and Germans were constantly on the edge not knowing where or when attacks might happen.

French repressive forces also radicalised over the years, culminating in the infamous *Milice*. Joseph Darnand, an extreme collaborationist who had sworn an oath to the Waffen-SS, created the *Milice* in January 1943, a political paramilitary force based on the Nazi model. Men of his kind had been kept at bay in 1940, but in December 1943 he was made head of police. He was minister of the interior in the last weeks of Vichy from 14 June to 19 August 1944, in fact, before fleeing to Sigmaringen along with France's greatest collaborators such as Laval and the writer Louis-Ferdinand Céline. The *Milice* received weapons from the Germans, were generally seen as in their pay, and carried out manhunts of Jews, communists, and resisters across France. They became renowned for their crimes in certain regions, such as in Haute-Savoie in the Alps with the tragedy of the *Maquis des Glières* in March 1944. Léon Werth wrote:

> When the Militia was created, I thought, and the peasants thought, it was a residue of the Legion, a Legion reinforced by policemen and the unemployed who volunteered 'for the bread.' We didn't see the reign of Darnand coming, the militia guiding the Germans or killing people themselves, supplying them with Frenchmen to kill, like presidential gamekeepers flushing game for invited sovereigns.[71]

The *Milice* were central to this eruption of violence in the last months of the occupation.

Landings, Violence, and Liberation

No one knew when, or where, but amidst the daily routines and struggles, the idea that Allies would soon be landing somewhere along France's coast was becoming increasingly hard to ignore. The Allies had been planning a landing in northern France for a long time. On 19 August 1942, Canadian regiments, as well as British regiments and some American and French soldiers, had been sent to land in Dieppe. Operation Jubilee, as it was called, was a resounding failure, with over half of the 6,000 men either killed, captured, or wounded. These losses made it tragically clear that any kind of landing in Western Europe would require formidable resources. The Allied invasion of North Africa a few months later, however, showed that landings could be successful.

A rough idea of Operation Overlord was sketched out at the Casablanca Conference in January 1943. The Allies would need to combine their naval, territorial, and aerial forces to land in north-western France, but where exactly? The Pas-de-Calais region was the closest to the British coast, but it also had the strongest German defences for this very reason. In late June and early July, at a conference in Scotland, the British agreed that the American plan to land in Normandy was best. Two tactical cities were immediately flagged: Cherbourg, with its deep-water port, and Caen, with its network of road and rail communications and its surrounding landscape ideal for air bases. They would need to be taken immediately. The following months involved the careful planning of a multi-faceted attack which required the cooperation of the navy, territorial, and aerial forces of Britain and the United States. The French were not involved in planning the landings, and de Gaulle was only informed of the operation on 4 June, two days before the Allies arrived on French shores (he was not happy about this). Meanwhile, General Eisenhower had been made supreme commander of the Allied armies in December 1943, and would lead one of the most famous military attacks of the twentieth century.

Discussions between the different armies were not always easy as each had its specific objectives, and other strategies were also integrated to make these highly risky landings a success. A misinformation campaign was launched to give the Germans the impression that they were planning to land in Nord-Pas-de-Calais, while a simultaneous Soviet push on the Eastern Front in the summer of 1944 would mean that Hitler was facing a double-fronted attack and could not mobilise resources so easily.

What was certain is that *everything* had to be thrown at these landings, and nothing could be left to chance. As a result, the landings would coincide with an enormous bombing campaign, one which was specifically aimed at immobilising railway networks across France. The BCRA set up a series of coded plans in 1944 to hinder German movement and defence as much as possible: the *plan violet* would target telephone lines; the *plan bleu* the electrical system; the *plan tortue* the roads; and the *plan vert* would target the railways. The latter was linked to the Allied Transportation Plan aimed specifically at railways, a tactic which had been successfully used in the Italian landings and which Eisenhower believed would work well again in France. But there were reasons to have serious reservations about this plan: for one, 80-90 per cent of the railway service would need to be destroyed in order to assure the plan's success. If railway destruction might be good in the short term to prevent German movement, in the long-term it was deeply problematic for the economic reconstruction of France. In any case, the Allies only planned to destroy 30 per cent of the railway infrastructure. Moreover, aerial bombings were inaccurate at best, frequently falling on civilian homes and workplaces. What kind of effect would this have on morale? As historian Olivier Wieviorka has written, the British War Office estimated 80–160,000 victims, half of which would be deaths.[72] Anthony Eden worried that the French population in general, and the railway workers specifically (who were likely to be the most affected by this), would turn against the Allies as bodies piled up and homes fell to the ground. Churchill was deeply concerned by these civilian deaths, but the Transportation Plan was ultimately accepted as a military strategy. The reason was simple: the landings were such an incredibly difficult operation that absolutely all strategies which might aid their success needed to be fully implemented. Almost a quarter of the bombs which fell onto Europe in the Second World War would fall on France; the very large majority of those would fall in 1944 alone, killing over 35,000 people and leaving hundreds of thousands stranded.

The success of Operation Overlord depended heavily on environmental factors. The troops needed enough space and the right weather to allow for a successful landing. Shrouded in total secrecy, the plan was to disembark in France on 1 June, when the tide was right. But bad weather pushed this back by a few days. On 4 June, while thirty-nine divisions waited to be launched across the Channel (men immobilised, waiting, increasingly anxious), Eisenhower was informed that the weather conditions were much worse than planned. Should they call the whole thing off, at least for now?

But morale was delicate and logistics were complicated: in the early hours of 6 June, Eisenhower decided to launch the operation regardless. The consequences of this would be felt: on the journey the wind blew hard, the waves were high, and the men were sick. At the landing, the tide rose far faster than anticipated and men drowned and materials were lost in the deep waters. In the air, 50 per cent of planned flights were cancelled. And still, the landings were an incredible success. The

British landed at Gold and Sword beaches; the Canadians at Juno; the Americans at Utah and Omaha. Omaha saw the highest casualties, but even that landing was surprisingly successful. On 6 June 1944, the Allies broke through the Atlantic Wall.

The Battle of Normandy would prove harder and longer than expected. The news of the landings had spread like wildfire on 6 June and feelings of euphoria and excitement were everywhere. But for a long time the town of Bayeux, taken on 6-7 June 1944, would be the only victory. After a very successful landing and after breaking past the Atlantic Wall with fewer casualties than anticipated, the Allies were suddenly brought to a halt and struggled to seize their major targets, Caen and Cherbourg. Tanks were stuck in the sand, hedgerows made swift action extremely difficult, and the Allies did not manage to uproot the occupier as quickly as they had thought. A stalemate situation emerged, and the hope of liberation began to disappear. 'Let's admit it: we're not happy and filled with joy, as we had hoped,' Léon Werth noted in his diary on 7 June. 'They're in Le Havre and Caen – so near. And for us, everything is just as it was. No more than if they had landed on some Pacific island.'[73] Liberation had seemed within arm's reach, but throughout June and most of July people in France were still wondering when – or even if – liberation would become a reality. Eventually, the Allies seized Cherbourg, and after several gruelling weeks they took Caen, which was only fully liberated on 19 July.

In the meantime, an intense bombing campaign was unleashed on these targets bringing thick clouds of dust, roaring flames, and countless deaths of civilians who had been woken by sounds in the early hours. Paulette Osouf described the bombing of her home in Coutances:

> My younger sister grabbed a hold of Papa's arm and yelled, 'I'm scared! I'm scared!' Papa had just enough time to reply, 'There's nothing to be afraid of. As long as we don't hear whistling, they're not coming our way.' And then we didn't hear a thing-it was finished, the third had our name on it. Three hundred and fifty

> Flying Fortresses bombed for twenty-five minutes, and we didn't hear anything. It's impossible to depict the state we were in. We hadn't fainted and we weren't sleeping, but we were unconscious.

After the bombing, she and her family emerged from the debris of their home: 'We were stunned. We had thought that our house was the only one that had been hit, but there was nothing left around it.'[74] By the end of July 1944, Caen, reduced to rubble with only a third of its population remaining in the city, was beyond recognition. But it was liberated.

If collaborators had been optimistic in June and July, by early August the writing was on the wall: the Germans had to retreat. Vichy's press and radio no longer referred to the imminent failure of the Allied landings but rather the inevitable destruction and devastation these 'liberators' would cause. Operation Dragoon in the south of France was launched in mid-August, once the foothold in the north was secure. The French army, led by General de Lattre de Tassigny, landed in Provence on 15 August and swiftly advanced northwards. Until the end, historian Henri Michel declared, Pétain and Laval refused to bring France into the war, whether on the side of the French or on the side of the Germans. Pétain was forcibly removed by the Germans from his apartments in Vichy on 20 August and, along with a few thousand of the most toxic collaborators, was brought to the Ruritanian castle of Sigmaringen in Germany, where he saw out the end of the war.

These were the highlights of the summer of 1944 in northern France; but to understand the story of Francesco Nitti, and to capture the complexity of the liberation, it is important to reflect on the explosion of violence in the summer of 1944, an explosion which went far beyond the battle front. There were, first and foremost, the bombings: relentless, deafening, terrifying, they had been intensifying since the end of 1943 but were fully unleashed in 1944. A total of 600,000 tons of bombs fell on France during the war, 22 per cent of the total dropped on Europe. In 1944 alone, 503,000 tons fell, causing over 35,000 deaths and thousands more casualties.[75] Bombings in the Paris region in March and April 1944 had been particularly destructive, and Pétain had seized this moment to attend a mass in honour of the victims. The crowds were large, and in this moment of mourning the popular support of the hero of Verdun seemed almost as strong as when he had first risen to power in 1940. After the landings, though, the bombing got worse, with Normandy devastated. A total of 19,000 Normans were killed during the invasion of Normandy, with tens of thousands more losing their homes. The photograph of an elderly woman being helped by an Allied soldier across the debris of Caen offers a glimpse into the despair that engulfed the most vulnerable population during the incessant air raids in northern France (see Figure 8).

The question of how intense the Allied bombing campaign should be had not been an easy one, for everyone knew that the mass destruction of infrastructure and civilian life went hand in hand with military bombing campaigns. Ethical issues aside, there was also the real fear that the Allied bombings would generate popular resentment which could become problematic once the Allied soldiers had landed and were advancing on French territory. After having caused such havoc, the Allies truly did not know what to expect when they landed in France. To what extent would the population resent them?

For many French people, the imminent threat of aerial attack went hand in hand with growing fears of execution and deportation. The camp of Souge, a military base seized by Germans during the occupation due to its key strategic location near Bordeaux, was the second largest execution site in France (after Mont Valérien) with a total of 259 executions. Although it reached a first peak in 1942 with ninety-nine executions, the number was even higher in the January–August period alone in 1944 with 102 executions.[76] Historians who have carefully tried to piece together the executions carried out after a death sentence in German tribunals show a clear linear progression as the war went on, with a sharp rise from February 1944.[77] This matched, of course, the repressive deportations which had become more frequent after the autumn of 1942 but exploded between January and August

1944. But there was the *Milice*, too, who were particularly punitive after the assassination of one of their leaders, Philippe Henriot. On 7 July they organised the assassination of the French politician Georges Mandel, one of the most fervent voices against signing an armistice in June 1940.

The days after the D-Day landings were thus marked by an unprecedented wave of murder and mass killing of resisters and even civilians. In spring 1944, one incident shocked the French and even some Germans: on the evening of 1 April, as the townspeople of Ascq in northern France were going to bed, eighty-six men were dragged in their bedclothes and marched to the railway line where they were executed by an SS Panzer Division.[78]

While this had been initially shocking, after 6 June this kind of reprisal became common policy. In some cases, prisoners were the first targets. On the day of the Allied landings, approximately seventy-five prisoners in Caen were executed, including three women. The handful who were spared remembered how the cells were emptied on that day, one by one, in a chilling and methodical manner.[79] Civilians were also on the receiving end of this violence. On 9 June, in the town of Tulle, around 100 men were executed and about 150 deported. On 12 July, in the town of Dortan, thirty-six villagers were tortured, raped, and executed by German forces. On 9 August, seventeen villagers from Saint-Julien-de-Crempse were executed by the German army. The list of towns goes on, all of them reflecting the explosion of German violence in retaliation for local resistance activity. The worst case of these 'martyred towns', as many would come to be known, was Oradour-sur-Glane, a sleepy village which had never seen a German until that summer. On 10 June, in retaliation for local *maquis* activity and the murder of an SS commander, 642 villagers were killed and the town burnt to the ground. The fact that children were now included in the victims was a striking turning point. Meanwhile, *maquis* groups were targeted specifically, with massacres on the plateaus of the Vercors and Glières in the Alps, where hundreds of *maquisards* had been preparing for action after the landings.

It is within this pattern of escalating violence that we can identify an acceleration in the deportation of French prisoners in the summer of 1944. It seems curious that Germans would bother deporting people en masse from France when the Allies were on their doorstep, but it is important to remember that this was not necessarily the mindset of June 1944. In the initial period after the D-Day landings, messages of German victory were coming loud and clear from Hitler, and the stalemate situation in Normandy for most of June, followed by the slow advance of the Allies in July, in no way suggested a successful Operation Overlord. The Allied commanders themselves were on tenterhooks until mid-July. The collaborationist press in Paris in those weeks only confirmed this picture of German optimism and Allied struggles.[80] The order during this 'optimistic' period was clear: military justice would continue as usual, albeit to a faster drumbeat, and dangerous prisoners would be evacuated to Germany.

By early August the mood was changing and German retreat was now inevitable. Still, the policy of emptying French prisons and camps continued, tightly binding itself to procedures for German evacuation. The most dangerous interns were identified for immediate deportation, but generally it was a somewhat chaotic formation of convoys that emerged as the circumstances allowed for little else, with interns from different prisons merged into single convoys. As the Germans evacuated they left with prisoners who were regrouped in Compiègne or in Paris, or sometimes were driven straight across the German border. On some occasions instead of being deported prisoners were executed on the spot. The historian Thomas Fontaine is clear: despite the messiness of this period, all of these convoys were methodically prepared, and it was only in the very last days, including at the liberation of Paris on 25 August, that spontaneous roundups and deportations took place. [81] The transports were often disrupted by bombardments and sabotage, and with the exception of some prisoners who the Swedish ambassador Raoul Nordling managed to save from deportation, all the convoys made it to Germany.[82] But some prisoners, like Nitti, managed to escape from the moving trains before the border, and would be saved from the concentrationary universe.

That summer of 1944 was a race against time: the quicker the Allies advanced, the sooner towns could be liberated, and the less likely it was that prisoners would be evacuated to Germany.

The liberation was not only a military affair, however: it was also a political one. The French National Liberation Committee (CFLN), created and headed by de Gaulle in Algiers in 1943, had been planning for the post-liberation for a long time. One of its main concerns was to prevent Allied control of France at all costs; they were not the only ones who feared that one occupier might be replaced by another. So one of the most infuriating things for de Gaulle was that as late as spring 1944, President Roosevelt was still refusing to accept that the CFLN would have government authority after the liberation. Churchill did not quite agree with Roosevelt on this matter, believing it would be impossible to side-line France completely from the liberation. However, an alliance with the United States outweighed that with France, and he could not force the situation. When the CFLN was renamed the *Gouvernement Provisoire de la République Française* (GPRF) on 2 June, just days before the landings, Roosevelt was still not acknowledging that the GPRF held any kind of authority. The Allied Supreme Commander was not as stubborn as Roosevelt, and for Eisenhower, de Gaulle was the clear leader of the French military forces, and the connection with the French resistance. Militarily, the French needed to be present, so if de Gaulle insisted that political recognition should come with this, then so be it. On 11 July, Roosevelt finally acknowledged the de facto authority of the GPRF.[83]

The political legitimacy of the GPRF was first made visible on French soil with the arrival of de Gaulle in Bayeux, the first – and for some weeks, the only – city in France liberated by the Allies. It was 14 June, almost four years to the day since he had last stepped foot in metropolitan France. The crowds did not go wild, but the event was symbolic. As towns were liberated, liberation committees popped up to remove the Vichyites and usher in the new government. In the 'red' city of Toulouse, known for its left-leaning politics, Pierre Bertaux was leading the liberation committee. Bertaux was a friend of Nitti, and the leader of the resistance group with whom he had been arrested in 1941.

It was the entry of French troops into Paris which symbolically signalled the end of the occupation, the end of the government in Vichy, and the return of republican order. The Allied armies had no military interest in Paris. As far as they were concerned they needed to seize a major port or industrial hub, not a symbolic capital. Entering Paris also meant having to address the food problem for the civilians there, which risked delaying their own advance.[84] Meanwhile, the Parisians were trying to take things into their own hands. Since the landings, the clandestine press had been urging individuals to take action and to join a mass insurrection.

The city saw a complicated power play between several different organisations. On one hand, the *Comité Parisien de Libération* (CPL) – created in October 1943 and part of both the CNR and the CFLN – had a strong communist slant. It was led by the communist André Tollet, who happened to be the head of the CGT trade union. There was also the CNR, who represented a broad spectrum of movements, parties, and trade unions. The third major player were the French Forces of the Interior under the general command of General Koenig but locally led by Colonel Rol-Tanguy. Made up of the *Organisation de Résistance de l'Armée* (ORA), the *Armée Secrète* (AS), and the *Francs-Tireurs-Partisans* (FTP), its Paris contingent saw the strong presence of communists. The question of the day was this: should the members of these groups begin an insurrection? For Tollet and Rol-Tanguy, the answer was clear: insurrection! But the GPRF saw things differently, and de Gaulle's representative Alexandre Parodi spent his summer trying to contain the threat of insurrection before the arrival of the Allies. Spontaneous action was extremely risky, with the catastrophes in Tulle and Vercors being prime examples. What is more, the importance of this group's lack of weapons could not be overestimated.

Despite the official orders of the GPRF, Parisians were itching to rise. On 14 July, a mass (if passive) demonstration encouraged Rol-Tanguy to think seriously about the insurrectional nature of the people of Paris. But it was a few weeks later, when German retreat was clear, that protests erupted. On 10 August railway workers went on strike, and strikes spread over the following days until 15 August, when the Germans started to disarm the French police and they, too, decided to go on strike. If Parisians seemed ready, this was not the case of the Allied soldiers. On 16 August, Chaban-Delmas received the devastating news that the Americans planned to circumvent Paris. As Parodi still tried to keep things in Paris under control, it seemed increasingly clear that, with or without the Allies, Parisians were rising. On 18 August, hundreds of leaflets signed COLONEL ROL were calling for an insurrection, and on 19 August, resistance groups decided to occupy the *Préfecture de Police*, at the very heart of Paris.

Between 19 and 25 August, two key things happened. First, the Swedish ambassador Raoul Nordling managed to negotiate a truce between the resistance and the Germans. It was initially supposed to only last an hour, but it ended up being extended. This does not mean it was fully accepted by the different factions of the resistance in Paris, though, and beneath this truce lay confusion, refusals, barricades, fires, shootings, and deaths (see Figure 9).

But it was a good sign that Von Choltitz – who had been put in charge of Paris after the SS's attempted assassination of Hitler in late July – was not going to go ahead with his initial orders, which had been to destroy Paris entirely. Second, the Allied command was persuaded to enter Paris. On 23 August, General Leclerc – who had won such great successes in Africa against the Italians and who had promised not to stop until the French flag flew over Strasbourg – and his 2nd DB took off in the direction of Paris. Paris needed to be liberated by French troops, the Allies agreed, and the fact that the 2nd Armoured Division – or *2ème D.B.* as it was known in French – had predominantly white, rather than colonial, soldiers was an important factor.[85]

And so Leclerc's division entered Paris on 25 August and the Germans surrendered. Later that day Charles de Gaulle arrived in Gare Montparnasse and went to the Ministry of War offices and the Police Prefecture before walking to the Hôtel de Ville, signalling a crucial political moment. At the Hôtel de Ville, surrounded by those who had been so instrumental in the insurrection of Paris, he made his famous speech: '*Paris, outragé! Paris, brisé! Paris, martyrisé! Mais Paris libéré!*'. The following day, as de Gaulle walked slowly down the Champs Elysées flanked by his political entourage, the crowds swarmed around the Place de la Concorde after four years of confusion, exhaustion, and longing. Shots were heard during the procession and a flurry of gunfire broke out at the Cathedral of Notre Dame, causing momentary confusion and panic. Yet even this commotion was unable to taint the parade's overwhelming success, and the celebration of liberated Parisians continued (see Figure 10).

What came after the liberation is less photogenic than those celebratory crowds in Paris. First, because of the violence of this period, the French had not unanimously resisted the German occupier, and a proportion of them, albeit small, had been fervent collaborators, either working zealously for the Vichy regime or directly with the Germans in Paris. In a wave of settling of scores, thousands of *Miliciens*, denunciators, and others were illegally shot in side-alleys, fields, and other locations. This savage cleansing, or '*épuration sauvage*' as it was known, affected between 10,000 and 15,000 people, a number which quickly surpassed the 984 death sentences delivered by the French courts.[86] Meanwhile, although exact numbers are extremely difficult if not impossible to obtain, specialists have suggested that approximately 20,000 women had their heads publicly shaven – the '*femmes tondues*' – for having collaborated with the enemy.[87] Photographs abound of these humiliating, public, and brutal exertions of male physical abuse of women, leaving contemporary viewers with a sense of unease and horror.

Second, because of the ongoing struggles of daily life, food remained a big problem and strict rationing continued for years. The French became one of the biggest recipients of humanitarian aid and food relief in those early post-war years. Other elements of daily life also continued to be seriously complicated, not least because the war was not yet over. For months after the liberation of the capital, Parisians could only use electricity for a small portion of the day. Meanwhile the rebuilding of towns bombed to rubble all across France would take years. All of this was compounded by the return – or not – of those who had been sent to Germany to work or been deported to the camps. The shadow of the dark years would continue to hover almost physically over France for several years; the memory of this period would then shape the entire post-war era.

The Stirrings of Memory

The memorialisation of the occupation years was an almost instant creation at both national and local level. Already in the autumn of 1944, survivors of internment and deportation were gathering to create associations, such as the women who created the Association of [Female] Resistance Prisoners (*L'Amicale des Prisonnières de la Résistance*, APR) which became the National Association of [Female] Resistance Deportees and Internees (*Association Nationale des Anciennes Déportées et Internées de la Résistance*, ADIR) the following July, or the National Federation of Deported and Imprisoned Patriots (*Fédération Nationale des Déportés et Internés Patriotes*, FNDIP) founded in October 1945, which later became the National Federation of Deported and Imprisoned Resistance Fighters and Patriots (FNDIRP). On 6 August 1945 Georges Bidault, then the Minister of Foreign Affairs, attended the first commemoration of the massacre of the *maquisards* in the La Luire cave on the Vercors to unveil a memorial plaque. A few years later, in July 1949, students from the elite Paris *École Normale Supérieure* (ENS) visited a school courtyard in the Vercors plateau where sixteen young men had been shot on 25-26 July 1944. Memorials, plaques, and pilgrimages to the sites of executed resisters and *maquisards* were common in this period, and the creation of grand, national memorials was as well: the *Monument national à la Résistance et aux Maquis de France du Mont Mouche* was erected in 1946, the *Mémorial du bois de Gentelle* in the Somme and the *Monument de la Résistance du Champsaur-Valgaudemar in the Hautes-Alpes* in 1947. The memory of Vichy France thus had a physical reality to it in the immediate post-war years, and it held society, culture, and politics in its grip. Whether it was René Clément's award-winning film *La Bataille du Rail* (1946), the medals of the *Ordre de la Libération*, or the communist slogan of the '*Parti des 75,000 martyrs*', the memory of resistance in France was impossible to escape in the late 1940s.

There has been much excellent literature on this topic, and specifically works by Henry Rousso and Laurent Douzou in the late 1990s which give a rich overview of the ebbs and flows of memory in post-war France.[88] They outline well how the memory of resistance dominated for several decades, at least until the late 1960s when, following May 1968, the death of de Gaulle, the hit film *The Sorrow and the Pity* by Marcel Ophuls, and the publication of Robert Paxton's *Old Guard, New Order*, a shift occurred which brought the reality of collaboration to the forefront of Vichy history and memory. This does not mean that the history of resistance disappeared completely, but rather that the memory battles shifted and the history of the resistance was revisited. The full extent of French collaboration, meanwhile, was being thoroughly examined. Former collaborators were brought to trial decades after the events and the extent of collaboration with regard to the Holocaust became more and more evident, and more and more public. In 1995 Jacques Chirac became the first French president to acknowledge the role of the French state in the deportation of 76,000 Jews from France. Since then, the memory battles have not disappeared fully, but they have softened over time, and with the emergence of studies which show life under German occupation as one of nuance, rather than defined by either heroic or ignoble behaviour.

Beneath this story of national memory lie the thousands of stories of individuals whether men, women, or children, who experienced war and occupation. In 1945 and 1946, a record number of personal accounts – 251 and 234 respectively – were published, showing the impulse to write down what people had experienced.[89] Nitti's account forms part of this literary explosion, and serves as an important reminder of the creation and maintenance of memory at grassroots level. But although it caused an initial stir – not least because it was considered a central piece for the trials against Nazi war criminals – the account was soon forgotten. It was only much later, in the late 1980s, that it resurfaced, and with it the story of the deportation train which Nitti had described with such intensity.

Part II

Nitti – A Foreigner in the French Resistance

The narratives that emerged after the Second World War were generally national ones, telling national stories with national actors and generating national memories and identities.[90] These national frameworks of Second World War history have not fully disappeared, but over time the borders of history and memory have become much more porous. The connections between people, structures, and beliefs in this period have become obvious in historical research, not least thanks to first-hand accounts which, like that of Francesco Fausto Nitti, brought to the surface the transnational connections of war-torn Europe.[91] (See Figure 11)

Nitti's account indeed sharpens the transnational picture of the war, showing how the history of Vichy France was not just a French story but one of global currents in the early-to-mid twentieth century. The ideological struggles between communism, fascism, and democracy in this period were tightly woven in everyday lives across France.

By introducing Nitti's life before, during, and after the war, this section thus tells a different story of Vichy France: one where the Spanish Civil War, antifascist exiles, and foreigners come to centre stage. For a long time after the war, the memory of Vichy France focussed mostly on resisters, and particularly on French male resisters. From the late 1960s, however, a cultural shift towards the history of collaboration allowed for new perspectives of resistance to emerge, such as those focussing on the plurality of resisters who included women and foreigners. In the early 1990s, when the *Musée de la Résistance et de la Déportation* in Besançon held an exhibition on foreign resisters, historians argued that these foreigners were not in the 'French resistance' as such, but rather part of 'the resistance in France', an argument Gildea also developed over two decades later.[92] Nitti's account is one of the sources which helps reveal this picture of otherwise anonymous foreigners who made up the resistance in France.

But this section is also an exercise in looking for the silences in history, and for the unspoken and unarchived emotions of the past. This short biographical account of Nitti's life is not exhaustive and there remain many unknowns; but such is the nature of all historical endeavour. After all, history is merely an *attempt* to reconstruct the past as best possible, and is in fact shifting, imperfect, and only partial. This is why it needs to be constantly re-written – but also perhaps what makes writing history such an exciting, creative, and delicate task. In a similar vein, personal accounts – be they diaries, letters, testimonies, memoirs, oral histories – should not be read in the quest of an absolute historical truth, if one were even to exist. They should be approached with sensitivity and generosity, with context and awareness. In doing so they can offer much more than precise details, and can hint at the mentalities, mindsets, and complexities of the past.

Piecing together Nitti's life was not straightforward as there is very little information about him. I started by looking at his own writings, not least his three accounts and recollections of his experiences under Mussolini, in the Spanish Civil War, and in the Second World War.[93] Secondary literature on this period of European history abounds, and reading it helped frame his own experiences within the broader story of the mid-twentieth century. These offered valuable information regarding specific moments and places of his life. Still, getting a sense of who he was remained difficult. However, if he is almost completely unknown today, recreating the network of people who surrounded him made clear that Nitti was part of elite, intellectual, political, antifascist communities in Italy, France, and Spain. The names of friends and family members, from Carlo Rosselli to Jean Cassou, showed his connection to some of the biggest political and intellectual actors of this period and allowed clearer inroads into his life. The memoirs of Jean

Cassou and Pierre Bertaux, the testimony of Louis Vaquer, the story of Silvio Trentin, the private archives of the Toulouse-based resisters Karl Oster and Denise Grosselle, the police and military reports in the French archives, the archives from the Shoah Memorial in Paris, and the memoirs and testimonies of other Phantom Train deportees were invaluable in painting a more intimate picture of this antifascist resister who escaped from a deportation train in 1944. A longer biography of Nitti was later written in Italian, but the desire in this book is to focus on Nitti's wartime experience, and also to get a better sense of his intimate life where we can. The photographs of his wife and sons during the war, published for the first time in this edition, add a truly unique dimension to Nitti's story and help make visible the lives of women and children during the war, voices and faces which are often much harder to get but which offer a different perspective on Nitti.

In reading Nitti's memoir alongside this range of primary sources, other important themes come to the surface, not least those of brotherhood and camaraderie. The intimate worlds he describes are worlds of men fighting, suffering, and talking together, a portrayal of a specific and masculine world in the first half of the twentieth century. For if his book is dedicated to his wife and to the women in the Phantom Train, they remain unnamed and generally unmentioned. This is not to say that women did not matter to Nitti, but as with many writings of this period, the narrative offers a certain performance of masculinity where women are less visible. This is not a criticism, but an important observation to bear in mind.

What is evident is that Nitti cared deeply about the friendships with his comrades in internment, exile, war, and deportation. Interestingly, there is evidence of the reciprocity of this feeling. First, in the generous preface of Jean Cassou, who describes his friend with great affection and admiration. But also in an official typed letter which Pierre Bertaux, then Commissioner of the Republic in Toulouse, sent to Nitti on 16 January 1945 regarding his friend Karl Oster. Beyond the letterhead and formal language, we see a simple line scratched in pen at the bottom: 'P.S. when are you stopping by to see me?' In French, the use of '*tu*', the informal 'you', signals their intimate relationship as well as Bertaux's desire to meet. In his account Nitti repeatedly lists the names of people who are completely unknown to us but who mattered to him in 1944, when he did not know their fates on that train. It is still difficult to know Nitti's full story, but this section highlights some of these bonds with people both known and unknown, with mostly men but also with some women, not least his wife.

Early Life

Francesco Fausto Nitti was born on 2 September 1899 in Pisa, Italy. He grew up in a close-knit family where Protestantism and liberalism were deeply entwined and where a fervent commitment to liberty was matched by an abhorrence of violence. His father, Vincenzo Nitti (1871-1957), was a pastor of the Italian Episcopal Methodist Church and held important positions in charitable organisations and the Church. His mother, Paola Ciari (1870-1932), who Nitti described as 'an angel in our house', raised her five children. Her own family had been among the first Protestants to arrive in Florence, and they had practised their devotion to God and to liberty in the shadow of the Grand Duke of Tuscany, who often persecuted this network of Protestant families. Regardless of living in a predominantly Catholic country and of the dangers this entailed, his ancestors had continued to live and act out their beliefs, a theme which is evident in Nitti's own life. On his father's side, Nitti's great-grandfather and namesake, Francesco Nitti, had been a renowned physician and surgeon. When he was sentenced to death by the Bourbons in the nineteenth century, he apparently 'faced his executioners with the cry: "Long Live Liberty!"'[94] Many of the men in his family fought for Italian independence, one of whom became a leader in the war of independence, the *Risorgimento*. Nitti himself became a soldier during the First World War. When Italy entered the conflict in May 1915, Nitti, only 15 years old, could not just stand by: '[t]he ideals which had formed my character impelled me to embrace the cause of the Powers who were fighting for liberty and justice.' At the age of 17 he enrolled in the army. Nitti's early years were thus shaped by the Christian values which Vincenzo and Paola practised so passionately, and by a love of democracy which ran through the generations of his family.

For the Nittis, the looming spectre of fascism after the First World War was thus an absolute tragedy. The rise of the Italian fascist dictator Benito Mussolini was swift and terrifying, with his March on Rome in 1922 marking the beginning of his authoritarian rule until his deposition in 1943. By initially promising land and the abolition of the army, Mussolini had attracted a lot of support; but his enthusiasm for violence soon set a very different tone. 'There were affrays all over the country and atrocious crimes were committed by the Fascists, who burned down newspaper offices, plundered private dwellings, and beat up and killed their political opponents,' Nitti recalled.[95] The atmosphere of violence not only horrified him but also impacted him personally. Nitti's uncle, Francesco Saviero Nitti, had become Italy's premier in June 1919 after the war, but he stepped down a year later in June 1920 as he failed to get majority support in his government. In 1922, Mussolini's fascist thugs ransacked his home and made several assassination attempts on him and his family. Like many antifascist Italians, Saviero fled to France to live in exile where he continued his passionate commitment to democracy in exile. His writings were translated into French, English, and German: in 1927, the English translation of his book *Bolshevism, Fascism and Democracy* (New York: The Macmillan Company, 1927) was described as a 'red-hot book' for vehemently denouncing fascism and critiquing bolshevism. An important theme in the politics of both uncle and nephew was that their enthusiasm for socialism was matched by their rejection of communism as well as fascism, these totalitarian systems which transformed the political spectrum of the interwar years and the twentieth century more generally.

As fascism was rising in Italy in the early 1920s, Nitti was studying law at the University of Rome and working in a bank to earn money. In his spare time he read the works of great Italian liberals of the *Risorgimento* such as Giuseppe Mazzini, the republican socio-democrat who had led the Italian revolutionary movement, or Alessandro Manzoni, the poet who embraced Liberal Catholicism and whose work was pivotal in the unification of Italy. He was part of '*Giovane Italia*', a student clandestine group who rejected fascism. But it was the assassination of the socialist politician Giacomo Matteotti in June 1924 that had a major impact on Nitti's life. Earlier in May, Matteotti had accused the fascist government of electoral fraud in the recent election and denounced the violence of their tactics. Days later, he was kidnapped and stabbed to death by the secret police. Matteotti's assassination shocked Italian society at large, and Nitti was especially affected after he met his widow, Velia Matteotti. He admired Velia and described her as 'a highly cultured woman, with great nobility of character'. On the second anniversary of Matteotti's death, in June 1926, he went to her house to drop off some flowers in homage.[96] It was then that he was approached by a detective who wanted to know more about him and his visit – after all, the Matteottis had been deemed enemies of Mussolini, and all those around them were thus labelled as potentially dangerous.

From that point onwards Nitti noticed that he was under intense surveillance, although he naively thought that the police would get tired of him. Yet on the morning of 2 December 1926, he was awakened by loud knocks on his door. When he opened it, four men were standing there, telling him to get dressed and go with them: 'When we stepped out into the street all was still, silent and deserted,' he recalled. 'I had no idea of what was awaiting me, but when I crossed the threshold of that house in which I had spent so many happy years I had a distinct feeling that I would not see it again.'[97] His instinct would be correct. Nitti was interned for several weeks in the Regina Coeli prison before he was informed that he had been sentenced to five years in a convict colony for subversive acts against the state. 'Can you inform me why I have been sentenced to five years' deportation without having been examined?' he asked the warder who had handed him the notification.

The warder shrugged: 'The law provides for no examination,' he answered.[98] At the time Mussolini had the power to arrest and intern all those suspected of challenging the state without any evidence. Fellow prisoners informed Nitti that one of the charges against him had been that he had held a far too 'scheduled' – routine, predictable, somewhat boring – life for a young man his age, 'with neither a wife nor a mistress' (although I believe he had already met his future wife, Ada, by this point). He was presumed to be a Freemason.[99] Someone later suggested that Nitti was deported not so much because of his own involvement in a secret antifascist society, or even his links to the Matteotti widow, but because of his connection to his uncle Saviero, 'one of the men most hated by Mussolini'.[100] Regardless of the reason, Nitti's first experience of deportation was about to begin.

Mussolini's Prisoner

During his time in power Mussolini deported criminal and political convicts to a string of islands between Sicily and Africa, convict colonies which were rife with poverty and where political prisoners lived under the constant surveillance of Fascist guards. This is where Nitti was destined to go, and he arrived on the small, rocky island of Lampedusa in handcuffs. During his deportation by rail and then boat Nitti had been chained to other inmates, sharing stories with them during their difficult journey. In Lampedusa they were housed in a barrack and lived a life of military precision. They were near a poor, desolate village where a few hundred common criminals lived and worked 'in a nauseous atmosphere of vice and moral degeneration'.[101] Relations with these men were difficult: drinking, brawls, and threats were daily rituals. Yet among the other prisoners Nitti developed strong alliances and friendships. They cooked together, cleaned, and set up a small theatre troupe to pass the time. In the evenings, they would read, write, and talk by the light of oil lamps before sleeping on the straw mattresses on iron beds. They could not, however, fully escape the violence of their guards. Nitti described Lieutenant Veronica, the man in charge, as a 'madman' with 'symptoms of persecution mania'. Guards rained blows on interns they believed to be conspiring, and one of them trampled and kicked an unconscious prisoner 'like an infuriated beast'.[102]

When the political convict colony of Lampedusa was shut down in February 1927, prisoners were sent to other islands in the Mediterranean Sea.[103] After more handcuffs, more chains, and days in an infested prisoner boat, Nitti arrived on the green, rich island of Lipari, near Sicily; renowned for its treacherous winds, it was, at least briefly, a relief from the arid scenes of Lampedusa. Five hundred convicts and their families lived on Lipari at the time, staying either in the communal barracks or, for those with a bit of money, in rooms or homes they rented from local inhabitants. The rents were exorbitant, as was food, and many of the political convicts had barely any money to their name. Some would bring their wives and children over, and they would live huddled together in basements with no air, light, or water. Nitti managed to live with his friend Umberto Pagani and his family, where he had a single room and some bookshelves.[104] New political convicts arrived on an almost daily basis: some were well known in political circles, some were even old friends. A network emerged around Nitti, a community of men who had fallen victim to Mussolini's repression for reasons both real and fabricated, symptomatic of the paranoid authoritarian regime which dominated Italy in those interwar decades.

The picture one gets of Nitti was that he was regarded as an intelligent, charismatic, and optimistic man well liked by his fellow prisoners; but towards the end of 1927, even he began to feel burdened by his circumstances. Nitti's usual intellectual pursuits such as studying, writing, reading, or teaching others, were no longer enough to sustain morale, and he became weary and anxious. It was around this time that he began to dream of escaping, and that he met Emilio Lussu (1890-1975) and Carlo Rosselli (1899-1937), who had recently arrived on the island.[105] Lussu was a Sardinian man of great principles with a glowing military record; Rosselli was from a family of wealthy Italian patriots and had distinguished himself during the First World War. Both were ardent antifascists and had spent many months in Mussolini's prisons before landing on this hellish island.

When Lussu and Rosselli met in Lipari in January 1928 they quickly realised they both wanted to escape. Nitti, so frustrated by this point, confided in them, and together they hatched a plan in absolute secrecy to escape the island by boat with the help of friends from the outside. After months of careful and patient preparation, this somewhat peculiar trio – 'the "modernist Jew" Rosselli, the lapsed Catholic Lussu, and the Methodist Nitti'– decided to escape in the summer of 1929.[106] Their first attempt failed, leaving Nitti 'gloomier than ever'. Yet soon they prepared a second attempt, successful this time: on 27 July 1929 they slid through the shadows past the guards, slipped into the water and swam swiftly and quietly to small boats off the coast. Hearts pounding, exhausted by their incredible feat, they watched the island disappear out of sight. When they caught sight of free land, '[t]he tiny band of prisoners threw discipline and discretion to the winds and gave themselves up to unbridled rejoicing over their hard-won freedom'.[107] They soon landed on the shores of southern France and made their way to the capital.

Fighting Fascism in France

When they arrived in Paris in early August, Rosselli, Lussu, and Nitti were the talk of the town. Nitti was reunited with his uncle, Saviero, and attended the many receptions organised in honour of their epic escape.[108] Everyone was fascinated by what they had endured: until then, no one had ever successfully escaped from one of Mussolini's convict colonies. Met with this enthusiastic welcome, Nitti set to writing about his conviction and escape. Indeed, one of the things that had concerned him on the convict islands was that the world did not know about the full extent of the violence and repression inherent to Mussolini's fascist state: '[E]ven America seldom hears the truth about Italy,' he had remarked.[109] Now was his chance to expose the violence of fascism. Nitti published his first book, *Escape*, in 1930, with the American editor G.P. Putnam who had offices in New York and London. The book was soon making a stir and the publisher received letters – presumably from fascist groups – threatening to bomb their New York office if they went through with the publication.[110] But G.P. Putnam went ahead with it and the book acquired an international, antifascist audience. Correspondence in 1932 shows that Nitti was very excited about translating the book into other languages, for his book was not just an escape story but a call to arms against fascism. '(E)ven if the Italian revolution comes in the summer, the book will have its effect! he wrote in October 1932. When it came out in French it was described as a vital publication shedding light on the horrors of fascism.[111] It was only in 1946, after the fall of Mussolini and the end of the Second World War, that the book was translated into Italian.

Nitti and his friends immediately folded into the Italian antifascist circles in Paris. At the time, Italians were the largest foreign community in France. There had been a steady stream of economic migration from Italy since the nineteenth century, but after the First World War the demand for foreign workers in France had grown even higher. A treaty set up under Saviero Nitti facilitated economic emigration as of 1921 and from the 1920s waves of Italian immigrants came to France, their numbers growing from approximately 400,000 in 1911 to 800,000 in 1931. If one were to add all of the unofficial migration as well, the number could easily be over 1 million. But if Italian migration was originally rooted in economic reasons, the rise of Mussolini triggered waves of political migration, not least to Paris. The French capital thus became a haven for Italian political exiles, known as the *fuoruscitti*.

Among the major political personalities to arrive in 1926–27 were Nitti's uncle, Saviero; Sandro Pertini, future president of Italy; and Pietro Nenni, national secretary of the Italian Socialist Party (PSI). They were generally well integrated into French social and political life, not least through common political interests on the left. The French Communist Party (PCF) created Italian language groups and edited the Italian newspaper *Riscossa*. Radical socialists in south-west France were welcoming to Italian political refugees, while French and Italian Leagues of Human Rights worked together on a number of projects. Unsurprisingly, Paris was described as the 'capital of Italian antifascism in exile' during the interwar years.[112]

In 1929, Nitti, Rosselli, and Lussu joined with a few others to found the non-Marxist antifascist group *Giustizia e Libertà*. The group was based around democratic, republican, and socialist principles; crucially, it was fundamentally transnational. Indeed, Rosselli believed that any kind of action had to be taken at an international level: only an antifascist Europe could properly respond to fascist transnationalism.[113] A major antifascist campaign had been launched in France in 1926, with international congresses of socialists and communists in Marseille and Lyon. This continued to develop over the course of the 1930s as authoritarian and fascist regimes sprang up all over Europe, and as political exiles from Russia, Germany, Spain, and Italy flocked to France to escape political repression and religious persecution.[114] Within this transnational, antifascist web, *Giustizia e Libertà* became the only non-communist group to build considerable influence both in Italy (clandestinely) and abroad.[115]

At *Giustizia e Libertà* Nitti had been in charge of developing rapports with other European and extra-European antifascist groups, as well as coordinating press and propaganda, and other general organisation. He was on a list of people suspected of terrorist activity but also acknowledged as someone '*très doué et capable*'. Aside from being involved in the movement, Nitti was a journalist for various papers including *Monde Latino* and *La Libertà* published in Paris, as well as the London papers *New Times*, *Review of Reviews*, and *New York World*. He also developed networks through the League of Human Rights and freemason circles. But over the years Nitti distanced himself from the movement. He was not the only one: some believed the movement was becoming too radical; others did not think it was radical enough. Criticisms, especially from the communists, painted it as a movement of bourgeois liberals disconnected from the masses.

The natural course of Nitti's own life also changed. If 1930 had been especially busy with the publication of *Escape* and the development of his political activities, it had also seen the arrival of his partner, Ada Ameriga d'Angelo, whom he had met through the Matteotti circles before his deportation. A passionate socialist, Ada, as she was known, was determined to join him in exile in France. After overcoming many hurdles, she arrived in France and they married soon after. They welcomed their first son, Vincenzo, on 4 November 1931 and their second, Josef, on 12 July 1934. With a growing family, Nitti needed to find a job. He began to work in an insurance company in Paris and was less able to get involved in *Giustizia e Libertà*. Many internal debates within the movement meant that not everyone agreed on the ways it should develop, and it is possible that Nitti's family obligations coincided with rising tensions within the movement. In 1933 he was offered a job managing a bookshop in the Dordogne, *Librairie Française*, and the family moved to Périgueux.[116] All seemed calm, at least for a while.

Political Divisions in 1930s France

The movement experienced a considerable blow when Rosselli and his younger brother, Nello, were murdered by the far-right French extremist group *Cagoule* in early June 1937. A crowd of 150,000 people attended the ceremony of their funeral, including Saviero. 'Before the remains of Carlo Rosselli, its beloved leader, and of Nello Rosselli, who was his true brother in the flesh, in faith, and in death,' they wrote, '*Giustizia e Libertà* lowers its mourning banner in an anguish equal to its profound indignation, to its will to continue the battle, which becomes all the more arduous as it is more elevated and sacred.'[117] The press coverage was intense in the following days, and the daily *Paris-Soir* reprinted extracts of their daring escape, taken from Nitti's account.[118] The assassination was not seen as just an Italian affair but had struck at the heart of European liberalism. While the murder of Matteotti in the 1920s had 'signalled the death of liberty in Italy', the murder of the Rosselli brothers 'signal[ed] the death of liberty in Europe'.[119] (See Figure 12)

The murder of the Rosselli brothers in 1937 revealed large cracks in the image of France as defender of liberalism, haven from virulent antisemitism, and heart of the European fight against fascism. As the spectres of authoritarianism and fascism swept across Europe, France had remained a republic throughout the 1920s and 1930s. Not only that, but while countries were closing their borders in the 1930s, France was a refuge for migrants across Europe, a home to political and religious groups escaping the extremism of communism, fascism, and Nazism.

This was not without consequence, however, and the arrival of foreigners combined with economic pressures led to spikes of extremism and violence. Already in the 1920s, the French Minister of the Interior, Albert Sarraut, was carefully watching the movements of all foreigners in France and keeping a particularly vigilant eye on Italian political emigrés in case they should stir up trouble. Sarraut had primarily wanted to avoid any sign of public disorder, but he had also wanted to ensure good relations with Italy, for antifascist demonstrations in France could potentially strain relations with Mussolini.[120] As a foreigner entangled in politics and *Giustizia e Libertà*, it was not such a surprise that the French police had Nitti under observation when he was in exile in France.

Anxieties about immigrants exploded after the Great Depression, however, which was felt later but for longer in France. During a period of economic difficulty and unemployment, the arrival of immigrants generated a rise of xenophobia and antisemitism which helped usher in the racist policies of the late 1930s and early 1940s. Right-wing extremist groups such as *Action Française* and *Cagoule* emerged, and although they never became mainstream, their impact on politics was deeply felt from the early 1930s onwards. On 6 February 1934, groups of far-right leagues held a violent demonstration outside the National Assembly, leading some to believe they had attempted a coup. The murder of the Rosselli brothers in 1937 was thus an important reminder that France was not immune to the transnational influence of fascist violence.

Indeed, if France remained a republic, tensions between the left and the right became omnipresent in French political life. The far-right fervour seemed to be calmed when the Popular Front coalition of the left-wing parties came to power between 1936 and 1938 under the leadership of the Jewish socialist Léon Blum. But if a huge popular movement had driven their rise to power, internal divisions between the different parties would soon allow cracks to appear within the coalition itself, exacerbating the tensions with political groups across the spectrum and ushering in an era of conservatism and toxic nationalism. After Blum was replaced by Édouard Daladier in 1938, and as Europe inched its way towards war, the government became even more wary of foreigners. Under the Daladier government in 1938, Sarraut would call for action against foreign 'undesirables', and laws on denaturalisation of French citizens and the opening the first detention camps for foreigners in France would mark a tragic change in policy.

Spain, Retirada, and Internment

The political tensions between democracy, fascism, and communism across Europe exploded in 1936 when the Spanish Civil War broke out. In July 1936 the Spanish army, led by General Franco, attempted a coup against the Republican government. Although not initially successful, a coalition of the military, conservative, traditionalist, and nationalist elements of Spanish society would spend the next two and a half years fighting the republicans. From the onset, France and Britain officially insisted that they would not get involved in this regional conflict. However, it was soon evident that conflict in Spain was anything but neutral: Portugal, Italy, and Germany openly supplied weapons to the Nationalists; thousands of antifascists from Europe and North America joined the Republicans in Spain; official non-interventionist claims by countries such as France were highly criticised and even circumvented. Even humanitarian aid had clear political contours.

The war in Spain absorbed those fighting fascism across Europe, not least Nitti and Rosselli. From the very beginning, Italians flocked to the International Brigades, specifically towards the Garibaldi Battalion. Jews, antifascists, and communists from all over also joined. Rosselli immediately became one of the leaders encouraging Italians to join, and along with Camillo Bernero and Mario Angeloni founded the *Colonna Italiana*. '*Oggi in Spagna, domani in Italia*'; today in Spain, tomorrow in Italy, he declared, marking himself as a leading antifascist in Europe and the greatest opponent of Mussolini. In November 1936, with the blessing of his wife and family, Nitti also joined the fight in Spain.[121] Over the next couple of years Nitti would join and lead different battalions, fighting in Sietamo in March 1937, before going to Codos, Lérida, and Ebro.[122] In his memoir of this period, *Il maggiore è un rosso*, written after the Second World War, Nitti recalled the deep fraternal links between the population and the soldiers. '[T]he Spanish had come to love and admire these brothers of faraway lands,' he wrote, and these brothers had been 'ready to offer limbs and life for the freedom of Spain'.[123]

By late 1938, as Franco's forces gained more and more ground, the situation had become irreversible and the republican government ordered foreign fighters to leave. It had a devastating effect on morale, Nitti recalled.

> All Spanish people … had come to know these foreign comrades and had loved those young blond-and-blue-eyed youths who came from colder lands, the brown and skinny Italians so similar to them, and the Portuguese and Argentinians, and the robust dockers from Flemish ports, who had all rushed into conflict

> and war and suffering and sacrifice alongside their Spanish comrades.[124]

While this extract romanticises the picture of republican and international fighters and does not capture the multi-faceted and more complicated relationships which were in play, there was more than a kernel of truth in this picture of international brotherhood and transnational camaraderie.

When Barcelona finally fell on 26 January 1939 the long retreat to France – the *Retirada* – began. In early 1939, almost half a million refugees from the Spanish Civil War arrived in France. Aside from the fact that this fuelled feelings of xenophobia, the French had been hit by a gargantuan housing problem for these refugees. Camps began to pop up all over south-west France, some set up in military sites or prisons, others made up from almost nothing. As the events of the late 1930s and early 1940s unfolded, many of these camps would be transformed into mass internment camps for foreigners and Jews. But already between February and July 1939 the hygiene conditions were appalling, and around 15,000 died in those refugee 'camps', generally of dysentery.[125]

Such was the case of the camp in Argelès-sur-Mer, where Nitti first arrived on his retreat from Spain.[126] It was a makeshift camp hurriedly set up on the beach *des Pins* in February 1939 to house Spanish refugees (see Figure 13).

The mayor of the town had never even been informed that a camp was going to be erected on his beach: one morning in late January, men from the *gardes mobiles* arrived and started to build a camp. 'Build', however, might have been overstating things: '… just a fence of barbed wire guarded by mobile guards to prevent refugees from spreading into nature. No sleeping facilities, no commodities. We welcomed the miserable straw which was ridiculously insufficient. The spectacle of these unfortunate people fighting for a fistful of straw was painful to watch and did not show much promise for the future.'[127] Over 100,000 refugees passed through Argelès-sur-Mer between February and June 1939: soldiers, International Brigades, and civilians. The 'Internationals', as they were called, organised themselves according to nationality and political affiliations. There were 540 Italians, over 100 of whom were identified as anarchists and were being carefully watched by the French police.

It is in these miserable conditions that Nitti recognised an old friend, Silvio Trentin. Trentin was an Italian antifascist lawyer and intellectual originally from Venice who had been living in France in exile since the twenties. In 1935 he set up a small bookshop in Toulouse, the *Librairie du Languedoc*, which became an antifascist hub from its inception, frequented by Rosselli, Pietro Nenni, André Malraux, Antoine de Saint-Exupéry, Emilio Lussu, and more (see Figure 14).

This is where Nitti and Trentin had met, as they both frequented these Italian antifascist circles tied to *Giustizia e Libertà*. In 1939, faced with the tragedy of the Republican collapse and the fate of so many refugees, Trentin had decided to go to one of the camps to offer his help. He had brought along his good friend Pierre Bertaux, a politically engaged academic and regular visitor at Trentin's bookshop. In his memoir, Bertaux recalled that one of the refugees in Argelès had instantly recognised Trentin: 'It was Francesco Fausto Nitti, nephew of President Nitti, who we were able to reach quite quickly,' he wrote. '[Nitti] would later play a role in our resistance network.'[128] (See Figure 15)

Indeed, the Second World War and the German occupation were around the corner and, as we will go on to see, the transnational antifascist networks which had been growing in France in the 1920s and 1930s would continue to exist and even thrive in the climate of underground resistance to the Nazis.

The French authorities in 1939 were highly suspicious of these new arrivals, and particularly of those who were politically engaged, such as Nitti. So after experiencing the deplorable conditions of Argelès, Nitti was sent to a disciplinary camp in the Château de Collioure in the spring of 1939.[129] Why, exactly, was he not simply released to return to his wife and sons? As mentioned above, the French authorities felt completely overwhelmed by this huge body of foreigners who seemed like an opaque mass of potentially dangerous political radicals. Keeping them in prisons, camps, and centres allowed the state to monitor them and keep things under control; indeed under Édouard Daladier – who had taken over from Léon Blum as prime minister after the collapse of the Popular Front in April 1938 – the French government became more and more authoritarian and xenophobic. With war looming, the control of foreigners was tightening.

We know nothing of Nitti's time in Collioure, but the prison was known for its horrible conditions. An old fortress, it had thick, cold, damp walls. The prisoners were put in cells – 'the darkest, coldest, least hygienic' – where there were 'no books; no papers; no news; no light'.[130] Prisoners slept huddled against each other to get a little warmth. They would do forced labour for twelve hours a day, the brutality of their Senegalese guards hovered over them, and hunger was a constant, oppressing concern. The conditions in those camps and the prisons of refugees from Spain outraged both those inside them and outside. A journalist from *L'Humanité* led an *Association pour la défense des séquestrés de Collioure*, and the prison became a major point of criticism from the Kominterm.[131] During his time there, Nitti's wife, Ada, was writing to Pietro Nenni, the Italian socialist also in exile, asking for someone to help her and her husband, 'Franz' as she called him.[132] Nitti was finally released from Collioure in August 1939, on the eve of another global conflict.

War and Resistance in Toulouse

Hitler invaded Poland on 1 September 1939, just days after signing a Nazi–Soviet pact with Russia. As Britain and France declared war against Germany over the next few days, the Second World War had officially begun. If this was a call to arms to all French people, what exactly did it mean for the foreigners who lived there, not least the Germans, Italians, Russians, and communists who were now on the enemy side? For Italians, it initially did not mean too much. At the time there were approximately 750,000 Italians living in France.[133] But at this point, Mussolini had not yet declared war on France. With news of war, some Italians returned to their home country, but thousands stayed, many volunteering to fight, such as Trentin (although he was turned down).

It was only when Mussolini declared war on France on 10 June that Italians were put in a precarious situation. Strict internment measures were swiftly put into place by the French government and popular opinion towards Italians generally took a sharp turn against them. This was short-lived, since fifteen days later an armistice was signed first with Germany and subsequently with Italy, but the results of these accords were also complicated for Italians. An Italian army of occupation was positioned in south-east France, and one of the terms of the Italian armistice was that antifascist Italians in exile in France had to be sent back. Many Italian emigrés were thus handed over by French authorities to the Italian government, who then interned them immediately.[134] Some managed to stay in France, escaping the surveillance nets and living in full or partial clandestinity. Others were sent to camps, often with other foreign antifascists.[135] Others still resisted.

The literature on Italians in the resistance is slim, but it so happened that one of the celebrated Italian resisters was Nitti's friend, Silvio Trentin.[136] A veteran of the First World War and university professor in law, Trentin had left Italy in 1926 when he refused to follow the fascist ideology which was now imposed on academics.[137] He discovered working-class life in France, initially as a farmer, preferring to settle in the rural south rather than Paris. More than anything, though, he was highly politically engaged. Rosselli had been a reference point of antifascism in Paris, but Trentin and his bookshop in Rue Languedoc were a landmark of Toulouse. Ada, Nitti's wife, remembered it as an intellectual and political epicentre where they regularly gathered: socialists, Christian democrats, intellectuals, young people, all would meet there to discuss the future of liberalism in Europe. During the occupation the *Librairie* would become a 'true home', wrote Bertaux, 'the only place where the flame [of democracy] still lived, faint but inextinguishable'.[138] Nitti's uncle Saviero had also been a regular in the Trentin household.

During the occupation, Trentin's bookshop became the hub of the first resistance group in Toulouse, the *Réseau Bertaux*. Pierre Bertaux, born into an academic family in Lyon in 1907, was a successful professor of German at the time. He had written a thesis on Hölderlin after his military service, and in his long stays in Germany for his research he witnessed first-hand the rise of national socialism. Back in France, he had continued working on his thesis but also entered politics with a brief political career in the Ministry of Education and Art before stepping down and continuing as a professor. With his German language skills, Bertaux became an interpreter and radio host in 1940 when he was called up to the front. After the defeat, he returned to Toulouse and was one of the first resisters to refuse to lay down arms. Together with his friend Trentin, Bertaux established radio contact with London and developed a resistance network. The *Réseau Bertaux* was thus born around a cluster of a few friends who met at the *Librairie du Languedoc*: Jean Cassou, who dealt with propaganda; Marcel Vanhove, in charge of information; Jean-Maurice Hermann, in charge of recruitment; Louis Vaquer in charge of escape routes; and Nitti, who focussed on action.[139] They were primarily concerned with relaying information to and from de Gaulle, the Free French, and the Allies, but in addition to creating information networks between France and London, they released propaganda and helped people cross into the Pyrenees. Their group was the first to organise parachute drops into the Free Zone.[140]

Beyond the *Librairie* on Rue Languedoc, resistance was bubbling throughout the city. From Maurice Jacquier, who set up the *Réseau Gallia*, which filtered information to London, to Ariane Scriabine-Fiksman and David Knut, who created the Jewish Army, or *Armée Juive*, in 1943, which eventually became the Jewish Combat Organisation (OJC), dozens felt compelled to act. Because of its geographical location, Toulouse lent itself well to escape routes and international networks, and several networks, including those run by the British spymaster Colonel Buckmaster and Pat O'Leary, were very active in the area. Marie-Louise Dissard was the only woman to lead one of these local networks, helping Allied airmen return to Britain. Resistance intensified over the course of the war and the risks were higher than ever. Albert Lautmann, a professor who Nitti befriended in the Phantom Train, started a local *maquis* in January 1944 before his arrest in May. Fiksman and Knut also encouraged many young Jews to join the *Maquis de la Montagne Noire,* one of the major *maquis* in the region which became a principal target for the Germans in summer 1944. Other local figures included Marcel Langer, leader of the 35th Brigade FTP/MOI of whom several members were deported alongside Nitti and Lautmann. Throughout the occupation Toulouse was thus a hive of activity for intelligence services, escape routes, and resistance activities more widely, with the *Réseau Bertaux* at the very origins of this.

Unfortunately, the successes of the *Réseau Bertaux* were short-lived: in December 1941, the members of *Réseau Bertaux* were arrested.[141] Nitti, Bertaux, Cassou, Vaquer, Vanhove, and others were initially held all together. In an interview from the seventies, Bertaux recalled the peculiar atmosphere of those early days of arrest where they were repeatedly told that they would never leave the prison alive and where nonetheless they sang songs of victory which rang out in the corridors – only half believing them.[142] After his trial on 31 July 1942, Nitti was sent to the military prison in Toulouse with Cassou before being transferred to Lodève prison on 19 August. Bertaux was condemned to three years, Cassou and Nitti to one. In November they were sent to Mauzac, another military prison, until the end of their sentence on 12 May 1943.[143] After their release Cassou was able to return to Toulouse; as a foreigner, Nitti would not be released so easily.

After the arrest of his friends Trentin established a new resistance group with Achille Auban, *Libérer et Féderer,* still based in the *Librairie du Languedoc.*[144] It consisted mostly of young socialists and some Freemasons who lived in the Haute-Garonne and who shared an ideological and political agenda. Beyond their concerns about the war and occupation, they had a vision of a post-war world, where federal structures could be developed to create a United States of Europe. Charles d'Aragon recalled meeting there with Cassou, Friedmann, and Jules Moch : 'At Trentin's, we entered an organisation which has since been long-forgotten but which managed to survive until the end of the war.'[145] The bookshop helped them form a resistance hub in Toulouse.[146] After the fall of Mussolini, Trentin returned to Italy to organise resistance on his home territory, but *Libérer et Féderer* would continue in Toulouse. Tragically, he was arrested in Italy and died before the end of the war due to ill health. The legacy he left in Toulouse, however, was to endure much longer. Trentin and his shop were landmarks in the town's history of antifascism and resistance. Today, a blue plaque on the site of the old bookshop explains its role during the Second World War, and one of the streets in Toulouse bears Trentin's name.

The stories of Nitti and Trentin make clear that resistance in Vichy France was part of broader currents of activism and defiance across Europe. Trentin's bookshop had embodied the continuity in all of this, explained Bertaux, 'Italian fascism, the war in Ethiopia, the war in Spain, Munich, the battle of 1940, maréchalisme under Pétain'.[147] Their stories shed light on the active role of foreigners in the resistance, who took on a number of roles within networks and organisations and who sacrificed their freedom and lives. It was a type of integration, too, as they melted into French resistance networks and were woven into the counter-currents of French society.[148] Italians were especially present in the *Francs-Tireurs-Partisans Main d'Oeuvre Immigrée*, the FTP-MOI, although few studies have explored this in depth.[149] Nitti's account helps retrieve many of these nameless and anonymous foreigners from the shadows.

Internment in Le Vernet Camp

Nitti and Ada were supposed to be reunited on 12 May 1943, when he and Cassou were released from prison, but as their wives were waiting outside to greet them, the two men were immediately arrested and sent to Saint-Sulpice prison.[150] Cassou was soon released, but Nitti, considered a dangerous foreigner, was transferred to Le Vernet on 3 July 1943. Ada would not see her husband again for many more months. Again, we know barely anything about Nitti's own experience during his time there, but some exceptional photographs of Ada and her sons during this period have recently surfaced. There is generally little information about Ada, but we catch fragments of her story in official and private archives. She was politically engaged, from the Matteotti circles to Trentin's Toulouse bookshop, and like so many wives of antifascist exiles was entangled in the intellectual life of the various political and resistance networks. She was also a devoted partner, following Nitti into exile, encouraging him to join the cause in Spain, visiting him in prison and camps, and pleading with Nenni to try to get him released.

While Nitti was detained in Mauzac and then Le Vernet, Ada was in Toulouse with her sons, and friendships became crucial in this period to support their small family. They had become excellent friends with Karl Oster and Denise Grosselle: he, a German anti-Nazi who had escaped to Switzerland in 1933 and joined the Spanish Republican Army in 1936; she, a devout, Catholic Frenchwoman born in Toulouse who worked in a watch-making shop on Place St Pierre. After the *Retirada,* Karl, like Nitti, was interned in France's southern camps, first Argelès-sur-Mer and then briefly in Gurs. He then managed to get work in Toulouse, met Denise on a tram, and fell in love. They, too, were resisters, and the couple developed a strong friendship with the Nittis. When 'Fausto', as they called him, was arrested, Karl and Denise helped support Ada and her sons. For aside from the emotional pain of separation, the hardships of daily life were exacerbated, not least in regard to the lack of money, which was a recurring problem for a single mother of two young boys. Photographs of Karl, Denise, Ada, and the boys give unprecedented insight into the intimate lives of the Nittis.[151] (See Figures 16 and 17)

Political and ideological networks were crucial for intellectual and resistance purposes, but on a personal and practical level they were also vital for emotional and material support. The risk of imprisonment was higher for foreigners, and alternative communities needed to build tight webs to allow individuals and families to survive the hardships of occupation. For years after the war, Ada and Denise would remain friends and continue to correspond.

Nitti spent a year in Le Vernet, and although we know barely anything of his own experience there, much has been written on the camp to allow us to imagine what life was like for him. Le Vernet was part of those networks of camps – many of them located in the south-west, near Toulouse – which became central sites of Vichy's surveillance and repression during the occupation (see Figure 18).

Over the decades these camps were used for multiple things, from receiving colonial troops or prisoners in 1918, to Spanish refugees in 1939 and later Jews and foreigners in the Second World War. The sites came to have long histories of detention, surveillance, and repression. After the defeat of France in June 1940, most Spanish refugees were evacuated and from mid-October Le Vernet was used to intern foreigners identified as 'dangerous' or 'extremist' by the government. It is at this point that the camp became a site of not only internment but also repression of these foreigners who, like Nitti, were deemed to be threats to national security.

Le Vernet stood out among neighbouring camps such as Gurs, Argelès, Rivesaltes, or Les Milles. First, because of its varied body of inmates with fifty-eight nationalities in the camp. Moreover, while all camps adopted a disciplinarian routine, the atmosphere was different in Le Vernet because its inmates were labelled as extremists.[152] By 1941, a clear distinction had been made between French 'hospital-camps' (Noé, Récébédou); emigration centres (Les Milles); internment camps (Argelès-sur-Mer, Rivesaltes, Gurs) and concentration camps (Le Vernet for men, Rieucros for women).[153] In October 1941 it was believed that in order to maintain order among this 'heterogeneous mass of undesirables', the camp directors had to create an atmosphere which combined a certain amount of support for the internees – communication, some support for frustrated or depressed interns, listening to complaints – with high levels of surveillance. Because these were 'dangerous' foreigners, maintaining order was the most important thing of all, and the surveillance system in Le Vernet was especially complex. Individual punishments were issued in combination with collective ones, and it was common to use the many different political factions against each other.[154]

With its combination of foreigners and political 'radicals', Le Vernet came to be known as the 'capital of European intellectual resistance'. A memorial to its victims in the local cemetery honours the 'antifascist fighters, known and unknown', who died for the people. It was the heart of European antifascism, with its string of anarchists, communists, or socialists who had roles in French as much as European resistance. A group of Italian anarchists was particularly well organised in Le Vernet, releasing a review, *Res Nova,* while there, and communists abounded to the point it was dubbed a Mini-Komintern. The camp also had a cultural pulse, often animated with public lectures or theatre performances produced in unique circumstances. Interns included many famous doctors, economists, authors, poets, or artists from Hungary (Arthur Koestler), Spain (Max Aub), and especially Germany (Rudolph Leonhard).

From Lipari to *Guistizia e Libertà*; from the Spanish Civil War to Trentin's bookshop in Toulouse; from the *Réseau Bertaux* to Le Vernet: Nitti's life articulates the wider story of this European, intellectual, antifascist elite.[155] It is a reminder of how Vichy's camps for foreigners acted as a link between the antifascist, anti-Franco struggles beyond France, and those struggles within France, against the occupier but also Vichy. Many, like Nitti, had started as antifascists or republicans in the war against Franco and would, after periods of internment and escape, take part in France's specific resistance and liberation struggles.[156] The photograph of Jakob Insel with his comrades in the Spanish Civil

War helps us visualise this link as he also became a resister during the occupation and was one of the deportees in the Phantom Train in 1944 (see Figure 19).

During the last couple of years of occupation – exactly when Nitti was in Le Vernet – a decrease in personnel and inmates across French internment camps was visible.[157] By the spring of 1944, there were only 8,800 people interned in French camps generally. This was not because conditions were easier, far from it; it was because more and more internees were being deported en masse to Germany after 1942. Over 4,600 internees were deported from Le Vernet between February 1941 and June 1944. Almost 2,000 left as forced (or possibly voluntary) workers and headed for Germany or the Channel Isles, and about 100 were repatriated to Italy at Mussolini's request. Unsurprisingly the latter were immediately interned in the fascist prisons there. Five convoys totalling 859 Jews were sent to Nazi extermination camps; 745 political prisoners were sent to Vichy's camps in Algeria; and 3 convoys totalling 833 people left for Nazi concentration camps. Among these three convoys were the last 403 prisoners in Le Vernet, who were deported on 3 July 1944: this was Nitti's Phantom Train.

The Phantom Train, 3 July to 28 August 1944

Throughout July and August the Phantom Train transported 724 people including 84 (11.6 per cent) women. The deportees from Le Vernet, Saint-Michel, and Fort du Hâ were an eclectic mix of twenty-four different nationalities, and only 40 per cent of them were French. Indeed, the majority were foreigners, especially from Spain (251) and Italy (71). During the transport about 160 (22 per cent) managed to escape, although some died in doing so and others were caught later on and deported once more. There are about 100 deportees for whom there is no information, but approximately 450 arrived in Dachau on the night of 28 August 1944. The Dachau concentration camp, just north of Munich, had been a concentration camp for political prisoners since March 1933 as part of the vast camp network established by the Nazis in the 1930s and 1940s, and had dozens of satellite camps around it. Over 200,000 people passed through Dachau, and more than 40,000 died there.[158] The women on the Phantom Train were sent three days later to Ravensbrück, while many of the men would later be sent to Mauthausen and its underground factories nearby: Melk, Gusen, and Ebensee. Only half (225) would return from deportation.

Amidst these mass deportations to Germany, Nitti's deportation train was exceptional in two ways. First, because of its timing after the Normandy landings and during the last weeks of occupation. Nitti was baffled when, on 2 July 1944, he climbed aboard a '40×8' cattle wagon in Raynal goods yard in Toulouse, barely four weeks after the Allies had landed on the Normandy beaches. It all seemed so irrational: '[W]hen the Allies had established a foothold on the European mainland and the whole transport system needed to be turned over to the German war effort, how could it be deemed a priority to move or deport us?' he asked.[159] Indeed, why was the train organised just as the Allies were arriving? Why would the Germans not simply flee themselves? Why were they bothering to deport hundreds and thousands of prisoners? One of the reasons Germans were deporting internees after the landings in Normandy was because Allied victory was still uncertain. After the initial success of the landings themselves, the American, British, and Canadian soldiers had taken weeks to liberate local towns and, crucially, the deep-port city of Cherbourg. Their second main target, Caen, was still under German control in early July. Even if the landings had dramatically changed things in early June, there was still no guarantee, at this stage, that the Allies would be victorious. Indeed if anything the German policy of repression escalated after the landings. Nitti had noticed this, and he identified their German escorts as a special SS Police Division commanded by First Lieutenant Schuster, an Austrian, and Second Lieutenant Weibel.

The second reason which made the Phantom Train exceptional was, of course, that it took almost two months to arrive in Dachau, becoming by far the longest deportation rail journey from France, and possibly throughout Europe. All camp survivor memoirs and testimonies mention the horrific conditions of their rail journeys to the camps, which, coming from France, typically took three days. There was no room to move, and there was barely any air to breathe. Smells, fluids, and voices mixed; those trapped inside were overwhelmed, humiliated, asphyxiated. In proportion to the time spent in camps the train journey was very brief and this tends to be mirrored in the space allocated to the train journey in individual memories. But its systematic presence in the camp narrative also speaks to its powerful impact on the bodies and minds of internees. Only a handful of memoirs are devoted to or framed by the deportation journey, such as Jorge Semprún's *The Cattle Truck*, the story of the 'Train of Death', another exceptional convoy which left Compiègne on 2 July 1944 and where 530 of its 2,162 deportees died during the three-day voyage to Dachau.[160] But the Phantom Train's journey took a much longer time and seems to have left a more pronounced mark on deportees' lives. Why, though, did it take so long?

The main reason for its extended and twisted journey across France was because of the Allied landings on 6 June 1944, which triggered a new phase in the war. Just a few days after the landings on the Normandy beaches, the Germans took control of Le Vernet camp as part of their plans to intensify repression. Jehan d'Armancourt, the camp director, was transferred due to his lack of cooperation and the prefect of Ariège received letters to get ready to evacuate the camp.[161] The most able prisoners were sent to forced labour, but the rest – the 403 detainees described as old, the sick, or the 'highly dangerous' – were to be sent to Germany. Nitti, of course, was among them. He managed to see Ada and his two sons one last time before the 403 were taken to the Caffarelli barracks in Toulouse on 30 June. There, the Le Vernet detainees were joined by 150 detainees from Saint-Michel prison. They were imagining every possible scenario at this stage; nothing, though, could have allowed them to believe for a moment that they would be on this train for almost two months.

On 2 July 1944, the 653 prisoners were ordered to board the train, but it was only on 3 July that the train set off. The journey was complicated from the start, and Nitti recalls its 'mysterious shunting manoeuvres' from the day it left Toulouse.[162]

It seems that he had some luggage with him, which included a small map that he used to try and figure out the routes. He also seems to have had a small notebook where he kept brief notes (which later helped with his account).[163] The train initially headed towards Bordeaux, leading many inside to believe it was going to Paris. The Germans probably had the intention of bringing the internees to Compiègne, 80 km north of Paris, as was the rule. But the train never made it far past Bordeaux and would, in fact, never get anywhere near Paris: bombardments and sabotages were constantly disrupting railway lines and the Germans were forced to skirt around the centre of France to avoid aerial attacks, sabotages, and military manoeuvres linked to the Allied landings. The detainees tried to track the direction but were constantly confused by the halts and changing of orientation.

The train initially inched its way towards Angoulême, over 100 km north from Bordeaux, with the intention of heading to Paris, but it soon came to a standstill. There, Nitti experienced one of the major traumatic moments of his journey: the bombing of Parcoul-Médillac on 4 July 1944. Those next to the ventilation openings caught glimpses of the planes, but it was the sounds of the planes, and the vibrations of the bombings, which were most terrifying.[164] The immobility was agonising: Nitti had been bombed before, in Spain, but he had had the freedom to run and hide. Here, as the planes circled above the train, the men were trapped inside, like 'sitting duck[s] waiting for the fatal bullet'. It was a 'deadly game', he explained. On 5 July, they were still there: there were no more actual bombings, but they could hear the planes coming. The Germans abandoned the convoy once more as they ran to hide in the vicinity. Meanwhile, the internees were left all day without water in the July heat, with wagons tightly sealed. They arrived in Angoulême on 8 July. 'I'll never forget the sight that greeted us!' wrote Nitti. 'The station had been completely destroyed. Once it got lighter, what we discovered were heaps of mangled locomotives and smashed wagons. Torn-up rails pointed their skeletal arms skywards. The buildings had been reduced to empty shells.'[165] The Germans decided to redirect the train back to Bordeaux, where they arrived on 9 July. By this point the 653 detainees had been trapped in the rail wagons for almost a week.

The train parked near the Bordeaux locomotive depot for three days, from 9 to 11 July. In the very early hours of 12 July, the wagons were opened and, in the darkness, the detainees were led to the Grand Synagogue in the city centre.

As Nitti entered the Temple, he paused to notice the magnificently carved doors; the 'white marble steps'; the pillars which 'bore the weight of the gallery above'. Nitti carefully recorded the extent German destruction: he counted how many branches have been broken from the menorah; the marble plaques 'which a hammer had smashed'; the 'magnificent organ' now 'out of commission'.[166] Nitti's father had been a pastor and he himself had been brought up in religious tradition and deep spirituality; seeing a sacred site destroyed like this would have weighed on him heavily. We can read in his description the full weight of Nazi antisemitism, which was interested not only in destroying the Jewish race, as he puts it, but in desecrating their entire culture. This sacred space had not only been destroyed physically but also spiritually, as it now served a very different purpose. Even portable toilets had been brought in.

The Jewish temple would become their prison for four weeks (see Figures 20 and 21). The prisoners initially welcomed the change: 'compared to what we have experienced as the train wandered on,' wrote Christian de Roquemaurel, a resister who had been detained at Saint-Michel, 'we were finally going to live in luxury'.[167] Nitti also welcomed this change of scene, at least in the very beginning: 'For the first time in ten days and nights,' he wrote, 'I was at last able to stretch my legs out fully.'[168] There were chess games and the Bible was shared around. Nitti immersed himself in the Gospels and the Acts of the Apostles.[169] A kind of community was set up, with exchanges of news – the thirst for news could never be quenched, and rumours circulated endlessly – but also goods through a black market. Yet their renewed optimism and faith in victory would soon wear thin. The suffocating heat of the cattle wagons had been replaced by a lice-infested prison, and they suffered terribly from hunger. Parcels from the Quakers and the Red Cross were all that kept them from starvation. Nitti dedicated three of the eight chapters of his account to this period in Bordeaux, capturing a unique moment of internment, intimacy, and tragedy.

Despite some optimism, brutality was everywhere in the synagogue. When a handful of detainees attempted an escape by hiding under some benches, they were tortured by their SS guards, made to stand motionless for hours.[170] More tragically still, ten comrades were taken away as hostages after German guards suspected some of trying to escape. Nitti's recollection of the departure of these men – among whom was the charismatic and wise Albert Lautmann and the young Meyer Rosner, barely 18 years old – is one of the most powerful testaments of the agonising entanglement of tragedy and brotherhood during the war: 'We watched them leave. They passed among us, shaking and gripping the sea of hands held out to them. They hugged and embraced those comrades they'd become particularly close to. I watched Lautmann cross to the door, walking fast and looking calm and almost serene.'[171] Nitti would later find out that they had all been taken to Souge camp, where they were executed on 1 August.

On 9 August, Nitti and his comrades left the synagogue and retraced their steps to the Bordeaux railway goods yard, once again in darkness. The ordeal of the Phantom Train was far from over and the determination of the Germans to bring detainees to Germany seemed limitless. And now, their convoy had grown: seventy-one detainees from the Fort du Hâ prison were added as they left Bordeaux. The direction was no longer north, that route was now impossible. The new plan was to head straight for Germany via southern France. The train took the direction of Toulouse again, heading east through the suffocating heat of southern France. It was these Fort du Hâ prisoners who would launch the first wave of escapes on 10 August. At first they were a handful, and many were not ready to take that leap of faith. That day Jean Barel escaped from his wagon; his father and brother, who chose not to follow him on, stayed on the train and would die in deportation. Lorenzo Barel, 48, died in Dachau on Christmas Day in 1944; Lino, 23, would die a few days later, on New Year's Day 1945, in Mathausen where he had been transferred.

On 12 or 13 August the train was stopped in Remoulins. 'This little corner of Provence is quite ugly,' one deportee would recall, but it was the heat which was completely unbearable.[172] The train was immobilised for days; a doctor, Léon Cigarroa, died inside his wagon; two other prisoners, however, managed to escape. The doors were occasionally opened to let detainees get some air; food was distributed, not least through the heroic efforts of Marie Damiani, who mobilised the Red Cross to help the prisoners. The constant roaring of the planes above would have continued to terrify those trapped inside, while news of the landings on 15 August – this time de Gaulle's Free French troops – in Provence would have brought in a whiff of hope.

The train left Remoulins on 17 August only to stop again the next day: 18 August would become one of the most memorable days of the journey for all included. The railways were so badly damaged in this region that the Germans had no other choice but to disembark the prisoners and walk them to another station where they could restart their journey. This was called a 'transbordement', and it was here that Nitti and the 750 others walked all day, about 17 km, from Châteauneuf-du-Pape to Sorgues. 'We walk through Château Neuf du Pape, the population is alarmed to see this strange procession. … And it is so hot.'[173] Men and women trudged forward weighed down by exhaustion, heat, and thirst. The Germans barked and hit them at any sign of potential disruption or escape. Locals watched, confused about who these people were, what they had done, where they had come from, and where they were going. Some were horrified and managed to approach the ghost-like shadows with small things to eat or drink, and some even helped a few escape. It was an agonising walk which marked both the detainees and the local community, and an annual commemoration of the march through Sorgues is held there each year under the leadership of the *Amicale.* At the end of the march on 18 August 1944, the detainees boarded another train.

The following day, 19 August, was marked by Allied bombings in Pierrelatte-Montélimar, causing some more escapes but also deaths in the wagons. The captives were better organised this time, however, quickly making tricolour 'flags' made up of scraps of jumpers, scarves, and shirts, which signalled to the pilots above that this was a prisoner train. The bombers took note and flew away, but fellow deportees had already died in another wagon, while others would die more slowly from their injuries over the next hours (see Figure 22).

Escape, 25 August 1944

By 22 August, over eighty prisoners had escaped from the Phantom Train. Escaping from a wagon was not so simple, and there are far fewer escape attempts than one would imagine.[174] There were several reasons for this. First, because Germans were on high alert and did everything to prevent escapes. Wagons were preferred to third-class passenger carriages precisely because they were easier for surveillance purposes, but a large number of German sentinels were still used to constantly survey the convoy. The SS carried out regular and intense searches to prevent prisoners from bringing tools into the wagons. Second, the threat of violence was constantly used. This is evident in testimonies from other mass convoys of this period. Germans regularly told deportees that entire wagons or even convoys would be shot if anyone even attempted an escape.[175] Most deportees did not question the seriousness of these threats, but testimonies reveal that these threats did not dissuade everyone. In Jorge Semprún's wagon, for instance, several young men, one of whom had belonged to an underground resistance unit, had smuggled tools with plans to escape: 'You have to hand it to them,' one deportee remarked. 'Sneaking those tools through all the searches, you really have to hand it to them.'

But sneaking in weapons to facilitate an escape did not necessarily mean they would be used. Indeed, debates over escaping were rife in the wagons as any escape would risk the lives of others. In Semprún's wagon, the call for escape was met with 'a chorus of protests', followed by an 'endless' discussion about German reprisals and orphaned children:

> The Germans would discover the attempted escape and take reprisals. And besides, even if the escape were to succeed, not everyone would be able to get away; those left behind would be shot. There were quavering voices that begged, for the love of God, not to try anything so crazy. There were tremulous voices that spoke to us of their children, their beautiful children who would be left orphans.[176]

Again, this is a common theme in testimonies of other deportation journeys: Louis Maury, who was deported on 14 July 1944 to Neuengamme, remembered how discussions of escape plans in his train ended in fights and anger.[177] When Annie Guéhenno voiced her intention to escape, some of the other women in her wagon forced her into the middle of it so that she would not attempt anything.[178] They were not wrong to be cautious: reprisals for escape attempts were swift, horrific, and particularly humiliating. Deportees were forced to undress, sometimes made to go into different wagons, other times to parade, completely naked, before local civilians.[179] At other times still, they were simply shot.[180] Ultimately in Semprún's wagon the escape failed to materialise. Men from another wagon had launched their own escape plan first, but the immediate repercussions – bursts of machine-gun fire, searchlights, deportees clubbed and forced to remove shoes – meant that those in Semprún's wagon had to ditch their tools.[181]

Debates about escape were also rife in the Phantom Train, especially at the beginning of the journey. Already in the synagogue, the small group of five who had tried to escape had been denounced by another prisoner. But back in the wagons, under the burning sun, Christian de Roquemaurel and Jacques Silberfeld became focussed on escape. But if some others joined them, others in the wagon were vehemently opposed, and tensions broke out: 'the communist majority spoke in a single voice and announced, after what was surely a democratic motion, that no one would escape from the wagon due to the risks that this would put on those who stayed behind.'[182]

But the length of the journey meant there were more opportunities for escape in the Phantom Train. Moreover, the successful escape of one detainee, Ange Alvarez – a communist resister of Spanish origin in the FTP who had been imprisoned in Saint-Michel – set the tone from very early on. On the very first day, he slipped through the skylight as the train rolled on. But it was really after Bordeaux that the Fort du Hâ prisoners started to attempt escape en masse; after all, they had not witnessed the repercussions of the escape attempt in the synagogue. A surge in escapes began on 18 August as the convoy walked through Sorgues. Being outdoors meant that some felt they could take their chances, and the help of some locals was equally important. Dozens more would then escape from inside the train before it reached the German border (see Graph 1).

Nitti was constantly thinking about escape, not least when walking through Sorgues, but he only raised it seriously on 24 August when their emaciated bodies had become barely recognisable and the descent into madness had firmly begun in the convoy. Not only that, but the proximity of the German border presented a new imperative: if there was any sliver of hope of escape, it had to be done in France. The German border was a cut-off point for all deportees from France: in another convoy the Jewish deportee César Chamay knew that any escape attempt needed to happen before Metz, which is very close to the German border, otherwise he would be in an unknown country, with a hostile population, no reference points, and no language skills. The chances of survival would have been close to none. Chamay managed to break the window bars and slip out before the border.[183] For Nitti, his thirst had also reached desperation by 24 August. When the train stopped because a railway line needed to be repaired after a visit from the *maquis*, the guards had refused to give them water. The thirst, which drove them close to insanity, also pushed those in Nitti's wagon to 'get to work' thinking of a final escape plan. If escape could be impromptu outside, such as when they were marching through Sorgues, from inside a moving train it needed very careful planning and was generally a collective endeavour.

If escape plans could, as explained above, create tensions among those inside the wagons, this was not the case in Nitti's wagon. Between 23 and 25 August, there were no debates at all, even as those who wanted to escape were cutting at the floorboards. The quasi comatic state of the severely dehydrated and emaciated men meant that many no longer cared enough either to escape or to face German repercussion. 'Most were simply too exhausted, physically and mentally,' Nitti recalled. 'Such an adventure was beyond them; they were resigned to whatever fate awaited them. Some were hardly even capable of responding to our invitation; their only answer was to bow their heads and murmur their good wishes.'[184] The process was highly organised, with precise discussions of how and when they should slip through the boards and lower themselves onto the tracks. In the wagon of de Roquemaurel the week earlier, the ex-railway worker Barrière had been able to describe exactly how they should ease themselves down to avoid injury or even death. The escapees were all given a number so that there was no confusion about who would escape when.

The tools of escape may have seemed random – scissors, knives, a nail file, and short iron bar – but each one had its use. The sound was relentless all night as they scratched away at the wooden floorboards. The prisoners also needed to dress for escape. They had stripped themselves almost naked from the very beginning of the journey but were now layering up again: shoes, hats, jumpers. Nitti even wore his tie.[185] They needed all the padding they could get, and then everything needed to be tucked into trousers and socks so that there could be no flailing garments. Urine became a valuable lubricant: in some wagons they urinated to soften the floorboards as they tried to cut through them; in another car one prisoner urinated on his jumper so he could stretch and slide between the window bars more easily.[186] After the escape, the plan was to walk in the opposite direction to the train, meet up nearby, and head to join the *maquis*.

Nitti remembered every detail of the moments before his escape: the sugar lump from a fellow deportee named Hyla; the incline of the train; the two comrades who held him up. Below them, 'the noise was deafening'. And then it was his turn. He squeezed through the gap; swiftly, he dropped onto the track, lying face down. There was pain in his knees, but he stayed completely still, as if paralysed by the 'thundering noise' of the train just inches above him. His arms were stuck to his side; his face was flat on the ground, probably digging deep into it. He first realised he was free by the feeling and smell of the country air. Everything about his first moments of escape was a contrast with the cramped and suffocating conditions of the convoy: the smell of the air, the immensity of the night. The 'sombre rumble' of the Phantom Train continued to sound across the sleeping land. It is with these words that Nitti ends his account.

Life After the Phantom Train

As Nitti watched the train light disappear into the darkness, he needed to focus on finding a safe place to hide. The deportees who had escaped from the train now had to rely on the local population to survive. Although the details of what happened are difficult to obtain, it seems that Nitti rested in the hermitage of Cuves in the Haute-Marne department before joining the group 'Charles', also known as the *maquis* de Varennes, on 28 August.[187] He was involved in the group's operations until the Allies arrived on 15 September, meaning he would have undoubtedly been involved in the attack on a train they carried out on 1 September, when twelve members of the group were killed. He returned to Toulouse after this, recuperating with his family and friends after years of separation and internment.

Nitti was immediately involved in building the scaffolding of post-war memory that began in the winter of 1944: commemorations, medals, awards, honours, ceremonies, associations, memoirs, testimonies, trials, publications, and institutions helped create a thriving commemorative landscape. Although no one knew what had happened to the deportees of the Phantom Train at this stage, a commemoration was held in Toulouse in the autumn of 1944 honouring the ten men – including Albert Lautmann – who had been taken from the Bordeaux synagogue and executed in Souge (see Figure 23).

It is possible that Nitti was in attendance, but what is clear is that on 1-2 December he and fellow Phantom Train deportees Jean de Pablo and Enrique Mauri y Forns founded the Amicale of Political Internees of the Vernet Camp (*Amicale des Anciens Internés Politiques du Camp du Vernet*), the association at the root of the Vernet camp memorial. Nitti began to write his deportation account shortly after that, probably in the autumn of 1944, for the earliest copy of the book is dated 1944. He published it with his old friend and fellow resister Louis Vaquer, who ran the small publishing house Éditions Chantal.[188] Another early copy was dated March 1945, again with Éditions Chantal, but unfortunately the records currently give us little more information about the context of the book's production and initial reception.

Across France there was also a desire to bring to justice German war criminals. On 1 February 1947 a newspaper article describing the 'tragic odyssey' of the Phantom Train asked for any witnesses who had seen the train and its guards to come forward: the 8th mobile brigade of war criminal services in Toulouse was looking for evidence to bring those in charge of the convoy to trial.[189] Around this time, the crimes of First Lieutenant Schuster and Second Lieutenant Weibel, who had commanded the escort, were brought to the attention of the Ministry of Interior. The extract from Nitti's book recording the agonising walk from Châteauneuf-du-Pape to Sorgues was considered as evidence:

> some of these deportees, of whom the most robust had to carry German packages, were brutalised, hit by the Germans escorting them when they tried to drink water or eat some grapes. It appears several deportees died of exhaustion during this journey or were killed by their escorts when they could no longer walk. Some may have even shot at civilians and at the deportees trying to escape. No food was distributed on that day.[190]

Locals were approached by the French gendarmerie in September 1946 to ask if they recalled anything, and while all remembered the infamous column of ghost-like figures who had walked through their town, most declared that they had not witnessed any actual violence between the deportees and their guards: 'I did not see that the deportees were victims of maltreatment', said railway worker Auguste D., 52 years old. 'Most of these men and women seemed exhausted, and their guards were rough,' another said, but 'I did not see the guards maltreat them, and I did not hear of any deaths amongst them.'[191] Such testimonies gathered in the late 1940s are in stark contrast to the testimonies of witnesses in the *Amicale du Train Fantôme*, showing the partiality of archival research, the elusive nature of memory and truth, and the opaque processes of gathering evidence and interviewing witnesses.[192] Still, they reveal a version of something which happened. Some witnesses, however, were more explicit, not least the wood merchant recruited to drive the invalids in his truck: 'One of the men I transported could no longer walk and had many wounds on his face. From what I understood he had just been subjected to bad treatment from his jailers and was in a lamentable state.' In 1947, the enquiry found that no one had died on the day and does not seem to have gone any further. Procedures against SS Friedrich-Wilhelm Dohse and Bachezr were later begun in the

Bordeaux military tribunal regarding the detention of the prisoners in the Bordeaux synagogue.[193] Dohse was eventually condemned in 1953.

Nitti and his family returned to Rome soon after the end of the war. He immediately became involved in politics there, keen to rebuild his country from the ruins of fascism and war (see Figure 24).

Nitti was put in charge of the returning 800,000 Italian deportees, became head of the National Association of Italian Resisters (ANPI), and was a municipal councillor in Rome. He also continued to write, not least his memoir of the Spanish Civil War *Il Maggiore è un Rosso* in 1953, and received the French resistance medal, the *médaille de la résistance.* Nitti continued to hold positions in the Italian government and within the Socialist Party until his death in May 1974, and during this time his connections to France also continued. In the early seventies he was still President of Honour of the *Amicale* of the Vernet camp, and his son, Joseph, would be president of the *Amicale du Train Fantôme* for a while.

It was only after his death that Nitti's account resurfaced and became a central component of the memory of the Phantom Train. Robert Silve, a resident of Sorgues, had been haunted by this story since childhood, and his parents remembered seeing the 700 ghost-like figures trudge through their small town. Robert had got hold of the 1944 edition soon after the war and although he had lost the book over time, he repeatedly discussed it with his wife, Edith. Finally, in 1987, he went to the *mediathèque* in nearby Avignon to look for the book. When it finally arrived thanks to a cross-library loan from Bordeaux, Robert realised he could not check it out to bring it home, so he and Edith decided to copy the entire book by hand. For a while they went to the *mediathèque* once a week, spending several hours transcribing the text before going home. Meanwhile, Jeannine Teissier had also spent years hearing about these prisoners, who her husband, Charles, had seen walk through Sorgues. In the late 1980s the two couples, who had known each other for many years, met over drinks only to realise that both Robert and Charles had been haunted by this same convoy of prisoners they had seen walk through Sorgues along the National 7 road, as it was then known. They joined forces and a chance encounter with Antoine Cayuela revealed that the train had ended up in Dachau.[194] Robert, Charles, and others – Jean and Jacqueline Simon, Jacqueline Nertz, and Max Bertrand – began to investigate the history of the convoy. They traced the list of names through the *Amicale* of Dachau and pieced together the whole trajectory of the Phantom Train through Toulouse, Bordeaux, Sorgues, and finally Dachau. They collected seventy-eight testimonies and published these in 1991 with *Études Sorguaises*, offering an exceptional range of sources and information which finally allowed for this mystery of the Phantom Train to emerge.[195]

The Phantom Train Association, or *Amicale du Train Fantôme*, was born in 1991, the same year that they inaugurated a memorial to the deportees outside the Sorgues train station (see Figure 25).

A series of books, and eventually documentaries, would piece together the incredible story of the longest-lasting journey of a deportation train to cross France, and the French writer Guy Scarpetta wrote a novel about his grandfather who was on the train.[196] The legacy of Nitti's account is well known among the circles of the *Amicale*. 'It's thanks to Nitti that the *Amicale* was born,' Jean-Daniel Simonet told me over lunch in Paris in November 2023.[197] We were in a typical brasserie, a stone's throw from the Rue de Rivoli and the Place de la Concorde. Jean-Daniel, son of Jacques Simonet and president of this *Amicale*, was sitting to my right. To my left were Hugues de Roquemaurel, son of Christian de Rocquemaurel, and then Corinne Brillié, daughter of Jacques Silberfeld. Their fathers were the resisters from Saint-Michel prison who escaped from the moving train shortly before Nitti. Across from her and next to Jean-Daniel was Guy Scarpetta, grandson of Guido Scarpetta. It seemed that their presence here was owed, in some way, to Nitti's account, which had been a guiding light in the research of the mysterious Phantom Train.

After the first inauguration in 1991, annual commemorations in Sorgues had continued to knit this community together, allowing them to exchange memories, words, acts of friendship, but also to remain silent, all of which helped make sense of what the survivors and their children had experienced. Now the second and third generations were next to me, with the shared experiences of their fathers and grandfathers. The mood was light and jovial in this Parisian brasserie where we ate Saint-Pierre fish and drank a glass of Chablis; but there were hints of more difficult times. About grandfathers who never returned from Dachau; about mothers who had been alone raising children for years while their husbands were absent; about fathers who never talked about this period. Hugues de Roquemaurel recalled how his father had made projects with a couple of friends in the train wagon, before escaping: 'They had business plans,' he said, 'to make jams!' This apparently compelled them to escape; this, and a slight madness – after all, to jump off a moving train was incredibly dangerous. Things did not always end well: when lowering himself to the track on 25 August, the Polish resister Stanislas Slowinski had both legs severed and died on the operating table of a nearby hospital. 'The beautiful message of this train,' they all agreed, was that differences faded, that people came together. Communists, anarchists, socialists – these things no longer mattered. De Roquemaurel, a Catholic, conservative aristocrat, had had prejudices, not least against socialists and communists, but his internment and deportation meant they eroded with time. Things had not always been so rosy of course, and tensions emerged. The fathers of Corinne and Hugues had come close to hitting each other, they explain, but in the end their bond over this shared experience was so powerful that it generated connections among the second generation.[198]

These gatherings do not, however, only offer a rose-tinted vision of the past. They are also spaces where more complicated memories and rapports emerge. For years one of the Phantom Train survivors kept the photograph of the *Milicien* who had arrested him in his bedside table: the photograph was of this *Milicien*'s dead body after he had been shot by resisters, a reminder of the violence and tensions within the French community itself. A descendant mentioned how his godmother had died when the Americans had accidentally bombed the beaches in Biarritz in summer 1944, alluding to American responsibility in the destruction of France: 'When the English bombed they aimed; when Americans bombed ...'.[199] The *Amicale* also had its own complex dynamic: when I attended the commemoration in August 2024, one woman commented to me in passing how she was exhausted by her husband's obsession with this train, and frustrations between some of the members became more clear. These observations are invaluable in allowing us to see beyond the veneer of commemoration. Memory is not perfect; it exists within contemporary social, political, and cultural contexts as much as it is rooted in a shared and tragic past.

***

Nitti's life is the story of transnational antifascism in the first half of the twentieth century, of the fight against Hitler, Mussolini, and Franco, and of foreigners in the French resistance. By contextualising his account, we expand the chronologies but also the spaces of resistance and open up important discussions about what it meant to defy, to transgress, to resist, during the Second World War. Meanwhile, the broader story of the account's afterlife offers insights into the development of memory cultures in France decades after the end of the war. In the 1980s and 1990s, threads of the story were pulled together by a range of written and oral testimonies, and the story of the Phantom Train has now become relatively familiar in France thanks to books, documentaries, and memorials. Nitti's testimony was at the heart of the post-war memory of the train, and the thriving *Amicale* is one of the great legacies of his work.

But there is also an intimacy to Nitti's account. Throughout the book Nitti names many of his fellow deportees, name after name: Arturo Zanoni, Marcucci, Ferri, Santi, Lanzati, Arlotto, Franco Beatrice. There was also Salavera, Francisco Franco-Bahamo, de Pablo, Albert Lautmann, Adelmo Pedrini, and many more. These names peppered throughout his book are interesting precisely because they are completely unknown to most readers. Thanks to Nitti these men are lifted, if only for a moment, from the anonymity of history. The names are like small memorials which reveal little-known historical actors and bring back to life those who were deported, those who died, and those who were dehumanised. But Nitti is not writing these names just for the reader, but also for himself. For at the time of writing Nitti did not know their fate: most, like Pedrini, ended up in Dachau. Nitti would have been fully aware of his privilege and luck that he had not only escaped but also survived. The burden of survival is heavy within these pages, within these lists of names. Ultimately, by listing the names of the men around him (for he generally does not name women in his account) Nitti reveals the intensity, intimacy, and pain of masculine bonds, brotherhood, and camaraderie in war. This intimacy is expressed in other ways, too, not least through the account's sensory language, as the final section of this introduction will show.

Part III

Sensory – A Sensorial History of Deportation

When historians or curators describe the past it can be somewhat odourless, with a 'strange stillness' to it.[200] We describe how things looked, how events unfolded, who was present (and who was absent), and we put forward these interpretations based on evidence as best we can. But recreating smells, sounds, tastes, and textures is more complicated. Whereas one can publish an image or photograph taken 100 years ago, we cannot reproduce a smell.

Or can we? In 1941, Lucien Febvre, the historian who founded the prestigious *Annales* school, warned readers against succumbing to the despairing complaint that there is nothing more to discover about the past. At times it may seem that every rock has been turned over, he wrote, particularly for some heavily researched periods of history; but approaching them from a psychological perspective, he suggested, would bring something new.[201] His insight still rings true today, and sources can often lend themselves to a multi-dimensional reading of senses, emotions, and affect in the past. Sometimes this is obvious – an instrument, an object, a recording – but most often it is more subtle, and it is up to us to approach the source differently in order to extract new meanings but also feelings and sensations. This has been done extensively by historians such as Alain Corbin, whose studies of sound and smell in French history have shaped an entire field. Anthropologists David Howes and Constance Classen as well as historians Ligh Schmidt and Mark Smith have written extensively on history and the senses, challenging the idea that sight was the most important of the senses in modern times. The highly visual elements of daily life in the modern era do not, they argue, downplay the other senses. Smith prefers to avoid talking of a strict hierarchy of senses, and, instead, to think about their intersection, where they are all at play and interacting with each other. This is especially clear in the case of deportation memoirs, accounts, or oral histories, but as Holocaust scholars Nikolas Wachsmann and Simone Gigliotti have pointed out, little work has been done on the sensorial world of deportation in the Second World War.[202] We regularly catch snippets of deportation in survivor testimonies; but Nitti's book is entirely devoted to the deportation experience, giving us a unique depth and breadth of evidence.

The real richness of Nitti's account lies in its rawness, a quality which lends itself well to sensory history. Written so soon after the events, Nitti retained and was able to communicate strong traces of smell, sound, taste, and texture. The way he talks about lice, about handshakes, about urine; these physical recollections threaded throughout his narrative give it an incredible power even eighty years after the events. This was not uncommon among the witness accounts published in the immediate aftermath of events, when memories and traumas were fresh. The detail of the physical destruction of sites but also bodies was often intense, explicit, and accusatory. Pierre Bourdan, a French journalist who followed the Allied advance into Normandy and northern France, and Marcel Picard, a war correspondent, pencilled the details of the horrors caused by Germans, a way of logging Nazi crimes which would need to be reckoned with after the war.[203] Nitti's own account as we have seen was used to build a case against Nazi brutality in the late forties. But this is more than a trial record, and Nitti brings to life the sensorial world of deportation. If the famous photographs of deportees in wagons are fixed and silent, Nitti's pages inject sound, smells, and tastes, no matter how horrific, into the past.

Sight

The night of 30 June, three days before the Phantom Train set out from Toulouse, Nitti could see the mess and tragedy around him. He was overwhelmed by the numbers, the anonymous mass of humans, this 'sea of heads and bodies'. The scene of 'dirty', 'untidy' men who were old or disabled was deeply unsettling. The reader can almost touch the artificial limbs Nitti describes which some had taken off and laid next to them. How would they ever survive this?

But once they boarded the train on 2 July, sight – often considered one of, if not the most, powerful senses – mattered less. Indeed it was very hard to see during deportation journeys, for the very simple reason that it was so dark inside the convoys, a darkness made worse when the window slits were boarded up: 'The existing lack of air and light is bad enough; now it'll be worse,' Nitti remarked.[204] They undressed in the shadows, their eyes slowly getting used to the darkness. Darkness was everywhere, when doors were kept closed (which was most of the time), but also when the prisoners walked through Bordeaux into the next stage of their ordeal. They had been ordered off the train in the early hours of 12 July, stepping out under a starless sky only to enter the darkness of the synagogue. In the Jewish temple desecrated by the Nazis things were not much better: 'the sun barely penetrated into our prison despite the large gallery windows'.[205] They spent four weeks in this *demi-ombre*, sometimes hearing the sound of machine guns being loaded and unloaded without ever knowing what exactly was going on. Life was 'colourless', and the low visibility in their synagogue prison served as a metaphor for their lack of clear sight in regard to their future.[206] Perhaps it was better this way; perhaps it was better that they did not see each other as they descended far down below the usual social conventions.

For all the darkness, solidarities were often indirectly expressed through a series of hidden actions, not least by local inhabitants. The gazes, signals, actions, and sometimes words of civilians were a lifeline. Two groups surface in particular: French railway workers, the *cheminots*, and women. If the role of railway workers was called into question in the 1990s vis-à-vis the deportations, in Nitti's account the relationship with *cheminots* was one of solidarity: 'Whenever they could,' he wrote, 'the

French railwaymen would signal to us and whisper what they'd gleaned from London on the wireless.'[207] Meanwhile, women were carers, helping the deportees at various stages of their journeys. On 3 July in Toulouse, before the train had set off, Quaker women approached the prisoners to 'distribute hot drinks and bread', looking at them 'with sympathy and compassion' while the German guards hovered over them threateningly. In Charmant, young women – probably from the *Secours National* – gave the detainees soup. Moral support could be seen in fleeting, secret glances: in the synagogue, a woman from across the street chalked bits of news on a board so that the prisoners could read them from the little windows which overlooked a side street. In Bordeaux, one woman had talked very loudly to her partner so that bits of news and encouragement could be overheard by the prisoners but not understood by their German guards.[208] In Valence, the stationmaster's wife did the same thing: when the Germans were not looking, she held up a piece of cardboard on which she had written that Paris was surrounded.[209] These actions were barely visible, but their importance was immeasurable.

Smell

Nitti's other senses are magnified in his account, perhaps because sight itself was reduced and meant he had to rely more on other senses; but also perhaps because deportation was in itself an all-encompassing sensorial trauma. First, there are the familiar smells which change. The odour of Roquefort cheese had always horrified de Roquemaurel, but now he was so hungry that he happily ate his piece. At another point in his voyage, he encountered a unique specimen of cheese, this time odourless: he chewed and chewed for a long time, as if chewing plastic. But it was 'indestructible', one could 'let it fall; it bounced back perfectly'.[210] Nitti recalls the smell of cigarettes as rare but delicious, and the absence of smoking was a real frustration for him and many others. Not all smells are described by Nitti, but one must imagine the deep smell of wood from the wagons' boards, or of burning and fire during the bombings.

More crucially, there were those smells which assaulted the deportees from the first hours of their journey, and which drew a clear line between their civilised past and the dehumanising agony they were now in. The smell of bodily excretions is still one of the relatively taboo topics of deportation, war, and the past generally, but it was a constant issue, and one of the first signs of the degradation of social mores. The deportees organised themselves well in one wagon, initially avoiding lying close to the '*tinettes*', or toilet buckets, but this kind of organisation could only last so long.[211] Changes in diet, hydration, and confinement meant that bodies were in turmoil, but they were also trapped in a narrow space for hours and days, only occasionally allowed to step out. Buckets soon filled up, were knocked over, and the smell of faeces, urine, and vomit would have soon been inescapable. This is one of the main reasons that incarceration smelled different from freedom. When the prisoners went out into the night in Bordeaux, on 12 July, it was dark but they nonetheless 'breath[ed] in the cool air of the night', the freshness was a contrast to the stale, pestilent air of the rail wagon.[212] After deportation in a confined space for hours let alone days, let alone weeks, nothing smelled so pure as a gust of air. Still, the smell of deportation was so strong that it penetrated the skin. In Angoulême, when the deportees were allowed a brief drink after their train had been bombed (when, according to Nitti, 'we were offered paradise'), Nitti managed to talk to a young woman from the Red Cross. She was standing at the door of their cattle wagon: 'She was disgusted,' he wrote, recalling the physical repulsion she would have been unable to hide as the smell of these deportees hit her.

Sound

If it was dark inside, sounds could still penetrate through the walls of confinement. Already imprisoned in the Caffarelli barracks, when Nitti was in the centre of Toulouse waiting to be deported, he could hear, but never see, the rumblings of the city around him.[213] Once aboard the train, in the darkness of the wagon, the deportees heard the deafening sound of planes before they saw them (if they ever did), these 'strident noise[s]' which 'tore the air' during the Allied bombings. Only those at the window slits told the others that planes were there. The air was 'shaking' and 'engines were screeching'; those inside had nowhere to escape.[214]

The sounds inside the wagons were different although similarly traumatic. Some people snored; some murmured; some hummed; 'a few Spaniards found the strength to sing'.[215] They went from threats, to philosophical conversations, to 'an endless concert of complaints'.[216] In Semprún's wagon there had been the terrified screams of those who thought they were dying, and the nightmarish ones which 'need[ed] to be silenced by any and all means'.[217] In the early part of his journey Nitti heard two women cry, wondering if they would ever see their children again.[218] The thirst, the heat, and the sounds of groaning penetrated deep into the souls of the men, changing them in unrecognisable ways: 'the desire sometimes seized one to kill those moaners', one said.[219]

Sounds were also treacherous and aroused suspicion. The sound of sawing was something the Germans listened out for:

> [German guards] who leap down and search the track every time the train stops, lighting their way with electric torches. Some pause occasionally to press their ears to the outside of the wagons, checking if they can hear anything of what we're discussing inside, though mainly they're listening out for the sound of sawing or the creak of a floorboard being prised up. We quickly realise what they're doing. The moment the guards reach our wagon, we go quiet.

The Germans were constantly listening out for 'sounds' of the *maquisards*, and the very word *maquis* struck a terrifying chord in them.[220]

Figure 1. A photograph of refugees in May–June 1940. An old lady is pushed along on a handcart, which holds all of her possessions, by the rest of her family, near Louvain in Belgium. The British Expeditionary Force (BEF) in France 1939–40, War Office official photographer, Malindine E G (Lt). (*Public domain, via Wikimedia Commons*)

Figure 2. Marshal Philippe Pétain in his office as vice-president of the Council in May 1940. On 16 June 1940, Pétain became head of the government and signed the Armistice with Germany in the following days. (*Public domain, via Wikimedia Commons*)

Figure 3. A portrait of Charles de Gaulle seated at his desk, probably in his office in London, c. 1940. Ministry of Information Photo Division Photographer. (*Public domain, via Wikimedia Commons*)

Figure 4. *Above left*: Alice Resch, Harriet Marple, Toot Blueland Van Oordt, Helga Holbek, and Ima Lievey from the Quaker delegation in Toulouse, 1943. (*Courtesy of the Mémorial de la Shoah*)

Figure 5. *Above right*: Damien Nardone, French resister deported on the Phantom Train on 3 July 1944. (*Courtesy of the Nardone family*)

Figure 6. German soldiers sitting at a café *terrasse* in Paris during the Occupation. (*Public domain, via Wikimedia Commons*)

Figure 7. This was the type of railway wagon used to deport Jews and non-Jews from France in the Second World War. Today, this wagon sits in Drancy, outside Paris, to commemorate and honour the victims of the racist and antisemitic persecutions, as well as the crimes against humanity, committed under the authority of the French state between 1940 and 1944. (*Public domain, via Wikimedia Commons*)

Figure 8. The consequences of Allied bombing in France were devastating. A British soldier in Caen after its liberation gives a helping hand to an old lady among the scene of utter devastation. July 1944. Captain E.G. Malindine, No. 5 Army Film & Photographic Unit. (*Public domain, via Wikimedia Commons*)

Figure 9. Bodies of Frenchmen executed in Vincennes on 20 August 1944. (*Public domain, via Wikimedia Commons*)

Figure 10. Enormous crowds at the liberation of Paris on 26 August 1944. (*Public domain, via Wikimedia Commons*)

Figure 11. *Above left*: Drawing of Francesco Fausto Nitti made on his last day of captivity in Mauzac, May 1943, by a fellow inmate. He thought he would be liberated that day, but was instead taken to Le Vernet camp. (*Frontispiece to the original 1944 edition of* Chevaux 8 – Hommes 70)

Figure 12. *Above right*: Italian antifascist Carlo Rosselli who founded Giustizia e Libertà in Paris with Nitti and was assassinated with his brother, Nello, by French fascists in 1937. (*Public domain, via Wikimedia Commons*)

Figure 13. *Below*: The camp at Argelès-sur-Mer where Nitti was held after the Spanish Civil War, April 1939. (*Public domain, via Wikimedia Commons*)

Figure 14. Trentin in front of his bookshop in Toulouse on Rue du Languedoc. Today a blue plaque marks this site, a reminder of its importance in the French Resistance and the fight against fascism. (*Courtesy of the Comune di Jesolo archives*)

Figure 15. *Right*: Portrait of Pierre Bertaux, head of the Réseau Bertaux which Nitti was part of. He became Commissioner at the liberation of Toulouse. (*Public domain, via Wikimedia Commons*)

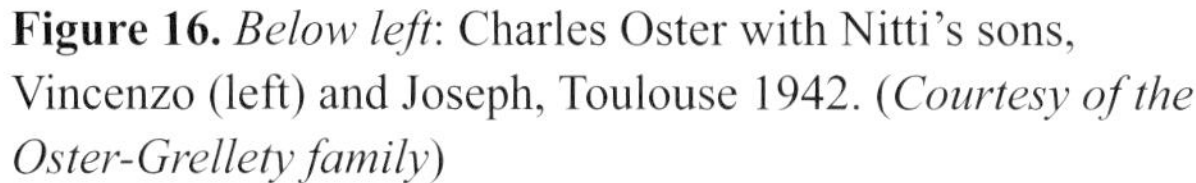
Figure 16. *Below left*: Charles Oster with Nitti's sons, Vincenzo (left) and Joseph, Toulouse 1942. (*Courtesy of the Oster-Grellety family*)

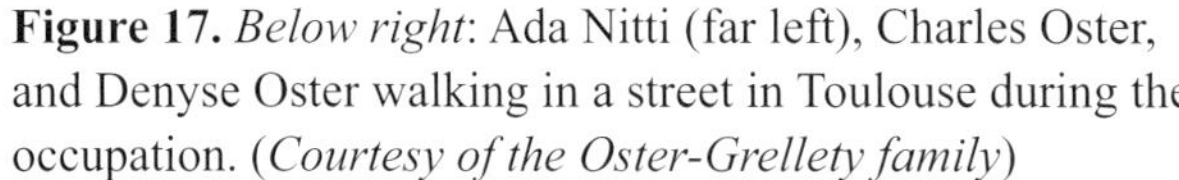
Figure 17. *Below right*: Ada Nitti (far left), Charles Oster, and Denyse Oster walking in a street in Toulouse during the occupation. (*Courtesy of the Oster-Grellety family*)

Figure 18. Internees behind the barbed wire at the Vernet camp, France. (*Courtesy of the Mémorial de la Shoah*)

Figure 19. Four Parisians who fought in the Spanish Civil War as members of the International Brigade. Jacob Insel, second from left, was a resister in the FTP-MOI and deported on the Phantom Train. He died trying to escape on 19 August 1944. (*Courtesy of the Mémorial de la Shoah*)

Figure 20. Grand Synagogue of Bordeaux where Nitti stayed from 12 July to 8 August 1944, desecrated by the Germans. (*Courtesy of the Mémorial de la Shoah*)

Figure 21. Another angle of the destruction in the Grand Synagogue of Bordeaux. (*Courtesy of the Mémorial de la Shoah*)

Figure 22. The bombing of the Phantom Train at Pierrelatte as witnessed from inside a wagon. Drawing from a post-war account, 'Jeunesse Héroïque. Il y avait un camarade. Biographie de François Lafforgue', Amis des F.T.P.F. (*Courtesy of the Mémorial de la Shoah*)

Figure 23. Ceremony in October 1944 for the Phantom Train after the liberation of Toulouse. In honour of those who were selected in Bordeaux and executed at Souge camp on 1 August 1944. (*Courtesy of the Mémorial de la Shoah*)

Figure 24. Vincenzo, Ada, and Josef Nitti in Rome soon after the war. (*Courtesy of the Oster-Grellety family*)

Figure 25. Monument in memory of the 700 deportees of the Phantom Train, Sorgues. Inaugurated in August 1991. (*Author's own*)

But because sound could travel through walls, it was also a way to stay connected to the outside world. The news was first and foremost a sound, one that the prisoners could not read or see: it was whispers – between themselves, with those on the outside like civilians and *cheminots* – which were much more than information. In the pestilence of these wagons wandering back and forth through southern France, where excrement and urine sloshed in hot, cramped, airless, dark spaces of confinement, news was a lifeline. And the deportees were hungry for it. In the synagogue, despite being cut off, they managed to grasp bits of news. The whispers of the lorry driver beneath the gaze of otherwise vigilant guards allowed them to hear about the outside world, about the Allied advance.[221] News gave them something to talk about, but also gave them faith. And as the train rolled on and escapes became more and more frequent, news travelled from wagon to wagon, a form of cultural resistance and defiance in a space otherwise meant to break them.

Taste

Deportees and camp survivors often comment on the awful taste of food; food which they nonetheless wolfed down for survival. Yet in the wagons of the Phantom Train which rolled on and on under a pitiless summer sun, hunger was secondary. It was thirst which was torturous, and this thirst had a taste and a texture. After Bordeaux, as the train headed back through Toulouse in early August, thirst was the dominant concern. 'For the previous thirty-six hours not a single drop of water had passed our lips,' Nitti wrote. 'The heat was intolerable. Many comrades had slumped to the floor barely conscious, so stifling were the conditions. In the foul, stinking air they gasped for breath through gaping mouths.'[222] The deportees were so dehydrated that they became oblivious to hunger.[223] Their tongues were dry, thick, and they could not salivate anymore: 'I can still see myself, my tongue covered in a kind of mud, licking the bars on the window to clean this sticky paste off which bothered my mouth.'[224] Damien Nardone recalled this agonising thirst in his short testimony: 'We were dying of thirst,' he writes. 'I saw some drink their own urine.'[225] Outside Nîmes, on 11 August, they were begging for water. The heat was crushing, the wagon airless, their bodily smells inescapable. In Nitti's journal, the entry for 24 August was a reminder of the sensorial overload: 'Heat. No water. No hope of escape.' That day, he wrote, was 'the lowest point of our wretchedness'.[226]

Touch

Because of the heat, bodies began to sweat immediately as they boarded the train in Toulouse. There was no kind of air flow, and the July heat was inescapable. On that platform in the Raynal sidings on 2 July, with the windows boarded up and the heat rising, the detainees removed their jackets and trousers, down to their underpants.[227] Raymond Levi, in a different wagon from Nitti's, talked about 50–70° around Nîmes, with bodies thick and shiny as they tried to eject the heat. It was unbearable. The texture of these semi-nude bodies crushed against each other was something they had never experienced before. Nitti paints a clear picture of this proximity, where the omnipresence of the sweat and skin of strangers broke all social norms and codes of conduct.

The prisoners were less packed in the synagogue of Bordeaux, but there they faced other problems. They lived in squalor, with straw which had been used by other prisoners before them and was ridden with parasites. With their fingertips they squeezed off the lice – three types of lice, according to one deportee. It was a daily obsession, a necessary practice: they were infested. Their skin crawled with them, and the scratching and squeezing never stopped. Nitti's references to lice often recur, revealing not only obsession but a form of physical torture and trauma:

> in the synagogue the infestation spread so fast that in just a matter of days everyone was contaminated. … Many of us didn't have a change of clothes to hand. … Therefore fresh clothes were out of the question. We'd wash our things in cold water only to find them still covered in lice. All that the water achieved was to stir them into life. Night and day, night especially, we scratched nonstop. Our fronts and backs looked as if they'd been flayed alive. The hunt for those creatures went on round the clock, a battle endlessly fought and lost.[228]

If touch could be repulsive, it was also the gateway to the deepest solidarities and intimacies. The ten hostages selected to leave the synagogue in late July – Lautmann, Peyre-Vidal, and others – walked through the row of their almost six hundred fellow deportees on their way out. As they walked, they took the hands of those comrades nearest to them, tightening their grip as they went through. Stunned, horrified, scared, broken, Nitti and his fellow detainees watched their comrades leave the synagogue in total silence with their fingers stretched out.[229] Their fate – execution in the camp of Souge – would only be revealed later. Nitti did not manage to shake the hand of his friend Lautmann; he was too far away. Days later, the bombing at Pierrelatte brought tragedy inside one of the wagons. One of the men inside, François Lafforgue, a resister from the 35th Brigade Marcel Langer in Toulouse, was hit during the bombing and died immediately: 'his head exploded, the brain jumped out,' one witness recalled. The Germans then opened fire on this wagon to prevent any escapes: '… Cries of horror echo throughout … Pierre lets himself fall on François's body. On the floorboards blood spreads in a slimy trickle. Jacques is wounded by an explosive bullet in the back. He dies slowly. … One by one the wounded die, drowning in blood. Comrades hold their heads in their arms. They learn their final words by heart.'[230] In this terrifying account re-told after the war, we are seized by the description of blood and bodies intertwined on the floor of the wagon, as dying men held on to each other in their final breaths.

Beyond the Five Senses

Certain themes come up in Nitti's account which bridge the sensory worlds. First and foremost is this unbearable heat which could be seen, felt, tasted, smelled. Already in the Caffarelli barracks, that first day, the heat was 'suffocating', the air 'heavy' and 'foul'.[231] On 5 July it was unbearable, crushing. Another theme is motion: as the train started and stopped endlessly, Nitti felt he was on a ship, with the rocking of the waves, the kind that makes one feel nauseous.[232] And, of course, there is sleeplessness. It started the night before their departure from the camp, from 29 to 30 June, and continued in the Caffarelli barracks.[233] Nitti's second chapter opens: 'We don't get a wink of sleep that night', the floorboards were 'bare' and dirty. Sleeplessness was a big problem, as it often is for soldiers in war. Nitti believed it caused them to go 'pale' and 'thin'.[234] This was not the case for all: Christian de Roquemaurel recalled falling into a deep sleep on the first night in the wagon, 'lodged between my companions'.[235] Nitti himself remarked that '[i]n that pestilential atmosphere, a good few of us managed to sleep, crouching and snoring in barely a square metre of space, legs curled up, arms pressed tight to our sides. Others conversed in low voices, yet others hummed tunes to themselves.'[236] As readers we start to imagine this sleep of bodies, scrunched up. Sleep, if it was reached, was made up of stiffness, entanglement, and stench.

Nitti's sensorial world is complex, made up of experiences which draw together and go beyond the five basic senses. This meets recent research on sensory patterns which show that there are, in fact, more than five senses. The vestibular sense – which measures movement, gravity, and temperature – and the proprioceptive sense – which gives awareness of the body – are now familiar concepts in neuroscience and physiology, although they have yet to be fully integrated into historical studies.[237] These terms, however, could refine our understanding of bodily experiences in deportation. The state of half-paralysis and semi-consciousness is, for instance, everywhere by the end of Nitti's journey. As the train headed towards Sorgues, the heat and exhaustion were mounting. One wagon had four or five people with tuberculosis, all of them constantly coughing, struggling to breathe. Older people had become barely mobile, bodies waiting to die, waiting for the release of death. The cadaver of one prisoner, a bank director, was unloaded at Nîmes: he had died of asphyxiation and starvation.[238] On 23-24 August, as Nitti was planning his escape, the bodies around him were only partly conscious, gasping for breath, hopeless under the heat. There was no more water by this point, no more food, their bodies shells, deeply weakened by the lack of food and air: 'We were barely recognisable as human beings,' Nitti wrote. 'Such supplies of food as we'd started out with had run out. What with the heat, the starvation rations, and the days and weeks we'd been cooped up together in a few square metres, our bodies were dissolving into ghosts. Our faces were death masks drained of all colour, our eyes dark hollows. Our beards were bedraggled, our clothes a collection of filthy tatters.'[239] The bodily afflictions had turned the prisoners into semi-conscious, filthy, shells – signs of madness in some of the people in Nitti's wagon were inescapable, while eruptions of gibberish highlighted the dysregulation of their nervous systems: 'Some of us were broken mentally, either existing silently in a private world of madness or transformed into gibbering wrecks.'[240]

The sense of time was also blurred throughout their journey. Nitti kept a daily journal which would have helped him not only maintain some sort of sanity and sense of self during the deportation, but also retrace his steps while writing his account. But it was hard to keep track of time. When Nitti describes the first bombings, he alludes to this sense of timelessness: 'It'll take longer to recount what happened next than the time it lasted,' he writes.[241] Time stops again during the Pierrelatte bombing a few weeks later: 'for several seconds – which seemed like hours – we remained frozen with fear'.[242] Nitti's sense of being 'rigid' with fear contrasts sharply with the drawings of one deportee who pictured the deportees with arms flailing, mouths, and eyes open, bodies writhing (see Figure 22).

Paying attention to the touch and sounds of violence raises interesting points about the combination of tensions and solidarity among the deportees themselves. Violence was not only experienced as a result of direct German aggression, but also within the wagons themselves. Nitti talks about the animated conversations about their potential destination in those early days of the journey, but there were other more serious confrontations.[243] The attempt to organise sleep rotas in Nitti's wagon did not prevent 'petty squabbles' from breaking out.[244] This was similar to the experience in Semprún's wagon, where one deportee had been complaining about the resisters, accusing them of terrorist acts against the French and of causing these deportations. One older man could no longer bear hearing his tirade: 'One suspicious move, just one, and I swear I'll strangle you,' he told him.[245] It was not uncommon to resort to violence. When preparing their escape, plan tensions with communists erupted in de Roquemaurel's wagon, and they came to blows to prevent him and a small group from trying to escape.

***

The sensory world Nitti describes is only a glimpse of what deportation felt like. Linking it not only to other voices from those within the Phantom Train but other mass convoys helps to identify patterns, but we must be careful to remember that this is only one version of the past, and that this account was written by a man who had published before. His profession as a journalist and his masculine perspective inherently shaped the narrative published in 1944; this is not to say it is not a true account, but rather that all personal accounts need to be contextualised. The sensory world of Nitti would have been different from that of, say, the women in the convoy, and we get no indication at all of what that would have been like for them. The women's experiences, while in some ways similar, would have been shaped by their gender. 'One of the women in my rail wagon was pregnant,' wrote Ginette Vincent Baudy. 'She gave birth to a little girl in Ravensbrück in precarious conditions and named her Chantal, who died arriving at Bergen-Belsen after an evacuation of mothers and their children. In fact, aside from three born close to our liberation, no child survived.'[246] Alice Bessou-Kokine, the wife of Meyer Kokine, was another pregnant woman in the Phantom Train. She gave birth to a son in Ravensbrück, who died at 10 days old. Meyer had managed to escape during the journey, but she died in the camp on 10 April 1945. If the physical experiences of the women in the Phantom Train are less known, they are no less real. We must listen even more closely to those silences of the archives.

What is perhaps most surprising is the human capacity for adaptation in those conditions. Nitti wrote:

> When I look back on that dark chapter which ended in tragedy for so many of our dear comrades, what strikes me most is human beings' extraordinary ability to adapt. Take ten men, shut them in a cell with very little food or water, and yes, they will suffer terribly. But bit by bit they'll adapt to the inhumane situation, they'll develop little habits, and as each day passes the harrowing pain of the first moments will diminish.[247]

This adaptation was an overlapping between sensory adaptation – an involuntary, decreasing response to sensory or constant stimulation – and habituation – the decreased response to something, especially over time. '[O]ne day follows another,' Nitti commented, until 'the acute suffering will become a matter of habit.' In some ways the dehumanisation of man is evident in his account. In deportation, 'the animal within the man was born again'. And when the prisoners collapsed on the dirty straw of the synagogue, they were 'like exhausted animals after an interminable trek'. Nitti was under no illusion, and as the weeks went on he understood that '[o]ur primitive animal side was taking over'. Yet the truth is they were still humans, and not animals; their sensorial world had drastically changed, but small signs of continuity and humanity had remained. 'Short of dying,' he wrote, 'humans get used to anything.'[248]

Amidst all of these reflections it is important to acknowledge the limitations of language. In our case we have the particular problem of translation. Language is cultural, shaped by the environment, beliefs, values, and experiences of a specific society at a specific time. To translate something from one language to another requires a mastery of both languages but also a sensitivity to their different rhythms. In his introduction, Nitti describes how the memory of the Phantom Train came to him and he uses the expression '*prendre corps en moi*'. There is no English translation which can adequately capture this expression. We have translated it as 'takes shape in me', which gives a very good sense of what was happening to Nitti; but the fact remains that the French version makes it much clearer that the memory of the Phantom Train is not just a mental memory but a full-body experience. This leads to a final point to bear in mind before reading Nitti's book: that language, whether French or English or any other, can only attempt to describe what the body feels. The language of the body is non-verbal, one which exists beyond words, and we can therefore never get the full picture of what happened in those railway wagons during that summer of 1944. Nevertheless, Nitti's book stands as a searing and unique account of the horrific deportation ordeals of the Second World War, that of the Phantom Train being unparalleled, as far as we know, in the length of time it lasted.

Notes

1. Francesco F. Nitti, *Chevaux Huit, Hommes Soixante-Dix* (Toulouse: Éditions Chantal, 1944). References to Nitti's text will refer to the current translation in 2025, unless they refer specifically to the 1944 edition.
2. Primo Levi's memoir was translated into English by Stuart Woolf in 1958 over a decade after its initial publication in Italian in 1947. It was then translated in German and the publication of subsequent editions propelled it to international acclaim, becoming one of the most important texts about the Holocaust. Primo Levi, *If This Is a Man* (London: The Orion Press, 1959).
3. The noun we have chosen to describe Nitti's book is *account*, rather than *diary* or *memoir*. It is not a diary, since the daily log Nitti managed to keep of the two-month ordeal is now barely visible. Nor is it a memoir, as memoirs cover a full or a significant part of a whole life, properly digested and considered at a distance in time. By contrast, Nitti wrote this testimony mere weeks after his escape from the Phantom Train, and months before the fighting ceased and the war ended. His vivid account of that deportation journey just as the liberation of France was underway underscores the unique value of immediate first-hand testimony, such a precious resource for the historian.
4. Jorge Semprún, *The Cattle Truck* (London: Serif, 2005); Charlotte Delbo, *Auschwitz and After* (New Haven and London: Yale University Press, 1995); Charles Rist, *Season of Infamy: A Diary of War and Occupation, 1939–1945* (Bloomington, IN: Indiana University Press, 2016); Raymond-Raoul Lambert, *Diary of a Witness, 1940–1943* (Chicago, IL: Ivan R. Dee, 1985); Léon Werth, *Deposition 1940–1944, A Secret Diary of Life in Vichy France* (Oxford: Oxford University Press, 2018); Hélène Berr, *The Journal of Hélène Berr* (London: MacLehose, 2008).

5. Nitti, *Chevaux Huit* (1944) 17.
6. *The Phantom Train: Deporting Prisoners from Occupied France—The Account of Francesco Fausto Nitti, 1944*, introduced by Ludivine Broch and translated by Martin Sorrell (London: Pen & Sword, 2025) 136. Thereafter Nitti account (2025).
7. Simone Gigliotti, *The Train Journey: Transit, Captivity and Witnessing in the Holocaust* (New York: Berghahn Books, 2010) 159.
8. Archives Nationales (AN): F/7/14747. Nitti (Francesco Fausto) Journaliste et écrivain; 1936–1938.
9. To understand more about the lead up to the Second World War and the impact of the Munich Accord and the Nazi–Soviet pact, read Jean-Pierre Azéma, *From Munich to the Liberation (1938–1944)* (Cambridge; New York: Cambridge University Press, 1984).
10. Winston S. Churchill, *The Second World War, Vol. II Their Finest Hour* (London: Penguin Books, 2005) 38.
11. A rich and detailed study of this is Hanna Diamond, *Fleeing Hitler: France 1940* (New York and Oxford: Oxford University Press, 2007).
12. Julian Jackson, *France: The Dark Years, 1940–1944* (Oxford: Oxford University Press, 2003) 121. Jackson is an authority on this period and *The Dark Years* should be read alongside his recent works on de Gaulle and the Pétain trial.
13. Churchill, *Their Finest Hour* (2005) 159.
14. Jean Claude Barbas, ed., *Philippe Pétain: Discours aux Français (17 juin 1940–août 1944)* (Paris: Albin Michel, 1989) 57–58.
15. A recent study explores the Italian question in great depth during this period. Karine Varley, *Vichy's Double Bind: French Collaboration between Hitler and Mussolini during the Second World War* (Cambridge: Cambridge University Press, 2023).
16. Daniel Cordier, *Alias Caracalla* (Paris: Gallimard, 2009) 27.
17. Julian Jackson, *De Gaulle* (Cambridge, MA: Belknap Press of Harvard University Press, 2018) 128.
18. Azéma, *Munich to the Liberation* (1984) 39.
19. Henri Amouroux, *La grande histoire des Français sous l'occupation: quarante millions de pétainistes, Juin 1940-Juin 1941*, Vol. 2 (Paris: Robert Laffont, 1977) 78. The lawyer and politician Jean Odin was

one of those eighty men who voted 'no'. He wrote a book about this originally published in 1946: Jean Odin, *Les Quatre-vingts* (Conseil Général de la Gironde, La Presqu'île, 1997).

20. Few works explicitly on the National Revolution have been published in English, but these include: W.D. Halls, *The Youth of Vichy France* (Oxford: Oxford University Press, 1981); Eric Jennings, *Vichy in the Tropics: Pétain's National Revolution in Madagascar, Guadeloupe and Indochina* (Stanford, CA; Great Britain: Stanford University Press, 2001); Miranda Pollard, *Reign of Virtue: Mobilizing Gender in Vichy France* (Chicago, IL.; London: University of Chicago Press, 1998).
21. Chris Millington, *France in the Second World War* (London: Bloomsbury, 2020) 46.
22. Jean Guéhenno, *Journal des années noires, 1940–1944* (Paris: Gallimard, 2002) 87.
23. *Le Train Fantôme: Toulouse, Bordeaux, Sorgues, Dachau* (Études Sorguaises, 1991) 19.
24. The question of prisoners of war was a major one as several works have shown, not least Robert Paxton, *Vichy France, Old Guard and New Order, 1940–1944* (New York; Toronto: Norton Library, 1975) and Sarah Fishman, *We Will Wait: Wives of French Prisoners of War, 1940–1945* (New Haven, CT and London: Yale University Press, 1991). The experience of colonial prisoners of war in Second World War France was studied extensively in Raffael Scheck, *Hitler's African Victims: The German Army Massacres of Black French Soldiers in 1940* (Cambridge: Cambridge University Press, 2010).
25. See the recent study by Claire Zalc, *Denaturalized: How Thousands Lost Their Citizenship and Lives in Vichy France* (Cambridge, MA: Belknap Press of Harvard University Press, 2020).
26. Speech by Marshal Pétain, 30 October 1940 in *Pétain: Discours aux Français* (1989) 95.
27. Paxton, *Vichy France* (1975) 314.
28. Ulrich Herbert, 'Forced Laborers in the Third Reich: An Overview', *International Labor and Working-Class History*, 58 (2000) 192.
29. Guéhenno, *Journal* (2002) 82.
30. Ibid., 41.

31. Shannon Fogg, *The Politics of Everyday Life in Vichy France: Foreigners, Undesirables, and Strangers* (Cambridge: Cambridge University Press, 2009) 41.
32. Jean Dutourd, *Au Bon Beurre* (Paris: Gallimard, 1972).
33. Simone Martin-Chauffier, *A bientôt quand même …* (Paris: Calmann-Lévy, 1976) 209–10.
34. Robert Gildea, *Marianne in Chains: in Search of the German Occupation of France 1940–45* (London: Pan Macmillan, 2011) 153–57. Gildea's book offers a unique window into everyday like in Occupied France.
35. Berr, *Journal* (2008) 48–59.
36. See Chapter 2 of Martin Thomas, *The French Empire at War 1940–1945* (Manchester: Manchester University Press, 2007) 38–69.
37. Jackson, *De Gaulle* (2018) 145–46; Eric Jennings, *Free French Africa in World War II: The African Resistance* (New York: Cambridge University Press, 2015). Jennings and Thomas have written extensively on the French colonies during this period and their books are a wealth of knowledge.
38. Azéma, *Munich to the Liberation* (1984) 75.
39. Cordier, *Alias Caracalla* (2009) 27.
40. Agnès Humbert, *Résistance, Memoirs of Occupied France* (London: Bloomsbury, 2009) 5.
41. 'Boches' was the pejorative French term for Germans.
42. La Contemporaine: F/DELTA/RES/0797/IV/11/dossier 77/8 (1987) – Témoignage de Ginette Vincent (née Baudry) 1987, 1.
43. Humbert, *Résistance* (2009) 41.
44. Henri Frenay, *The Night Will End: Memoirs of the Resistance* (London: Abelard-Schuman, 1973) 12–13.
45. Azéma, *From Munich* (1984) 75.
46. H.R. Kedward, *Occupied France: Collaboration and Resistance, 1940–1944* (Oxford: Blackwell, 1985) 46.
47. Stéphane Courtois, Denis Peschanski, and Adam Rayski, *Le Sang de l'Étranger: Les immigrés de la M.O.I. dans la Résistance* (Paris: Fayard, 1989); Robert Gildea, *Fighters in the Shadows: A New History of the French Resistance* (London: Faber & Faber, 2015).

48. H.R. Kedward, *In Search of the Maquis: Rural Resistance in Southern France, 1942–44* (Oxford: Oxford University Press, 2003) 13.
49. Kedward, *In Search of the Maquis* (2003) 33–34.
50. See Raphaële Balu, 'The French *maquis* and the Allies during the Second World War', in Ludivine Broch and Alison Carrol, eds, *France in an Era of Global War, 1914–1945* (London: Palgrave Macmillan, 2014) 192–210. Along with Balu, Claire Andrieu and Guillaume Piketty are doing fascinating work on this at the moment.
51. John Sweets, 'Mouvements Unis de la Résistance', in François Marcot, ed., *Dictionnaire historique de la Résistance* (Paris: Robert Laffont, 2006) 134.
52. Guillaume Piketty, 'Economie morale de la reconnaissance. L'Ordre de la Libération au péril de la sortie de Seconde guerre mondiale', *Histoire@Politique*, 3(3) (2007) 5.
53. Jackson, *De Gaulle* (2018) 337.
54. Laurent Douzou, *La Résistance française: une histoire périlleuse: essai d'historiographie* (Paris: Seuil, 2005); Laurent Douzou, *Le Moment Daniel Cordier: Comment écrire l'histoire de la Résistance ?* (Paris: CNRS éditions, 2021).
55. Kedward, *In Search of the Maquis* (2003) 89.
56. La Contemporaine: Témoinage de Ginette Vincent, 1987, 1.
57. Ludivine Broch, 'Colonial subjects and citizens in the French internal resistance, 1940–1944', *French Politics, Culture and Society*, 37(1) (2019) 6–31.
58. Gemma Caballer, '"Pour la renaissance des villages abandonnés": Quaker Humanitarian Aid in a France at War', *Quaker Studies*, 24(1) (2019) 125.
59. Personal Archives Family Nardone: 'Récit de Damien Nardone'.
60. Olivier Wieviorka, *The Resistance in Western Europe, 1940–1945* (New York: Columbia University Press, 2019) 1–6.
61. Récit Nardone.
62. Its second principal mission was to ensure that Germany got all the required resources it needed from France.
63. The French administration is organised at local level by departments, and each department has its own prefecture and prefect, as well as sub-prefects within that.

64. Thomas Fontaine's doctoral thesis is unpublished at this stage but is the authority on the topic of repression and deportation in occupied France. Thomas Fontaine, 'Déporter: Politiques de déportations et répression en France occupée, 1940–1944', doctoral thesis from Université Paris I, Panthéon-Sorbonne (2013) 274–76; 285; 389-91.
65. Fontaine, 'Déporter: Politiques de déportations et répression' (2013) 298.
66. Lambert, *Diary* (2007) 128; 138.
67. Thomas Fontaine, 'Chronologie: Répression et persécution en France occupée 1940–1944', Mass Violence & Résistance, Sciences-Po, [online], published 7 December 2009, http://bo-k2s.sciences-po.fr/mass-violence-war-massacre-resistance/fr/document/chronologie-ra-pression-et-persa-cution-en-france-occupa-e-1940-1944, ISSN 1961-9898.
68. Ludivine Broch, 'Professionalism in the Final Solution: French Railway Workers and the Jewish Deportations 1942–1944', *Contemporary European History* 23(3) (2014) 359–81.
69. Eight prefectures that housed internment camps were affected: Rhône (Vénissieux), Haute-Vienne (Nexon), Pyrénées-Atlantiques (Gurs), Tarn-et-Garonne (Septfonds, Brens) Haute-Garonne (Noé, Récébédou), Ariège (Le Vernet), Pyrénées-Orientales (Rivesaltes), Bouches-du-Rhône (Les Milles, others in Marseille).
70. Cited in Anne Grynberg, *Les Camps de la Honte* (Paris: La Découverte, 1991) 297.
71. Werth, *Deposition 1940–1944* (2000) 275–77.
72. Historians Wieviorka and Overy offer excellent analysis of bombing campaigns over France and Europe more broadly. Olivier Wieviorka, *Normandy: The Landings to the Liberation of Paris* (Cambridge, MA and London: Belknap Press of Harvard University Press, 2008) 129; Richard Overy, *The Bombing War: Europe 1939–1945* (London: Penguin, 2014).
73. Werth, *Deposition 1940–1944* (2000) 279.
74. Mary Louise Roberts, *D-Day Through French Eyes, Normandy 1944* (Chicago, IL, and London: Chicago University Press, 2014) 83–84.
75. Wieviorka, *Normandy* (2008) 131; For more numbers see Olivier Wieviorka, Julie Le Gac, Anne-Laure Ollivier, Raphaël Spina, *La France en chiffres – De 1870 à nos jours* (Paris: Perrin, 2015) 608.

76. '1944, un dénouement victorieux mais meurtrier', Association du Souvenir des Fusillés de Souge, Accessed via https://www.fusilles-souge.asso.fr/.
77. Jean-Pierre Besse and Thomas Pouty, *Les fusillés. Répression et exécutions pendant l'Occupation (1940–1944)* (Paris: L'Atelier, 2006).
78. Ludivine Broch, 'Martyred Towns at the Liberation: The Case of the Massacre d'Ascq' in Broch and Carrol, eds, *France in an Era of Global Wars, 1914–45: Occupation, Politics, Empire and Entanglements* (London: Palgrave Macmillan, 2014) 50–72.
79. Archives Départementales du Calvados (ADC): 726W/16909/2. Exécution des prisonniers politiques de la prison de Caen.
80. Henri Michel, *1944: La Libération de Paris* (Brussels: Complexe, 1990) 21–25.
81. Fontaine, 'Déporter: Politiques de déportations et répression' (2013) 1033–36.
82. Raoul Nordling, *Sauver Paris:* mémoires du consul de Suède (1905–1944) (Brussels: Complexe, 2002).
83. Jackson, *The Dark Years* (2003) 552.
84. Michel, *1944* (1990) 16.
85. Wieviorka, *Normandy* (2008) 314; Matthew Cobb, *The Resistance: The French Fight against the Nazis* (London: Simon & Schuster, 2009) 265–6.
86. Marc Bergère, *L'Épuration en France* (Rennes: Presses Universitaires de France, 2018).
87. The leading authority on this topic remains Fabrice Virgili, *Shorn Women: Gender and Punishment in Liberation France* (Oxford: Berg, 2002).
88. Henry Rousso, *The Vichy Syndrome, History and Memory in France since 1944* (Cambridge, MA: Harvard University Press, 1991); Douzou, *La Résistance française* (2005); Philip Nord, *After the Deportation: Memory Battles in Postwar France* (Cambridge: Cambridge University Press, 2020).
89. This is based on the EGO 39–45 database, a project conducted by the Centre de Recherche d'Histoire Quantitative (CRHQ) and the University of Caen which regroups all published testimonies related to the Second World War. See CRHQ: ÉGO 1939-1945, Écrits de guerre et d'occupation, Accessed via http://www.ego.1939-1945.crhq.cnrs.fr/.

90. A good book on this topic is Pieter Lagrou, *The Legacy of Nazi Occupation: Patriotic Memory and National Recovery in Western Europe, 1945–1965* (Cambridge: Cambridge University Press, 2000).
91. Recent works showing this shift include Bob Moore, *Survivors: Jewish Self-Help and Rescue in Nazi Occupied Western Europe* (Oxford: Oxford University Press, 2009); Wieviorka, *Resistance in Western Europe* (2019); Claire Andrieu, *When Men Fell From The Sky: Civilians and Downed Airmen in Second World War Europe* (Cambridge: Cambridge University Press, 2023).
92. Philippe Joutard and François Marcot, *Les étrangers dans la résistance* (Besançon: Le musée, 1992) 10; See Gildea, *Fighters in the Shadows* (2015) 1-19.
93. Nitti wrote about his escape from Mussolini's convict island in 1930, *Escape*; about his ordeal in the cattle wagons in France in 1944, *Chevaux Huit, Hommes Soixante-Dix*; and a recollection of his time in the Spanish Civil War in 1953, *Il Maggiore è un rosso.*
94. Francesco Fausto Nitti, *Escape. The Personal Narrative of a Political Prisoner Who Was Rescued from Lipari, the Fascist Devil's Island* (New York: G.P. Putnam's Sons, 1930) 22.
95. Ibid., 23–24.
96. Ibid., 23–26.
97. Ibid., 33.
98. Ibid., 50–51.
99. Ibid., 54.
100. Emilio Lussu, 'The Flight From Lipari', *The Atlantic*, July 1930.
101. Nitti, *Escape* (1930) 78.
102. Ibid., 120.
103. Since 2015 Lampedusa has been used by the European Union as a centre for migrants.
104. Nitti, *Escape* (1930) 151.
105. Lussu, 'Flight from Limpari' (1930).
106. Stanislao G. Pugliese, *Carlo Rosselli: Socialist Heretic and Antifascist Exile* (Cambridge, MA: Harvard University Press, 1999) 93.
107. Lussu, 'Flight From Lipari' (1930).

108. Pietro Ramella, *Francesco Fausto Nitti: L'uomo che beffo Hitler e Mussolini* (Rome: Aracine, 2007) 73.
109. Nitti, *Escape* (1930) 169.
110. 'Putnam Tells Police of Threat on Life; Letters Seeking to Prevent Publication of Nitti Book Givento Officials', *The New York Times*, 18 January 1930.
111. *Bulletin d'information édité par la concentration antifasciste italienne,* Paris, 20 March 1930, 3.
112. Bruno Groppo, 'Entre immigration et exil: les réfugiés politiques italiens dans la France de l'entre-deux-guerres', *Matériaux pour l'histoire de notre temps*, 44 (1996) 30.
113. Arnd Bauerkämper and Grzegorz Rossoliński-Liebe, eds, *Fascism without Borders: Transnational Connections and Cooperation between Movements and Regimes in Europe from 1918 to 1945* (New York: Berghahn Books, 2017) 16; Another useful resource for this is Hugo García, Mercedes Yusta, Xavier Tabet, and Cristina Clímaco, eds, *Rethinking Antifascism: History, Memory and Politics, 1922 to the Present* (New York: Berghahn Books, 2016).
114. Groppo, 'Entre immigration et exil' (1996) 27–35.
115. John Larner and Giuseppe Nangeroni, 'Justice and liberty, an alliance of republicans, democrats, and reformist Socialists founded by Carlo Rosselli and others in 1929', *Britannica.*
116. Ramella, *Nitti* (2007) 71-88.
117. *Giustizia e Libertà*, year IV, no. 25, June 18, 1937.
118. Nicolas Violle, 'La réception de l'assassinat des frères Rosselli dans la presse populaire parisienne', *Matériaux pour l'histoire de notre temps,* 57 (2000) 42–49. The Rossellis have received substantial attention, and their memoirs were re-published on the 80th anniversary of their murder.
119. Pugliese, *Rosselli* (1999) 229.
120. Olivier Bataillé, 'Fascistes et antifascistes à Toulouse: l'Italie déchirée dans le Sud-Ouest (1925–1945)', in *Le Midi dans la nation française. Actes du 126 Congrès national des sociétés historiques et scientifiques*, Terres et hommes du Sud, Toulouse, 2001 (Paris: Editions du CTHS, 2002) 211.

121. Ramella, *Nitti* (2007) 91–93.
122. Groppo, 'Entre immigration et exil' (1996) 30.
123. Francesco Fausto Nitti, *Il Maggiore è un rosso* (Edizioni Avanti, 1953) 203.
124. Ibid., 204.
125. Monique-Lise Cohen and Éric Malo, eds, *Les camps du Sud-Ouest de la France, 1939–1940* (Toulouse: Privat, 1994) 27.
126. Refugees were initially sent either to Argelès or to Saint-Cyprien.
127. Pierre Bertaux, *Mémoires Interrompues* (Asnières: PIA, 2000) 170.
128. Ibid., 167–71
129. The Argelès camp memorial has a lot of information on these internationalists. See Mémorial du camp d'Argelès-sur-Mer, Accessed via https://www.memorial-argeles.eu/fr/. See also Grégory Tuban, *Les séquestrés de Collioure: Un camp disciplinaire au Château royal en 1939* (Perpignan: Mare nostrum, 2003); Grégory Tuban, *Camps d'étrangers: Le contrôle des réfugiés venus d'Espagne (1939–1944)* (Paris: Nouveau Monde, 2018).
130. Frédéric Vergès, 'Une journée à l'enfer de Collioure', *L'Humanité*, 14 May 1939.
131. Grégory Tuban, 'Collioure Un "bagne fascist" en France', *Retronews*, 28 May 2018.
132. Patrimonio dell'Archivio Storico, Senato della Repubblica, Fondazione Nenni: 'Unità 671, Nitti Ada', Accessed via https://patrimonio.archivio.senato.it/inventario/scheda/pietro-nenni/IT-AFS-051-000675/nitti-ada.
133. Joutard and Marcot, *Les étrangers* (1992) 28.
134. Groppo, 'Entre immigration et exil' (1996) 29; Karine Varley explored the Italian occupation in great detail in Varley, *Vichy's Double Bind* (2023).
135. Joutard and Marcot, *Les étrangers* (1992) 29.
136. A major publication which raised the complexity of the experience of Spanish and Italian migrants is Pierre Milza and Denis Peschanski, eds, *Exils et migration: Italiens et Espagnols en France, 1938–1946* (Paris: L'Harmattan, 1994). The chapters by Gianni Perona and Pierre Milza are particularly resonant.

137. Silvio Trentin, *Le Maitron, dictionnaire biographique du mouvement ouvrier et social*. Accessed via https://maitron.fr/trentin-silvio/.
138. Bertaux, *Mémoires* (2000) 95.
139. Ibid., 132.
140. For more information on the Réseau Bertaux, see the Mémorial François Verdier Forain, Accessed via http://francoisverdier-liberationsud.fr/.
141. Service Historique de la Défense (SHD), Vincennes: GR 28 P 4 220 / 10 – Nitti.
142. Institut National de l'Audiovisuel (INA): Interview with Pierre Bertaux, 21 August 1974. Accessed via https://www.ina.fr/ina-eclaire-actu/video/i07344814/pierre-bertaux-resistant-a-toulouse.
143. Bertaux became Commissaire de la République de la Libération in Toulouse, a role he took over from Cassou and which saw him propelled not only into the final events of the liberation, but also into the politics of the liberation which involved tensions with de Gaulle. See SHD: GR 28 P 4 220 / 10 – Nitti.
144. Paul Arrighi, 'Silvio Trentin et le mouvement de résistance libérer et fédérer: de la résistance vers la révolution', *Guerres mondiales et conflits contemporains*, 226(2) (2007) 121–30.
145. Charles d'Aragon, *La Résistance sans héroisme* (Geneva: Tricorne, 2001) 104–05.
146. Trentin, *Le Maitron*. See also Nicola Cacciatore, 'Missed connection: relations between Italian anti-fascist emigration and British forces in Egypt (1940–1944)', *Modern Italy*, 24(3) (2019): 265–79.
147. Bertaux, *Mémoires* (2000) 95.
148. Joutard and Marcot, *Les étrangers* (1992), 12–13.
149. Ibid., 70–1. Studies have tended to focus on Trentin and Eusebio Ferrari, member of the Organisation Secrète (OS). On the role of Italian exiles in antifascist movements see Fabio Fernando Rizi. *Benedetto Croce and Italian Fascism* (Toronto: University of Toronto Press, 2003).
150. SHD: GR 28 P 4 220 / 10 – Nitti.
151. Personal Archives Rosemarie Oster-Grellety.
152. 'Les Carnets d'Ariège' in Cohen and Malo, *Les camps du Sud-Ouest* (1994) 45–48.

153. Tuban, *Camps d'étrangers* (2018) 245–46.
154. Denis Peschanski, *La France des Camps* (Paris: Gallimard, 2002) 300–05.
155. 'Les Carnets d'Ariège' in Cohen and Malo, *Les camps du Sud-Ouest* (1994) 49–51.
156. Tuban, *Camps d'étrangers* (2018) 319; 323.
157. Tuban and Peschanski make this especially clear in their works.
158. A very useful overview of the Nazi concentration camps, including Dachau, is Nikolaus Wachsmann, *KL: A History of the Nazi Concentration Camps* (London: Little Brown, 2015).
159. Nitti Account (2025) 143.
160. These numbers have been gathered from the entry 'I.240 Transport parti le 2 juillet 1944 de Compiègne et arrivé le 5 juillet 1944 au KL Dachau', in the memorial book created by the Fondation Mémorial de la Déportation (FMD) *Livre-Mémorial*, Vol. 2 (2004) 1081–177. The FMD have also made an online resource.
161. Laurent Lutaud and Patricia Di Scala, *Les naufragés et rescapés du "train fantôme"* (Paris: L'Harmattan, 2003) 25–26.
162. Nitti Account (2025) 158.
163. Ibid., 192.
164. Ibid., 156.
165. Ibid., 159.
166. Ibid., 167.
167. Personal Archives Family de Roquemaurel: Christian de Roquemaurel de l'Isle, *Voyage au centre de ma vie* (1986) 246.
168. Nitti Account (2025) 167.
169. Ibid., 174.
170. Récit Roquemaurel (1986) 251-52.
171. Ibid., 180.
172. Marie Bartette, 'Les étapes d'une déportée', *Le journal d'Arcachon*, 45 (juin 1945). Accessed via https://htba.fr/marie-bartette-les-etapes-dune-deportee-1/.
173. La Contemporaine: Témoinage de Ginette Vincent, 1987.
174. The most detailed work on this topic is Tanja von Fransecky, *Escapees. The History of Jews who Fled Nazi Deportation Trains in France,*

Belgium and the Netherlands, translated by Benjamin Liebelt (New York: Berghahn Books, 2019).

175. FMD: Joseph Onfray, *Tragédie de la Déportation* (1954).
176. Semprún, *The Cattle Truck* (2005) 27.
177. FMD: Onfray, *Tragédie* (1954).
178. Annie Guéhenno, *L'épreuve* (Paris: Bernard Grasset, 1968).
179. FMD: Jacques Adam, 'Impressions et souvenirs de 23 mois de déportation chez les nazis'. Deported 22 January 1944 from Compiègne to Buchenwald.
180. Bernard Le Chatelier, *Matricule 51306: memoires de déportation* (Paris: La Bruyère, 1984).
181. Semprún, *The Cattle Truck* (2005) 28.
182. Récit Roquemaurel (1986) 253.
183. Mémorial de la Shoah, Centre de Documentation Juive Contemporaine (CDJC): DLXI-1, testimony of César Chamay.
184. Nitti Account (2025) 196.
185. Ibid., 197.
186. Récit Roquemaurel (1986) 243–65.
187. SHD: GR 28 P 4 220 / 10 – Nitti.
188. Ramella, *Nitti* (2007) 231.
189. 'Le train fantôme', *Le Messin*, 1 February 1947, 4.
190. AN: 19880016/8/2 Haute-Garonne. Crimes de guerre commis par les allemands en Haute-Garonne. Dossier 15205/4839. Transfèrement en allemagne de prisonniers politiques. (affaire du train fantôme) (1946-1947) Exposé des Faits.
191. Ibid., PV de renseignements sur un convoi de déportés ayant quitté le train à Roquemaure. 1–2.
192. It is possible to explore the website and database of the *Amicale du Train Fantôme*, Accessed via http://www.lesdeportesdutrainfantome.org/.
193. AN: 19880016/4/2 Corrèze. Crimes de guerre commis par les allemands en Corrèze. Prisonniers dans la Synagogue de Bordeaux.
194. *Le Train Fantôme* (1991) 9–10.
195. Interviews with Edith Silve and Jeannine Teissier, 18 August 2024.
196. Guy Scarpetta, *Guido* (Paris: Gallimard, 2014).

197. Interview with Jean-Daniel Simonet, 14 November 2023.
198. Interviews with Hugues de Roquemorel and Corinne Brillié, 14 November 2023.
199. Interview Simonet, 2023.
200. Peter A. Coates, 'The Strange Stillness of the Past: Toward an Environmental History of Sound and Noise', *Environmental History*, 10 (2005) 636–65.
201. Lucien Febvre, 'La Sensibilité et l'histoire : Comment reconstituer la vie affective d'autrefois ?', *Annales d'histoire sociale (1939–1941)*, 3(1–2) (Jan.–Jun., 1941) 5–20.
202. Alain Corbin, *Village Bells: Sound and Meaning in the Nineteenth-century French Countryside* (New York; Chichester: Columbia University Press, 1998); Alain Corbin, *The Foul and the Fragrant: Odor and the French Social Imagination* (Cambridge, MA.: Harvard University Press, 1986); Constance Classen, *Worlds of Sense: Exploring the Senses in History and Across Cultures* (New York: Routledge, 1993); Leigh Eric Schmidt, *Hearing Things: Religion, Illusions, and the American Enlightenment* (Cambridge, MA: Harvard University Press, 2000); Mark M. Smith, *Sensory History* (Oxford: Berg, 2007); Nikolaus Wachsmann, 'Lived experience and the Holocaust: spaces, senses and emotions in Auschwitz', *Journal of British Academy*, 9 (2021) 27–58; Simone Gigliotti *The Train Journey: Transit, Captivity and Witnessing in the Holocaust* (New York: Berghan Books, 2010).
203. Pierre Bourdan, *Carnet de Retour avec la Division Leclerc* (Paris: Payot & Rivages, 2014); Marcel Picard, *J'étais un correspondant de guerre* (Lille: Janicot, 1946).
204. Nitti Account (2025) 149; See also Semprún, *The Cattle Truck* (2005) 37–38.
205. Ibid., 173.
206. Ibid., 180.
207. Ibid., 163.
208. Ibid., 150; 159; 175.
209. Ibid., 191.
210. Récit Roquemaurel (1986) 247.
211. Ibid., 244.
212. Nitti Account (2025) 165.

213. Nitti Account (2025) 147.
214. Récit Roquemaurel (1986) 245.
215. Nitti Account (2025) 160.
216. Récit Roquemaurel (1986) 254.
217. Semprún, *The Cattle Truck* (2005) 29.
218. Nitti Account (2025) 145.
219. Récit Roquemaurel (1986) 254.
220. Nitti Account (2025) 151.
221. Ibid., 174.
222. Ibidi., 192.
223. Récit Roquemaurel (1986) 253.
224. Ibid., 245.
225. Récit Nardone.
226. Nitti Account (2025) 192.
227. CDJC: CCXXXVI-62 Déposition non datée de Raymond Lévy sur les circonstances de sa déportation de la prison Saint-Michel de Toulouse et de son évasion du 02/07/1944 au 25/08/1944.
228. Nitti Account (2025) 169.
229. Ibid., 180.
230. CDJC: DCCXCIII-64 Tracts contre l'oubli des horreurs de la guerre. Claude Urman. *Jeunesse Héroïque. Il y avait un camarade. Biographie de François Lafforgue*, ed. Association des Amis des F.T.P.F. (Strasbourg) 21–22.
231. Nitti Account (2025) 146.
232. Ibid., 158.
233. Ibid., 145.
234. Ibid.
235. Récit Roquemaurel (1986).
236. Nitti Account (2025) 160.
237. Nicolas Wade, 'The Search for a Sixth Sense: The Cases for Vestibular, Muscle, and Temperature Senses', *Journal of the History of the Neurosciences*, 12(2) (2003) 175–202; Gerald Wiest, 'The origins of vestibular science', *New York Academy of Sciences* (2015) 1–9.
238. Nitti Account (2025) 183.
239. Ibid., 192.

240. Ibid., 193.
241. Ibid., 155.
242. Ibid., 187.
243. Ibid., 153.
244. Ibid., 158.
245. Semprún, *The Cattle Truck* (2005) 28.
246. The spelling errors for names of places are in the original version. La Contemporaine: Témoinage de Ginette Vincent, 1987.
247. Nitti Account (2025) 160.
248. Ibid., 160; 168.

The Phantom Train

By Francesco F. Nitti

To my wife Ada and the womenfolk
of my comrades on the Phantom Train

Preface by Jean Cassou

Francesco Nitti has become something of a specialist in stories of escape. They form a literary genre of their own and their exponents need the special qualities that Nitti revealed in his previous book, the account of how he and two equally remarkable comrades, Lussu and Carlo Rosselli, escaped from their prison on the island of Lipari. The subsequent death of Rosselli will forever be on the head of that monster, Il Duce. Today though, in the present book, Nitti takes us with him on a journey to freedom through very different straits, not treacherous rock-strewn seas this time but down between the wheels of a train of railway wagons speeding by just centimetres above his body lying flat on the track. I defy anyone to read this straightforward, unadorned account without shuddering in sheer horror and amazement. Nitti tells a heart-stopping story of how certain people have faced up to what we are having to live through. It's a remarkable record of suffering and fortitude.

Between his first and second escape, Nitti endured exile in France and war in Spain, where he served as an artillery officer in the Republican Army. He was all too familiar with the wretchedness of exile, for which Cacciaguida prepares Dante with such eloquence. After Spain, next it is in France that Liberty was crying out for rescue before it was too late. Unwavering in his commitment to our cause, the indomitable Nitti joined the Resistance movement, which had been steadily growing from roots of irrational hopes and dreams. Nitti and I were members of the same Toulouse cell, and it was on the same December day in 1941 that we were arrested.

Over a period of months we were moved from one prison to another – Toulouse, Lodève, Mauzac – as was the publisher of this book, our dear and courageous friend Louis Vaquer. Eventually, on the same day, Nitti and I were released. But the Vichy police were not going to stand for that. On the other side of the barbed wire fence where our wives were waiting for us, so were the gendarmes, brandishing handcuffs. So off again we went, Nitti and I, to continue our fraternal conversation in the Saint-Sulpice-la-Pointe camp. A month later, I was released, and I returned to my law-breaking activities. But first I'd had to go through the sad business of saying farewell to Nitti. As a foreigner, he was being transferred to the internment camp at Vernet.

Anyone who has experienced life in prison knows that no friendship can compare with those forged behind bars. Nitti was much loved by his fellow prisoners. Spirited, strong-willed and generous-hearted, he had a special aura about him. Every blow which Fate dealt him he met with the detached curiosity, patience, and grace of the well-bred gentleman who prefers to meet the enemy's every new trick with laughter rather than tears. It was these qualities which made him such a comforting and reassuring companion. He made us understand more clearly than ever that our struggle was a just one. With him, we saw the comedy as well as the sheer effrontery of mankind's basest deeds. He helped us rise above our circumstances. He breathed the pure oxygen of truth, and he made us breathe it too. If, as I do, I believe that Italy will rise again; if, as I do, I have faith in the Italian people; and if their country's last twenty years under fascist rule seem one huge and hideous lie, an un-Italian aberration (unlike Nazism, a phenomenon that is altogether German), it is thanks to the likes of Francesco Nitti and to that native Latin intelligence which is the very antithesis of the grotesque, monstrous fraud currently imposed on Italy; and to that country's great, age-old, deep-rooted tradition of which its people fully understand they are both the heirs and the defenders; and it is thanks equally to the republics of the fifteenth century, and to Garibaldi, Mazzini and Manin ... No squalid little upstart, no puffed-up mediocrity can ever or will ever tarnish the jewelled splendour that is Italy.

On his deathbed, looking back over his life in that slightly wry fashion of his, Heinrich Heine murmured, 'But when all's said and done I *was* one of liberty's true warriors.' I hope that one day I myself will be able to make the same claim! And you, Francesco, my friend, my comrade-in-arms, my companion-in-suffering, you who will continue to take the fight wherever Liberty finds itself in peril, not just in Italy but also in our beloved Spain and France – you more than any of us will have earned the right to utter those same words of Heine's with the quiet and more than justified pride which your smile never quite manages to conceal.

Jean Cassou

Introduction

A few days ago I was returning home from Paris by train. Comfortably settled in a second-class compartment between an old man with a white moustache and a generously-proportioned woman reading a romantic novel, I was dozing. We were fast approaching Châteauroux.

At some point, I was overwhelmed by a sudden and strange vision. I was on another train, quite unlike the present one. I closed my eyes, and as I listened to the rhythmic clickety-clack of the wheels on the rails, I said to myself:

> Open your eyes again and you'll find yourself squatting on your haunches in a different vehicle on a different train, the Phantom Train, which wandered about for more than two months before finally disappearing over the German border. You'll be back on the floor of that putrid wagon among seventy near-naked comrades, your body squeezed tight against theirs, curses and groans filling the contaminated air. Then the train comes to a halt. Our guards, big brutes from the *Feldgendarmerie*, run back and forth, calling to one another. They're armed with grenades and machine-guns. They yell, they bark out threats. Once they've reassured themselves that the doors of the cattle-trucks we're confined to have remained properly locked, they march up and down on either side of the train. We're in a siding outside some big station. Strings of wagons full of war materiel stand on the adjacent tracks. It's August,

> and the heat is terrible. Our wooden wagon is a furnace. The sweat from all these bodies crammed together in such a small space is streaming down and mingling with everybody else's. We're parched, our mouths are bone-dry. There's hardly a breath of air. We'll be staying put for a few hours or a few days. Then, after a series of incomprehensible manoeuvres, the train will be off again. We'll make it to some other station where, whether it's big or small, we'll come to a halt yet again ...

I open my eyes. I'm still in my comfortable carriage on the express from Paris. The old gentleman is asleep, the large woman is tucking into a tasty-looking sandwich. Is my nightmare over?

I'm haunted by the memory of the Phantom Train. It really did exist; it's a fact. Seven hundred human beings did suffer, scream and weep inside it. The fact is that today, at this moment, those men and women are in Germany behind the barbed wire of concentration camps in the depths of brutal winter, deprived of food and clothes and warmth.

My thoughts never stray far from them, my companions in suffering and misfortune, and I write these lines thinking of them. As I visualise them, each and every one forever etched on my memory, I murmur a few words of hope:

'Be brave, comrades, stay strong, and soon we'll all be together again.'

Chapter 1

The entry for 6 June 1944 in the log which I've kept religiously through thick and thin right up to today reads: 'The Allies have landed in northern France. Down here, all remains calm. We await developments nervously.'

'Down here, all remains calm ...' The *here* was Vernet, the concentration camp in Ariège reserved for foreigners, where acts of reprisal the whole world now knows about were carried out. I'd been there since 3 July 1943, following a year in military prisons at Toulouse, Lodève, and Mauzac in the Dordogne. Among my fellow inmates were Pierre Berteaux, Jean Cassou, Louis Vaquer and Marcel Vanhove. We'd all been tried and sentenced together in 1942. At the end of my sentence, Jean Cassou and I had been transferred to the camp at Saint-Sulpice-la-Pointe, in the Tarn. Then, as a foreigner, I'd been interned in Vernet, and to my great sorrow, separated from my dear comrades.

By the time I got there, Vernet was no longer quite the nightmarish place it had been in 1939, '40 and '41. During those years, it had been run with an iron discipline. For months on end, there'd been a shortage of food, and the cemetery had steadily swollen with row upon forlorn row of fresh graves.

In 1943, the people running the camp saw that the march of history was inexorably changing direction. Surveillance squads of gendarmes and uniformed guards were deployed to keep watch inside the camp as well as beyond its perimeter. The rest of the personnel comprised a police superintendent and several plain-clothes inspectors and officers. In overall charge of the camp were the commandant and his deputy.

Having experienced military prison, I didn't find the discipline too harsh. Food was neither interesting nor plentiful, but we got by, especially in the summer months. We were allowed family visits as well as food parcels and clothes.

I'd asked to be given some work to do, and had been made camp librarian. I spent my days among Vernet's several hundred books, classifying and cataloguing them to facilitate their distribution round the various sectors of the camp. At that time there was the B sector for political prisoners; the T sector for workers; the C sector was the hospital wing. This last one included those internees whose files were being assessed or for whom there wasn't as yet any clear reason to detain them. I myself was housed in the hospital wing, following an illness of several weeks. I shared a small room in a long hut with a Spanish officer, Lieutenant Colonel Salavera. We became great friends. Salavera was about sixty years old; he was fit for his age, and he held himself in the erect military fashion, shoulders back. A career soldier, he was one of that select band of courageous officers in the former Spanish army who remained loyal to the Republic when Franco rose against it in 1936. He'd tell us about the most interesting moments in his career, the campaigns in the Rif War, the various battles he'd fought, and the injuries he'd sustained. I was particularly struck by his account of the occasion in Barcelona in July 1936 when almost single-handedly he'd prevented his regiment of infantry from mutinying against Spain's legitimate government. Our main topic of conversation was the war now raging across the world. Well into the night we'd go over the scraps of news which came our way, doctored, of course, by the Vichy press, and we tried to predict what would happen next. The prospect of an Allied invasion kept our thoughts occupied for many a long hour. When would it happen? On which bit of the French coast? What would be the Allies' strategy? Then, on 6 June, when the landings did take place, we went wild with joy. We were desperate to know more. What had the Allied forces gone on to do afterwards? Our emotions were running high. That was also true of those guards who often brought us the latest news from London which they'd heard on the wireless. Naturally, they were petrified that what they were doing would be discovered. Among the guards was a unit of Darnand's *miliciens* sent to spy on staff as well as prisoners. On the morning of 9 June (all bad things happen on a Friday), scarcely three days after the Normandy landings, I was awoken by a comrade who rushed into our sleeping quarters panting for breath.

'Get up,' he shouted, 'the Germans have taken over the camp.'

Still half-asleep, we looked at this bearer of bad news with considerable distrust. The fact is that silly hoaxes happened all the time in Vernet. There were certain internees who spent their entire time dreaming up fake news. We called them Radio Latrine. (Readers may not know what latrines are like in prisons and camps; just ask any former inmate.) The comrade who'd awoken us was getting on in years, and had been a journalist all his working life. Everyone knew how desperately keen he was to *appear* well informed – one of the deceptions common in his trade. He liked to tell us how he'd spent a lifetime fighting for peace, writing books and newspaper articles, joining every peace campaign going. Now having to live with the marvellous results of his heroic efforts, we'd often come close to thumping him.

However, that morning of 9 June, it was genuine news he was bringing. I went to the window and saw that for once what our journalist was saying was true. On the far side of the barbed wire, 100 metres from the huts, helmeted German guards had already taken up position.

We got dressed quickly and went outside. All around, groups of internees had gathered. Everyone was in a state of agitation, talking, arguing, exchanging views, second-guessing what was going to happen. As for our own guards, we found out an hour or so later that they'd been disarmed at first light by the Germans, who'd arrived at the camp gates in lorries. The gendarmes were relieved of their guns, revolvers, and automatic rifles, and then confined to Sector B, the one for political prisoners. The same happened to the other guards, to the police and the camp's office staff. The prisoners held in Sector B were transferred to Sector T to make room for the new inmates, the uniformed men who up to that point had formed the camp's surveillance corps. The whole operation had been carried out by a company of *Landsturm* reservists under the command of a captain. The company was composed of older men unsuited to combat at the front. Later, we were able to talk with some of them through the barbed wire. They told us that they'd been declared unfit for service four or five times, but at their last medical they'd been given non-combatant duties. They were under the command of junior regular officers, most of whom wore the insignia of the Russian campaign. They were cruel and vicious, and they terrorised their own men.

A new life began. The camp became disorganised, the first few days especially. All services ceased. Provisions arrived only every fourth day, when the German commandant allowed two or three of our erstwhile guards to fetch them in. All internees were confined to their respective quarters, even those the camp's French staff had allowed to work in sectors other than their own. Family visits continued to be permitted but only under the watchful eye of the German soldiers. So it was that I had the joy of being reunited with my wife and family, though these visits would be the last occasion I'd have any contact with them for a very long time – something I couldn't have guessed then. Only one of the camp's French staff stayed on in post: Monsieur Vernet. This man, who by pure coincidence shared his name with the camp itself, was at that point its deputy commandant. The commandant himself had left for Vichy a few days earlier. We never saw him again.

It seems Monsieur Vernet, who spoke fluent German, was of Austrian descent. During the time the Germans ran the camp, he went nowhere without an armed escort. Apparently, the Ariège *maquis* wanted him dead or alive. Monsieur Vernet was the only senior official to continue co-operating with the Germans right up to the time we left the camp. He's currently in prison following his capture shortly after the liberation.

On 18 June, representatives of the *Organisation Todt* came to the camp. When I'd arrived in July 1943, there were about a 1,000 internees. Eventually, the figure rose to 1,500, but fell again following the deportation of a very large number of Jewish prisoners, men, women, and children. In May 1944, the Gestapo bundled all remaining Jews into lorries, prodding and hitting them with their rifle butts. They were then conveyed to Toulouse, where a train was waiting to transport them to Germany. The *Organisation Todt* had already made several visits to the camp, and taken away the majority of internees after a cursory medical examination, so that by June 1944 we were down to around 400 internees, nearly all of them sick, old or wounded. Roughly 100 were amputees, most of whom had lost limbs in the Spanish Civil War. On 18 June, the *Organisation Todt* rounded up the last remaining men still able to wield a shovel. I managed yet again to avoid the medical. The sixty or so prisoners deemed fit left for Toulouse three days later. We heard later that part of their group was transported to Germany and the rest to northern France. Those of us who remained at Vernet thought that the Germans wouldn't consider us worth bothering about. Would there really be any point in relocating the old, the maimed, the amputees? At a critical time like this, when the Allies had established a foothold on the European mainland and the whole transport system needed to be turned over to the German war effort, how could it be deemed a priority to move or deport us? Logic was on our side. But German logic was nothing like ours, as events would very quickly prove.

On Thursday, 29 June, I had the joy of seeing my family once again. We met in the camp's visiting room, situated in a wooden hut near the entrance. Close by, sub-machine guns poked their barrels through the slats in a block of concrete. I wasn't aware that our masters had already decided on our fate. But I did have forebodings that forlorn June day. Rain had fallen in the morning; then a few rays of sunlight pierced the clouds. But still the sky hung low and overcast, grim as the adventure we were about to embark on.

At 5 p.m. I embraced my wife and children. I was on my way back to my quarters when I heard the rumour that was running round: we were leaving the next day. In camps and prisons, it's always the inmates who are the first to spread the news. This piece of information was accurate. Most of the night was spent packing our belongings. We didn't get to bed until the small hours, and then none of us could sleep. Going round and round in our heads was the prospect of a fresh, unpredictable crisis in our lives, bound to be awful. The following morning, Friday, 30 June (for the superstitious, another Friday), we were up at dawn. Our luggage was ready. The official order to leave arrived. The evacuation of the camp began at 8. The German soldiers packed us together in an alley opposite the camp's office block. There, a fleet of lorries and buses was waiting. M. Vernet and a few of his subordinates were standing alongside the German officers. He did a roll call, reading from the three lists he'd drawn up himself. One was of internees considered to be the most dangerous; the second, those held for reasons yet to be determined; the third, those arrested for infringements the administration deemed minor. Soon, the first convoy of lorries left for Toulouse. Each lorry had a German escort and a few French *miliciens* on board. It was not until the afternoon that the camp was completely empty. I was on the last lorry to leave. A *milicien* with the face of a spiv was sitting close to me, all the while fidgeting with his gun, obviously keen to make an impression. We looked at him with no more than curiosity. He was the typical fascist specimen: arrogant, stupid and cowardly.

By 6 p.m., we were at the Caffarelli police barracks. We disembarked among rows of soldiers armed to the teeth. We were shut in a shabby room on the first storey. Seated on the floor were the 400 comrades who'd left before us. A sleepless night ensued. There'd be plenty more of those in the future. That night it hit home that we'd become nothing more than objects entirely at the mercy of the Germans, items to be got rid of, no longer living, breathing human beings.

Chapter 2

We don't get a wink of sleep that night, 400 of us sitting or lying on bare, unswept floorboards. The first light of day allows us to take stock of one another. We're the picture of exhaustion and fraying nerves. The wives of two Spanish comrades are here with them. All four had arrived in the Noé camp a few weeks ago. Then the order was given to transfer them to Vernet, where our convoy of lorries was expecting them. The two women are in tears, thinking of their children who've not been allowed to leave Noé. Will they ever see them again?

I'm standing in a corner looking at a sea of heads and bodies. Next to me there's an elderly bearded man hunched up on his suitcase, which isn't properly closed. Dirty clothes are poking out of it. His face is waxen. His seventy-five years weigh heavily on him. Close to him are a few Spaniards sitting in the untidiness our night here has created. They're disabled. Two of them have removed their artificial limbs, which lie beside them like worthless discarded objects. The big friendly Asturian called Artime is talking to his comrades with his usual gusto, which makes him sound almost violent. He waves his stump around in the air. He lost his right arm in the final year of the Civil War. I've always thought that he must have acquired extra exuberance and bonhomie in compensation for this loss. He's young and strong, the epitome of vitality and an example to us all. I take another look round this motley crowd of the sick, the injured, and the incapacitated. There's a very small minority of fit and healthy youngsters. I try to weigh up our chances of making it to wherever it is we're supposed to be going. It will all depend on the duration of the journey and the type of transport provided. I can't begin to think why Greater Germany's version of the New Order would want to include the sort of rag-tag bunch we are. 'Providence' certainly can be unfathomable.

Yesterday evening a junior *Wehrmacht* officer made two announcements: one, we'd be leaving in the morning; two, on no account must we go anywhere near the windows, let alone open them. The guards have been ordered to fire on us without warning. As for when our journey will begin, it won't be this morning. Rumours are circulating. Soldiers have been overheard saying that our departure has been delayed until a few hundred more prisoners arrive from the St-Michel prison. The plan is to put them on the same train as us. The windows stay shut and we're suffocating. The air in the room is heavy and foul. The portable latrines placed at our disposal contribute their own delicate fragrance. A few of us have managed to peep down into a side street where a number of women have been watching our windows. Our men used sign language to indicate what was happening. Some caught sight of their wives, others their daughters, roaming around outside the Caffarelli barracks, hoping to witness our departure, which seemed imminent. Later on, in the afternoon, we prisoners are re-organised; one half of us will be transferred to quarters opposite the place where we've been so far. That will make more room. I'm in this group. I take my share of the straw which our comrades are distributing. We get our 'beds' ready for the night to come. I find myself among the group of senior Spanish officers. The highest in rank are Colonel Velasco and Colonel Blasco, both getting on in years, as well as the ever-spritely, ever-smiling Colonel Redondo. Colonel Velasco was tutor to Francisco Franco-Bahamonte, currently the new

Spain's führer, at the Toledo Academy of Infantry. In 1936, when Velasco was commander of a regiment in Valencia, he did what he considered his duty as a loyal soldier of the Republic by not switching sides. He commanded various battalions right through to the end of the war. In February 1939, he crossed into France. He and a group of Republican career officers were arrested by the Gestapo, and spent three months in Perpignan Citadel before being transferred to Vernet. They're all here now. I'm impressed by their high morale and the dignity and courage with which, despite their age and the state of their health, they've faced so many ordeals.

This afternoon, we're allowed to go downstairs to have a wash, overseen by two lines of soldiers. We run towards the water as if towards the most precious nectar in the world. As for food, we've each been given a chunk of bread plus some noodles cooked in unsalted water. Thankfully, we've all got some food of our own. We'd been permitted to store a certain amount at Vernet, and with the help of Mlle Paule Mourret, director of Social Services at the camp, the French Red Cross has also sent us jam, gingerbread, and biscuits. So long as the journey ahead isn't too lengthy, we can hold out. In the evening we go down into the yard. Only a wall separates us from the boulevard that runs in front of the Caffarelli barracks. We can hear the noise of trams and cars, children's voices, all the familiar sounds of the Toulouse where I was living and where my loved ones will remain. Around 7 p.m., a Gestapo staff car arrives and three uniformed men get out. A few minutes later, we're told that we'll be leaving tomorrow morning at 6. We must gather our belongings. We'll be joined by a sizeable cohort of female prisoners and 150 other detainees from the same gaol.

This is how our journey begins: at 6 a.m., we're bundled into lorries and coaches. The men who do the shoving wear death-heads on their caps, and they're not exactly gentle. They keep prodding us with their rifle butts, and we scramble aboard to the accompaniment of 'Scum! Dogs!' shouted in French and about as affectionate as these gentlemen will get. We make our way across Toulouse, which is still half-asleep in the pale early light. At the Raynal railway yard we have our first encounter with the men who are going to be our escort for many a long week.

[NITTI'S FOOTNOTE: *Our German escort was part of an SS Polizei division, which specialised in anti-terrorism. It was made up entirely of professional policemen,* Schupo *or* Schutz-Polizei. *Before France, they'd 'worked' in Russia, Italy and Yugoslavia. The head of our escort was an Austrian Oberleutnant (first lieutenant) called Schuster. His adjutant had the rank of Meister (second lieutenant in Schupo). His name was Weibel. As for surveillance on the journey, an armed guard took up position at the door of every wagon whenever we stopped at a station or in open country. Between each pair of guards there was a Pendel-Posten, or mobile post, made up of men carrying machine-guns.*]

There are about 150 of them, loudmouthed jumped-up thugs in *Feldgendarmerie* uniforms. Half of them are youngsters, the other half older, 40 and upwards. Rank and file men, solid and well fed, bursting with good health and the sheer joy of serving Hitler's Greater Germanic Reich. A good 50 per cent are sporting the Nazi insignia, especially the numerous young SS. One by one we alight from our lorries and are promptly shut into cattle trucks, a long line of which is waiting for us.

Because I'm one of the last to arrive, I find that half the trucks have already been locked and chained. I and some others are pushed into the nearest one available. The door is quickly slammed shut. We count how many we are: sixty. We think it's too many for such a small wooden vehicle hardly big enough for forty.

But this is relative luxury, as sixty will soon become seventy, then seventy-five ... The heat is starting to affect us. Instructions have been shouted that the windows must remain shut. Already, we're stifling. A German speaker among us calls down to the guards to tell them what it's like. They hurl abuse at him, but a few minutes later the order is given that we can open the windows, but on no account must we position ourselves next to them, even less try to look out. If anyone disobeys, the windows will be permanently boarded up.

We try to settle ourselves. We sit on the floor, which is streaked with cement powder. In no time at all, we're white as bleach. This particular wagon must have transported cement to build the infamous impregnable Atlantic Wall. Today, it's carrying a different kind of cargo which no doubt our escort considers of much less value.

We look through little gaps in the side walls of the wagon. We can see officers in discussion with French and German railway personnel. Then we hear banging coming from the adjacent wagons. We wonder what on earth it can be. We soon find out; a couple of gendarmes arrive to nail planks across the slats of our two windows. The existing lack of air and light is bad enough; now it'll be worse. We begin to sweat. The walls and the roof are heating up even further. We remove our jackets and trousers. We're down to our underpants. Around midday, the instruction comes that we must surrender our knives, scissors, razors, nail files, and any blunt instruments in our possession. What was not dangerous in Vernet has become so here. A guard shouts: 'Everything will be returned to you in Germany.' How very kind of you! I'll happily hand over my beautiful new Swiss penknife in return for never having to clap eyes on your charming country!

Our first night aboard the train has passed. Monday, 3 July, and we're still in the Raynal yard. Around 10 a.m., women volunteers from the Quakers pass down the length of the train. One by one, the wagons are unlocked, and the women distribute hot drinks and bread. They look at us with sympathy and compassion. The guards stick close to them, monitoring their every word and movement. The distribution is quickly done and we're shut in again. There's shouting, blasts on whistles, guards running up and down. Some of them take to their motor cars and disappear. Finally the train shakes into life and starts to move. It's midday. Adieu, Toulouse ....

By early evening, we've arrived at Bordeaux. The train comes to a halt in the marshalling yard, whereupon a violent thunderstorm suddenly erupts. Naturally, the rain gets into our wagon. We get wet, but the heat stays just as stifling as before. The sweat is pouring off us. In this Turkish bath we must be shedding kilos. We spend the night of 3-4 July parked on a disused track. At nightfall, the doors of our wagons are opened, we're each given some water and allowed to get out to attend to our most pressing business, as it's tactfully put. In groups of four or five, we're taken to the boundary wall and told to get on with it. The guards don't let us out of their sight. They're carrying rifles and machine-guns. Some have grenades. We've already ascertained that our escort team is heavily armed with plenty of automatic rifles and a large arsenal of ammunition, including grenades.

I take advantage of this evening sortie to have a good look at our train of horror. It's made up of about thirty wagons. After every fourth or fifth one, there's a third-class carriage for the gendarmes. Other vehicles contain provisions, munitions, straw and packing crates. Further to my right, I see more squads of gendarmes taking prisoners off the train and across to the same wall, which encircles the entire marshalling yard.

'Those are the lads from St-Michel,' whispers a comrade who's squatting next to me.

‘How many are we in this train altogether, do you know?’

‘About 650, including forty women. The Caffarelli barracks were full of prisoners, male and female. I managed to snatch a few words with a couple of them. They said that every prison around is chock-a-block and there’s nowhere to put new arrivals. They’re using this train to get rid of a few. There’s no way we can speak with the St-Michel prisoners yet, but when we can it’ll be very instructive. They’re bound to have lots of news to impart.’

‘Stop talk!’ yells one of the Germans. ‘Get again to the train!’

We don’t wait for a second invitation. They’re looking for any pretext to do us some damage. We’ve already been warned that if there’s any attempt to escape, ten prisoners from the wagon concerned will be shot. The train sets off into the night. On and on we go, passing through sleeping stations scarcely visible in the feeble light of a lamp briefly waved from the platform. After an hour, the train comes to a halt and does some incomprehensible shunting. It changes track two or three times. It starts, stops, starts again. What does it all mean? We try to find out by listening at the tiny gaps in the blocked-up windows and the walls of the wagon. It’s futile. All we can hear is steam escaping from the locomotive, the whistles of other engines passing by, things shouted in German by guards who leap down and search the track every time the train stops, lighting their way with electric torches. Some pause occasionally to press their ears to their side of the wagons, checking if they can hear anything of what we’re discussing inside, though mainly they’re listening out for the sound of sawing or the creak of a floorboard being prised up. We quickly realise what they’re doing. The moment the guards reach our wagon, we go quiet. We post lookouts by the window. Eventually, the train gets under way again.

‘We’re heading back to Bordeaux,’ says one of our lookouts.

He's right. One hour later we're back in the yard where we started. More manoeuvres, more false starts, more halts, more starts. Then it's complete silence except for the footsteps of the guards pacing up and down.

Chapter 3

4 July, 7 a.m., we set out once more from Bordeaux, heading northwards in the direction of Angoulême. Our destination and likely itinerary are what we've been mostly talking about from the start of our ordeal. At Vernet, some guards in the know had confirmed that we'd be heading towards Compiègne. Then, at the Caffarelli barracks in Toulouse, the rumour went round that we'd be going straight to Germany and one of the camps the Reich had set up for political prisoners. As for our route, given that we were in Bordeaux, the majority of us thought that it would go through Angoulême, Poitiers, Tours and Paris. Our forthcoming journey was indeed our main talking point.

But opinion was divided. Some of us believed, quite reasonably, that it wasn't credible the Germans would send us on a route as strategically vital as that one through Tours just when the fighting in Normandy was at its most intense and Allied planes were pounding the railway network behind the German frontline. Others said that the Germans would risk it anyway. Agreed, it might have been a different matter if our train had been carrying armaments or aircraft engines. On the other hand, since we were no more than 'enemy terrorists', just meat to be processed, why hesitate? Maybe you're right, came the reply, but what about our escort? There were 150 Germans on board with no desire to get blown to bits by the RAF.

Around 10 a.m., we reached the little station of Parcoul-Médillac on the outskirts of Angoulême. There, our train parked itself in a siding, and there we remained for most of the day.

We were roughly 200 metres from the station buildings. Silence all around; no passengers, no staff. At about 4 p.m. we heard a muffled sound in the sky, coming from the west. Almost immediately, five spotter planes appeared. They flew over our train at an altitude of a thousand metres or so, and vanished to the east. It was then that we witnessed a disgusting spectacle which later would become quite normal. The whole of our escort, all those brave SS and *Feldgendarmes*, so courageous when it came to beating and insulting us, abandoned their posts and scurried away the moment they saw RAF planes in the sky. Obviously, they thought the whole area was about to be blanket-bombed. On both sides of the train, we saw those valiant men hare off, darting this way and that or crouching down among the vines. The first to flee was the commander in chief, followed by his underlings. In their mad dash each man had managed to grab something: a bag, a suitcase, a leather briefcase, a rug, a rifle. They quickly made it to safety about 200 metres from the train, then set about a 'reconnaissance' of the sky. Only a few of our escort stayed put on the railway track, one every 50 metres. Once they'd checked that the wagons were securely shut, they found their own hiding places from which they could keep an eye on the train, weapons at the ready. A group of four or five of them set up their machine-gun behind some hay bales stacked some fifty metres from the train, next to a hut. We watched all these goings-on with mounting concern. The Germans' frenzied flight was the surest way to make the planes return.

'We'd better brace ourselves,' someone in our wagon shouted, 'the planes will be back soon. They must have spotted the gendarmes jumping down and making a run for it. The pilots are bound to think the train is full of German troops.'

'That's right,' said others, 'a train of sealed wagons doing nothing outside a country station wouldn't interest those planes if they were looking for a more important target further off. But dozens of fleeing Germans in uniform means they're sure to return.'

The distant sound of explosions told us that the planes must have dropped some bombs somewhere. Minutes later, they reappeared, flying lower this time in formations of two and three, and heading our way.

'That's it,' someone yelled, 'they're coming for us.'

It'll take longer to recount what happened next than the time it lasted. First, the planes flew over the train east to west, then four of them turned and circled in a wide arc while a fifth one peeled off and headed straight for us. The crackle of gunfire ripped through the air. The men hiding behind the bales of straw opened fire on the plane, which then swooped low over our locomotive and sprayed it with bullets. The plane rose again and continued to circle above us like a merry-go-round, still firing its gun, always flying width-wise across the train, never down its length. We heard cries coming from one of the wagons close to ours, then more machine-gunfire. We thought it was our own wagon which was being hit. The noise of the plane's engine was deafening. It was flying very low, scarcely higher than the telegraph wires. It rose then dived again, guns blazing. Next, we heard an explosion which we took to be a small bomb. Then the plane climbed high and rejoined the others which were continuing to circle, waiting. Finally they all vanished, heading west.

To be machine-gunned in open country by an aeroplane is not particularly pleasant, to say the least. I'd endured the same thing many times during the Spanish Civil War. But I'd always been able to choose where I ran to and threw myself to the ground or lay low in a ditch or took shelter behind a tree. That way, at least I had the illusion that I wouldn't be spotted by the pilot. However, to be in some remote station, cooped up in a wooden box on wheels, knowing that it and all the others either side of you are in the cross-hairs of a plane which can toy with you for as long as it likes and that you're a sitting duck waiting for the fatal bullet that will end the nightmare – that deadly game of cat-and-mouse is pure and utter terror.

When we heard the first burst of gunfire, all sixty in our wagon dived to the floor. Many of us instinctively grabbed suitcases and boxes and held them over our heads in the vain hope they'd give us protection. Between two rounds of gunfire, there was much talking and shouting and swearing.

'Those bloody Germans! First they run for it, then they open fire and all hell is let loose!'

'Bastards! They're making the plane retaliate on *us*!'

'Look out! Lie flat, it's coming back! ... Panic over, it's gone.'

As soon as the noise of the plane's engine had subsided, we ran to the windows. Everyone wanted to see, everyone was talking, yelling, asking questions. The first thing we saw was a German policeman lying face down on the ground directly outside our wagon. Two of his colleagues were attending to him. There was a pool of blood. Moments later, Dr Van Dick, one of the Vernet contingent, arrived on the scene. He'd been fetched from his wagon to tend the wounded. We watched on as the badly injured soldier was taken away.

From what we learnt later, it seems that after the Germans opened fire, the plane machine-gunned the locomotive to put it out of action. Then the plane turned its attention to the train itself, spraying the front wagons with bullets, killing three of our comrades and seriously injuring several others. One German was wounded, the one lying by our wagon. He'd tried to fire his machine-pistol at the plane which had wheeled round and opened up on him. On the ground in front of our wagon we could see the row of pockmarks left by the bullets. Dr Van Dick attended to the

German then walked down the length of the train, banging on the door of each wagon.

'Any wounded in there?'

If the answer was yes, the gendarmes heaved open the door and the victims were brought out. For quite a while we watched the comings and goings of Germans and French railway staff as well as the civilians and police who'd gathered over by the station. An ambulance arrived and took away the most seriously hurt. We got no further news that day of the comrades who'd been evacuated. Later, we heard that after the first wave of shooting, prisoners in other wagons had waved scarves and handkerchiefs out of the windows to attract the pilot's attention. Having swooped down low, the plane had circled several times over the train and then stopped firing. The pilot must have realised it was full of deportees.

Thursday, 5 July [*TRANSLATOR'S NOTE: in fact, a Wednesday*], the sky was overcast and the heat was unbearable. At 10 a.m., there was another alert but this time we didn't see any planes. We guessed that RAF planes couldn't be very far away since our guards embarked on the same 'running race' as the previous days. They disappeared into the fields and the vineyards and didn't return to the train until evening. We, however, remained firmly bolted in our wagons and without water.

Our ordeal got worse, mainly because of the lack of water. No one slept a wink that night. I've never felt the want of sleep as badly as I did on that train. It was physically impossible for sixty people to stretch out in such a confined space. There was scarcely room even to sit. We had to take care not to extend our legs too much and invade our neighbours' space. Did I say space? All through the day and then the night, near-naked body was pressed tight against near-naked body, sweat pouring and intermingling. By 4 a.m., we were running out of air. The heat was as fierce as if it was midday. The walls of the wooden wagon had had no chance to cool down. That hellish box was a furnace. We tried to devise a sleep rota, groups of twenty at a time who'd stretch out from, say, 10 p.m. to 1 a.m., or 1 to 4 a.m. The remainder would sit or stand awaiting their turn. As in any community, there were arguments and petty squabbles. Several of our number were getting on in years, worn out, unwell, their nerves in shreds. The first glimmers of dawn revealed a sprawling mass of emaciated figures, white as ghosts. Our beards and hair were growing long and straggly. We were fast becoming the classic picture of fugitives on the run.

We spent the next night laid up at Parcoul-Médillac. It wasn't until 6 July that we set off in the direction of Coutras. The mysterious shunting manoeuvres started up again. Why would we be going to Coutras? A thousand and one theories flew around. A change in the itinerary? The *maquis*? We'd overheard guards saying that Resistance units were now fully in action. Bridges and tracks were being blown up, entire trains too. Knowing that the Germans were petrified was some small recompense at least for the nightmare they were putting us through. They lived in mortal fear of the *maquis*. When night came, they mounted a guard of two or three men who scanned the darkness and shouted '*Halte*!' every time they heard anything suspicious.

From Coutras we started out once again for Angoulême. Our train was turning into a rudderless ship, borne by the waves towards the shore, then swept back out to sea, tacking and veering under full sail towards some distant and unknown harbour. Our guards gave the impression of not knowing or understanding anything. The only duty of the captain was to find a way into port. We stopped at Charmant, a small station near Angoulême. In our dire situation this respite felt like a ray of sunshine. We stayed put for two days. The wagon doors were opened for a few hours, and we were brought water. A *Secours National* [National Assistance] van arrived from Angoulême. The young women aboard them dished out provisions. Most welcome of all was the hot soup. In the early evening a violent storm broke out, and once more we got drenched. The floor of the wagon flooded. At around 11 p.m., we set off yet again and at dawn on 8 July we entered Angoulême station.

I'll never forget the sight that greeted us! The station had been completely destroyed. Once it got lighter, what we discovered were heaps of mangled locomotives and smashed wagons. Torn-up rails pointed their skeletal arms skywards. The buildings had been reduced to empty husks. Teams of workmen were moving back and forth along the track, carrying shovels and pickaxes, trundling wheelbarrows. When our train came crawling out of the mouth of the tunnel and into the station, they must have wondered if they were hallucinating.

We remained all day at Angoulême, parked in a remote siding. Then off we went again back where we'd come from – Bordeaux.

Chapter 4

When I look back on that dark chapter which ended in tragedy for so many of our dear comrades, what strikes me most is human beings' extraordinary ability to adapt. Take ten men, shut them in a cell with very little food or water, and yes, they will suffer terribly. But bit by bit they'll adapt to the inhumane situation, they'll develop little habits, and as each day passes the harrowing pain of the first moments will diminish. Add another ten men, give them a bit less bread and just one glass of water, the suffering will begin again, this time worse. Then, as one day follows another, the acute suffering will become a matter of habit. They'll bear it. Short of dying, humans get used to anything. That was true of us; locked up in our mobile prison, sixty bodies in an area scarcely sufficient for forty, deprived of air, appallingly maltreated, unable to rest or sleep, slowly we were getting used to the horror of it. Our primitive animal side was taking over. In that pestilential atmosphere, a good few of us managed to sleep, crouching and snoring in barely a square metre of space, legs curled up, arms pressed tight to our sides. Others conversed in low voices, yet others hummed tunes to themselves. A few Spaniards found the strength to sing. It is said that the Spanish like to sing – especially when things are going badly.

I was among comrades I'd known for years. The one I discussed our situation with the most was Pedrini, a born optimist possessed of a great and unshakeable faith in the future. During the whole of our terrible ordeal, he'd come up no matter when with the right words to calm us and give us strength. For him, the outcome was never in doubt: the Germans would not be able to get us to Germany. He assured us the nightmare would soon be over. Given the general state of things out there, a train like ours couldn't possibly get through. So we must bide our time, and go on believing.

There were also comrades who liked to make a joke of things. 'What we are is The Roving Commissioners for Junk & Trash, sent out to list all the scrap material we can find,' said one Italian. 'Which is why we're concentrating our efforts entirely on wrecked stations and abandoned machinery.' Or else, 'Our German hosts are giving us a conducted tour of France so that we can judge for ourselves just what they're up against.'

It was true. We could see with our own eyes just how effective the Allied bombing raids had been. That little phrase, 'Roving Commissioners for Junk & Trash', was soon doing the rounds of the other wagons. Our train, the harshest of prisons, had one thing in common with a regular gaol: despite being strictly forbidden to make contact with prisoners in the other wagons, we managed not only to communicate with them but also to organise a fairly effective and accurate news service. That was normal enough in a gaol, but in ours it felt strange. What we wanted to have news about more than anything else was the progress of the war. Our hunger for information about the fortunes of the Allies following the D-Day landings is what kept us going. That's not difficult to understand. It wasn't simply some abstract interest in the politics of it; it was what kept our hopes alive. In that summer of 1944, our liberty, our very survival, depended on the Allied advance into France. Our train was one of the last, if not *the* last, of the convoys of political prisoners trying to make it out of the country. Our fate rested in the hands of General Eisenhower's troops; if his brave soldiers and his formidable air force could push forward at speed, destroying the railway network which the enemy depended on, severing the lines and wrecking bridges, we ourselves would stand a real chance of remaining in France. And then there was the *maquis*. I've already alluded to the panic which the mere mention of that word caused our guards. They convinced themselves that there were *maquisards* everywhere. And indeed, the fact that our odyssey lasted as long as it did, that we spent so many long days and nights stuck in wayside stations, wasn't down only to the damage caused by Allied air raids, but also to the delays created by our courageous comrades in the *maquis* who were operating in all the areas we passed through. How often did we overhear our escort talking about them! They said that there were 'terrorists' all around. We heard them swapping bits of news, and we'd often pick up that it was the *maquis* in such and such a place who'd brought our train to a halt. Because a bridge had been blown up, or several hundred metres of track had been reduced to a tangle of scrap metal, the train had had to wait for the repairs to be carried out, and that had meant a bit more time won for us. Our suffering may have been immense, but we bore it in anticipation of the greater prize: freedom.

Every wagon had one comrade who could act as interpreter. Interpreters were of supreme value. Other comrades were given different tasks: nurses, carriers of water and fetchers of such food as we were allowed. Passing up and down the train every day as they did, they functioned as bearers of news. In addition, we picked up bits of information here and there: at station water fountains when we replenished our cans, or from the odd civilian or railwayman we came across as we walked along the track. A large informal news network had mushroomed in the country. All the civilians we encountered knew they could pass us information without fear that we'd betray them. Whenever they could, the French railwaymen would signal to us and whisper what they'd gleaned from London on the wireless. Our main danger was the constant watch the German escort kept on us. They were a brutal and suspicious lot. They forbade any contact between us and the outside world. Often I saw the railway workers who were bringing us water get beaten back with rifle butts. The Germans' fear was that every civilian, every station employee, could be a *maquisard* or a 'terrorist'. On top of that they knew that they were surrounded on all sides by the enemy. The *Bahnhof* railwaymen drafted into the German army controlled every station, and the Gestapo or the *Wehrmacht* every town and village. But Germany's enemies were all around. The Germans knew all too well that they were walking a minefield. A look, a smile, the wave of a hand in our direction could be a signal. It was in such an atmosphere that news of the war regularly travelled the length of the mud-coloured serpent we were living in. We were able to communicate from one end of the train to the other and get the latest news. Our old comrades from the St-Michel prison, the brave freedom fighters who'd joined us on our Train of Woe after long months spent in the Gestapo's cells, informed us that among their number was a group of backroom staff from the French police, some brave *Résistants* such as Subra, a divisional commander in Toulouse; and Heim, chief inspector in Cahors. There was our dear Borios, who would later lose his life in the Souge camp. There were others too, including Professor Lautmann from the University of Bordeaux; Peyre-Vidal, an engineer with the Highways and Bridges Department of Ariège; and several non-French nationals, mainly Spanish and Italian.

The first person to escape was one of the French prisoners in the St-Michel contingent. On our sally to Angoulême, the young man jumped from a narrow gap in the window space. Despite the darkness, the guards spotted him. The train was stopped, an intense burst of gunfire followed, but in vain. Under cover of night, our comrade got away. We salute him. As the first one out, he'd set the example which in due course several more passengers aboard the Phantom Train would follow.

We remained in the goods yard at Bordeaux for three days: 9, 10, and 11 July, on a track near the locomotive depot. Adjacent to it was the parcels office, piled high with boxes and packages. Its employees – women as well as men – kept coming and going. Often they looked in our direction with pity in their eyes, but it was almost impossible for them to speak to us. The weather was fresh but humid, the sky overcast; it had recently poured with rain. The 10th was day nine of our incarceration. Our nerves were in bad shape. We were pale and thin through lack of sleep. We still had a small amount of the food we'd brought with us from Vernet. All that the Germans gave us were four dry biscuits per day, the width of two fingers, and a teaspoon of unsweetened jam. Thank heavens the Bordeaux *Secours National* arrived! The doors of our wagons were opened for half an hour and we were given bread and hot broth. The young women of the *Secours National* watched us, shock and fear etched on their faces, as if we were pirates or convicts. True, we weren't a pretty sight: straggly beards, tangled and matted hair, drawn features, hollow eyes, slow movements. Scarcely the picture of decency for well-bred young ladies.

A new rumour started to circulate. According to what some soldiers had said, we were going to remain in Bordeaux. Then further details emerged: we'd be taken from the train into the city and locked up in some barracks while we waited to set off once more. On 11 July, de Pablo let me know that this was correct, broadly speaking, though it was a church or possibly the city's synagogue we'd be shut in, where we'd be held for a month waiting for another batch of prisoners to join us before our train set off again.

De Pablo was a lieutenant colonel in the Spanish army. He was fluent in German, which was why he'd been able to have proper exchanges with our escort. One young officer in particular, a Nazi true believer, enjoyed talking with de Pablo. When he was on duty during the long pauses in stations, he'd listen to de Pablo explain the Spanish Civil War to him, telling him things he found hard to believe because, as a dyed-in-the-wool Nazi, he had all the 'facts' he needed to know; the rest he ignored. One day, de Pablo gave him a lesson on the correct use large battalions should make of artillery, and the young officer listened open-mouthed, astonished that a 'red', a 'Spanish Bolshevik', could teach him anything about military matters. It was he who gave de Pablo the official news that we were to be taken somewhere in Bordeaux, and swore him to secrecy.

And that's what happened. On Wednesday, 12 July we were awoken at 2.30 a.m. The yard was in pitch-black darkness; at that stage of the war blackouts were strictly enforced in Bordeaux. We were ordered to get down from the wagons and gather on the platform. We were surrounded on all sides by guards armed to the teeth with machine-pistols and rifles and grenades.

Our escort had been strengthened by a large deployment of gendarmes from the Bordeaux garrison, plus a Gestapo unit. We stood there with our bags and cases, gazing at the starless sky, breathing in the cool air of night, such a change from the stench inside the wagons!

There's shoving and shouting; it's our lovely guardian angels pushing us around, arranging us in groups of five, yelling in bad French: 'Sort yourselves out! Get on with it!'

We start walking through the silent yard. We reach a set of railings, pass through an opening, cross a bridge, then find ourselves in front of the St-Jean passenger station, unlit and deserted like an abandoned house. The streets are quiet. All the windows are shut, there's no one about. The only sounds are of 600 people trudging slowly along, and the soldiers' repeated cry of 'Move it! Move it!'

I look at the station with its great awning which I've passed beneath so often in happier days. How many times have I come to this city where I have so many friends! How often have I walked along these streets, trodden these pavements, gazed in these shop windows! Who'd have guessed I'd be seeing it again in the present circumstances, in a convoy of deportees surrounded by vicious guards marching us towards an unknown fate. There's Place de la Victoire with its arch, its buildings! There's that avenue whose name I try hard to remember without success! It's easy to lose bits of the memory after days like those we'd had to endure. A first-floor window is open, and a shadowy figure leans out, observing us. Immediately, threats are shouted and the window closes. We continue marching. Our female comrades head the procession, laden like us with luggage. They get pushed around and prodded to make them walk faster. The idea is to get us inside a secure location as quickly as possible. We pass in front of a large building on our left. Next to its main doors there's a sentry-box painted in German colours. The soldier on duty watches us pass by, and is curious.

'Terrorists?' he asks a guard marching alongside me.

'Terrorists, that's right,' comes the reply. The sentry is satisfied; we've been captured, so Germany is safe.

Then we're there. Our crocodile comes to a halt where there's a narrow street to our left. I've since learnt that it was rue Labirat. A few metres away stands the Grand Synagogue, requisitioned by the Germans, who've turned it into an overflow gaol. The Hâ fortress is already full, and the other potential locations for us in Bordeaux are also overflowing with prisoners. So the synagogue now serves as a holding pen for a number of prisoners. We're admitted into its courtyard in groups of ten; we climb a few stone steps, cross a second courtyard, and that's where finally we enter our new gaol.

Bordeaux's Jewish place of worship comprises a vast prayer hall and a number of smaller annexes. The building in which we were going to reside for the next several weeks had been transformed almost out of recognition by the use the Germans were putting it to. At the far end was the bimah, reached by a series of white marble steps. Two rows of seven pillars each, one either side of it, bore the weight of the gallery above. Also at the far end, facing the bimah, there was another gallery furnished with several rows of wooden benches. At the main entrance to the building were three magnificently carved doors of walnut wood. Inside, immediately behind, were two marble plaques which a hammer had smashed. Two branches of the menorah had been broken, reducing the number to five. On one of the walnut doors was an inscription which we hoped would be providential: 'Blessings on you when you enter, blessings on you when you leave.'

All around was evidence of the depredations caused by the Germans. On the right, the magnificent organ was out of commission. A thin layer of dirty straw had been spread over the stone floor. At the end by the entrance doors a collection of portable toilets had been installed for our use. As the destroyers of the Jewish race, the Nazis considered that both by desecrating the synagogue and turning it into a prison for their enemies, they were giving vent to their hatred twice over. We laid ourselves down at around 4 a.m. and I fell immediately into a dreamless sleep. For the first time in ten days and nights, I was at last able to stretch my legs out fully. All around me everyone was already snoring. Further up, on the bimah, groups of slumbering figures looked like dark stains on the white of the stone and the walls. Two light bulbs illuminated this huge improvised camp, 650 souls collapsed on the straw like animals exhausted by a trek that never seemed to end. Up above us on the side and end galleries, rifles at the ready, the gendarmes were the governors of our sleep.

Chapter 5

This is how the next phase of our odyssey began. From 12 July to 9 August we remained in the Bordeaux synagogue. By the time we left, already we'd reached the conclusion that we were stuck there for good. Two things epitomised our time there: first, we got worse physically, as did the conditions we were living in; second, whatever the day served up, we became more and more certain of our ultimate victory. From the moment we arrived, we knew we'd be facing real hardship even if our stay turned out to be short. There was a total lack of hygiene. We were allowed one wash per day in the interior courtyard under the vigilant eye of the gendarmes. But those morning ablutions were no match for the lice. In no time they were everywhere. We had, in fact, occasionally been visited by the wretched things in the train. But in the synagogue the infestation spread so fast that in just a matter of days everyone was contaminated. How to fight them off? We only had cold water to wash our clothes in, and next to no soap. Many of us didn't have a change of clothes to hand. It was all in the luggage which had been confiscated and stacked in an upstairs gallery. The rest of our possessions we'd had to leave at Vernet, so they were gone for good. Therefore fresh clothes were out of the question. We'd wash our things in cold water only to find them still covered in lice. All that the water achieved was to stir them into life. Night and day, night especially, we scratched nonstop. Our fronts and backs looked as if they'd been flayed alive. The hunt for those creatures went on round the clock, a battle endlessly fought and lost.

The food was disgusting. One of the German barracks in town had been given the task of feeding us. Three times a day, a lorry arrived laden with cauldrons. Every morning, we were each given half a litre of dark hot water they called coffee. Midday, it was a plate of hot water coloured yellow this time, in which swam two or three bits of vegetable peel and some potatoes. There was a repeat performance in the late afternoon. We each received about 200 grams of bread. We couldn't have survived without the small food parcels that the Red Cross and the Quakers sent us every week, containing some spice bread and biscuits, and a little bit of butter. Those parcels kept us from starving. We were woken at 6 a.m. Feeding times were midday and 4 p.m. We were allowed to move around the prayer hall, which had been divided into two sections by a length of barbed wire.

Thus, we were reunited with comrades from St-Michel. Among the first I greeted was Professor Lautmann, a man who'd always impressed with his dignity, intelligence, and wisdom. He, Salavera, Velasco, and other friends, and I spent many an hour squatting on the straw, swapping stories of our experiences. We discovered we had friends in common. Lautmann spoke in his very measured way; only once did he get at all loquacious, telling us how in 1940 he'd been an artillery officer, was captured, but with several fellow prisoners had made a daring escape. Often though, a cloud of melancholy would spread over his face. Once, when he seemed particularly sad, I asked:

'Are you unwell?'

'No, no more than any of us,' he replied. 'It's just a premonition that this business is going to finish badly for too many of us.'

I tried to be positive.

'You think so? Granted, for the moment you're part of a convoy making for Germany among people accused of serious or trivial things. And others too, like the ones from Vernet who pose no threat to anyone at all, given their age and physical condition. We'll leave for Germany or we won't, but up till that happens I'm certain we won't come to any harm.'

Lautmann was unconvinced. He remained pensive, shaking his head. Then he looked me in the eye, wanting perhaps to say something. But he thought better of it and wandered off.

At other times, too, I noticed that he seemed to be anticipating something and was preparing himself for it. But at that point nobody could have foreseen that he'd be proved right so soon.

There were several young prisoners in the St-Michel contingent. Many had been tortured by the Gestapo and bore the marks: burns, bruises, disfigurements of every description. One was a youth of 17, a *maquisard* who'd been caught red-handed carrying weapons. He recounted his story in a matter-of-fact way. I talked to him as if he was my son. He was still only a boy, but a determined, intelligent and big-hearted one.

Among my fellow Italians, I recall in particular Arturo Zanoni, Marucci, Ferri, Santi, Lanzati, Arlotto, Franco Beatrice, and a few others. Arturo Zanoni, who'd served as a high-ranking officer in the Spanish army, wasn't feeling too well at that stage. He always sat in the same place, reading. Though he had heart trouble, this great bear of a man with the smiling countenance was the very model of courage and optimism.

Marcucci was a wonderful artist, a product of the Academy of Fine Art. In Vernet we'd been impressed by the drawings and portraits he did to pass the time. But here, in the synagogue, he'd become grumpy, finding it hard to bear a life so devoid of beauty.

We organised a celebration for 14 July, France's national day. In the morning, three quarters or so of the inmates made themselves a tricolour buttonhole from bits of paper they fished out of their belongings. Peyre-Vidal stood on the steps of the bimah, and we listened in complete silence to him speak of his unswerving faith in our ultimate victory, and he asked us to remember those who had already laid down their lives in the struggle. The gendarmes, who'd woken up too late to what was going on, chose not to intervene.

Early in the morning of 15 July, we were herded into one end of the prayer hall. A junior officer, the head guard's right-hand man, began the roll call. He was a strange-looking specimen. Except for his height – he was short – he was the spitting image of the actor Erich Von Stroheim. He even wore his cap nonchalantly slanted over his left ear, the way Von Stroheim did in several of his films. (I say this with all due respect to that great actor, who, in fact, was anti-Nazi and a true gentleman.) The officer stood on the bimah steps to do the roll call. Alongside him were two of our number who acted as interpreters. As our names were called, one by one we moved to form two separate groups behind the officer. Several times he paused when there was no response to the name read out, and we had to remind him that such-and-such had been taken to hospital after the RAF had attacked the train or that another person had been removed to hospital straight after our arrival in Bordeaux. But there were two or three names we stayed quiet about, comrades who'd managed to escape a few days earlier. 'Von Stroheim' understood what our silence meant. He made the interpreters shout the question again: 'So nobody knows where X or Y is?' He tried to look menacing, but then he said: 'Oh, to hell with him!'

15 July was to be a day of much activity. At around 3 p.m., as we lay on the straw digesting the hot water which passed for a meal, we were startled by a command which was suddenly barked out. Our interpreters translated: 'On your feet! Everyone up! Get your belongings together and go out into the yard ten at a time!' Pedrini was standing next to me. Ever the optimist, he whispered: 'I told you they'd take us out of here. This place is a

danger to our health. We'll be going to some barracks somewhere. We'll be much better off there.'

I'd already done my luggage, such as it was: a small case and a bundle of this and that. I wasn't nearly as optimistic as Pedrini. He wanted to be one of the first out. He pulled me along behind him. We went into the yard. Three or four tables had been set up, at which sat a few gendarmes equipped with pens and paper. Straightaway, an officer from the Bordeaux *Wehrmacht* informed us in execrable French of what was going to happen.

'You will empty your pockets of everything, all your coins and banknotes. You will surrender all wrist and pocket watches. And all your rings except wedding rings. All fountain pens, cigarette lighters, nail files, all jewellery and valuables, and razors, razor blades, shaving soap, and brushes. You will hand over the tobacco, cigarettes, and matches in your possession.'

Pedrini and I were the first to present ourselves at one of the tables, where we had to relinquish everything on our person. In return, we were given a receipt written in German, and informed that we'd be reunited with all our belongings once we'd reached Germany. Every prisoner had to go through the same ritual. It went on until evening. Those of us who attempted to hide money or valuables were caught and beaten. Afterwards, we were returned to our places inside the synagogue. The cruellest loss was our tobacco.

Dark clouds filled the sky, and the sun barely penetrated into our prison despite the large gallery windows. This was a time of frequent air-raid sirens, though Bordeaux, in fact, never got bombed. We whiled away the time with endless games of chess, and we read the few books which remained in the synagogue. There was an Italian Bible which belonged to my friend Juan Mossolin. Juan, a lawyer in a northern region of Italy, was both a passionate believer in democracy and a devout Catholic. He and

I had lived at close quarters in Vernet and I'd often heard him debating topics with a combination of passion and forensic skill; that was his distinctive style.

Mossolin had installed himself on the top step of the synagogue's bimah. I can still picture him now, sitting with his baggage, reading his Bible and occasionally raising his head to peer at me through the monocle he usually sported. At certain fixed points of the day he lent me his Bible, thereby ensuring we each got time for a proper read. I revisited the Gospels and the Acts of the Apostles with a great deal of pleasure.

But our main concern was to keep up to date with the news. The Germans had established a tight ring of guards around the synagogue, allowing us no contact with the outside world. At first, it was impossible to lay our hands on any newspaper or catch wireless bulletins. But after a few days, we found a way of outwitting our guards. The prisoners ordered to go to the main entrance every day to collect the food from the lorry began to sneak us back bits of news. The lorry driver was a Spaniard who'd been given special dispensation to work for the Germans. Wily as a snake, he contrived to whisper bits of information to our comrades. It's amazing that so much got conveyed in the very few minutes available – and right under the noses of our supposedly vigilant guards.

We found other ways of getting news. Through one of the windows in the little rooms which overlooked a side street, we'd often seen a middle-aged woman watching us from her house opposite. One day, not at the window but discreetly from further back inside her room, she held up a slate on which she'd chalked news of the war, including about the Allies' advance. And another woman, who lived directly opposite the main entrance to the synagogue, would walk by every time a lorry delivered food, accompanied by a man she pretended to be addressing.

By speaking fast, she contrived not only to transmit the latest news but also to add words of comfort and support to cheer us up. In no time at all, every scrap of the news we'd obtained in these unusual ways had done the rounds of the synagogue. We all discussed everything at great length.

Eventually, we managed to get hold of some newspapers. Every day our gendarmes received copies of a German paper called *Soldaten Am Atlantik*, intended for the troops stationed on France's Atlantic coast. We managed almost every time to filch a copy or two, which the German-speakers among us translated into French. That's how we learnt of the attempt on Hitler's life, which, alas, had failed. One of our interpreters persuaded a German guard to smuggle us in some tobacco and French newspapers. Many prisoners had been able to secrete a bit of cash when our things were searched, and so could pay for the tobacco – at black market prices, naturally. I recall reading a copy of *Petite Gironde* which had cost someone 100 francs.

Our guards were a mixture of stupidity, fear, and brutality. They were frightened of us because we'd been described as dangerous terrorists who had not the slightest regard for life. They loathed us since we were the reason why they'd had to embark on such a long and dreadful journey. These gentlemen from the *Feldgendarmerie* had been despatched from Paris to Toulouse to take charge of us, having first been assured that the whole operation would take no more than three or four days. Several of them had womenfolk in Paris and elsewhere in France and were impatient to get back to them. Things weren't working out for them. They'd already had to spend ten days aboard our train getting machine-gunned by the RAF. The French had risen up against them. They had absolutely no idea when and how our journey would resume. One fact they knew for sure, though:

things may not have been too wonderful for us, but they were not much better for them. There could be no satisfactory outcome to the current situation. They saw that every day, every week, yet more obstacles were being placed in their path. We'd often catch sight of them in the outer courtyard where they had set up their guardroom, sitting on benches, looking dejected. They devoured the newspapers and they pored over maps, following the course of operations. They debated among themselves, alarm written all over their faces. They knew things were 'hotting up', as the expression goes. We hardly needed newspapers to inform us that the war was going well for our side; those men's worried expression said it all, which kept our hopes alive.

What happened on 24 July is proof enough of our guards' state of mind, which, as I've said, was a mixture of hatred and fear. At around 5 p.m., as we were quietly getting our bedding sorted out for the coming night, a dozen gendarmes and one of their superiors rushed into the prayer hall and amid much shouting and threats and pushing and shoving, herded us beneath a gallery close to the bimah. There we stood, several hundred of us, waiting to discover what these charming gentlemen had in mind. We soon found out. An interpreter relayed that a guard on duty outside the building had just heard the sound of a file scraping against the wall. It was made clear to us that if after ten minutes the file hadn't been handed over, next day they'd shoot ten of us. That would be just a start. As he was speaking, a gendarme set up his machine-gun on the central gallery, loaded it, and calmly pointed it down at us. No one uttered a word. The failing light threw shadows across our faces and all around the building. We stood there wondering what would be the consequences of this latest threat. The soldiers encircling us began to brandish their weapons, jostle and kick and insult us, hit us with their rifle butts.

Ten minutes went by. The threat was repeated. We were told we'd spend the entire night on our feet in a corner of the hall, after which we'd discover exactly how the matter was to be resolved. It was at this point that one of our comrades stepped forward, holding a spoon and a file substantial enough only to make some difference to a piece of wood. He explained that he'd been using it not to try to pierce the wall – laughable, given that it was two metres thick – but merely to give the spoon an edge sufficiently sharp to cut his bread. Anyone who's been in prison knows that it's a recognised trick to file down the handle of a spoon – if you happen to have a file, that is – or by rubbing it against a wall, transforming it into a makeshift knife which in a cell comes in extremely handy.

As soon as the explanation had been given and translated into German by one of our interpreters, the gendarmes fell on the culprit, snatched the spoon and file, and hauled him off somewhere for interrogation, hitting and insulting him as they went. Their leader told us that the matter wasn't over yet, that he'd not been fooled by the explanation, that the next day he'd report back and we'd all receive a severe punishment. He marched his men out, leaving us in the gathering gloom, shoved up against the wall, asking ourselves how else they'd use us for our entertainment value. All the while, the machine-gunner on the gallery had carried on loading, unloading and reloading his weapon and aiming it randomly at one section or another of the crowd of captives standing there like a massive herd of cattle. Every so often, the beam of his torch played over us, as if selecting a target. The sound of loading and reloading continued. I expect that by putting the fear of God into us our gunner was giving himself an enormous amount of pleasure.

We remained standing there until 11 p.m. We were beginning to flag when the order was shouted to return to our places, which were in complete chaos as the gendarmes had turned everything upside down and inside out. They'd rummaged around in the straw, emptying our cases, no doubt looking for weapons and ammunition. It took us a good half hour to retrieve our things in the dark and sort them out before we could even think of sleep.

Chapter 6

The lice were particularly busy last night ... That's how I begin my log for 31 July. It was a fine day. Shafts of warming sunlight reached us through the tinted windows of the gallery. Obviously, it was thanks to this new burst of warmth that our uninvited guests had become more aggressive. The sun brought out the colours of the rose window in the gallery, and we scratched and scratched like things possessed.

But the tragedy continued. That afternoon we watched on as ten of our comrades were marched off, possibly unaware they were about to make the supreme sacrifice. At around 4 p.m., one of our senior guards had entered, and through our interpreter ordered us to stop talking. Ten names were read out. They included Lautmann, Borios, Peyre-Vidal, and the boy of 17. They were ordered to pack their things because they were leaving. There was stunned silence everywhere. Our eyes were fixed on those men, worn down by pain and suffering, as they bent over the pathetic luggage which had kept them company thus far, containing whatever remained of the items so lovingly put in for them by a wife, a fiancée, a mother – and which now, after what we'd been through on our wanderings, were reduced to an assortment of bric-a-brac. We didn't know why these comrades were being removed, but we feared the worst, which the demeanour of our captors only served to confirm. Four or five gendarmes armed with automatic rifles kept us under surveillance as the ten men continued with their preparations. The guards harried them: 'Get a move on, get on with it!'

We watched them leave. They passed among us, gripping and shaking the sea of hands held out to them. They hugged and embraced those comrades they'd become particularly close to. I watched Lautmann cross to the door, walking fast and looking calm and almost serene. I was too far away to shake his hand, and the Germans hardly let us move a muscle. We remained in shock the rest of the evening. The following morning, our forebodings about our comrades deepened when we saw that their luggage had been left behind, piled up against a wall in the yard as though surplus to requirements.

It was only much later that we learnt of our comrades' fate. They'd first been taken to the Hâ fortress, and were among forty-six prisoners shot by the Gestapo at the Souge camp soon after in early August. They were led out twice to be murdered only to be brought back to the fortress as apparently there was no firing squad. It was only at the third attempt that Lautmann, Peyre-Vidal, Borios, and all the others were killed, facing the mass grave which had been dug for them.

Life in the synagogue continued, a sad, colourless life lit up now and then by scraps of encouraging news which raised our morale. The weather had turned bad again. Rain fell, the sort of August rain which refreshes nothing and only deepens the already sombre atmosphere. A little before 5 p.m. on Tuesday, 7 August [*TRANSLATOR'S NOTE: in fact, a Monday*] we were given the order to bring down all our luggage, which had been dumped in the central gallery. We piled it up in the synagogue's main corridor. We knew what this meant: we were leaving. An hour later, the women who'd been held all this time in their prison's hospital arrived and were shut in a room adjacent to the main building.

Our interpreters tried to discover what was happening. They found out that indeed we were leaving. At 2 a.m. on Wednesday, 8 August, [*TRANSLATOR'S NOTE: Tuesday*] we were ready and waiting when we were called as we hadn't had a wink of sleep all night. And so off we went, back along the same sleeping streets of Bordeaux we'd come in by. We observed the same buildings, the same squares, the same closed windows. Again, we had to march in ranks of five, pushed and shoved by the numerous guards surrounding us. At 4 a.m. we arrived on the same platform in the same part of the yard we'd left twenty-seven days earlier. The crack troops of the *Feldgendarmerie* were past-masters at filling and emptying trains of human cargo. They had the knack of how to herd a crowd. Occasionally, there was a bit of light which let us read the stencilled markings on the wagons we'd previously occupied, denoting the number of human bodies each one would now hold. The lowest figure was sixty but some said seventy. I was one of the luckier ones, bundled into a wagon marked sixty-five. The moment everyone was in, the doors were slammed shut. Dawn broke. Opposite, on the other side of the platform, there was another train exactly like ours. It appeared to be waiting. It, too, had figures chalked on the wagons. The same as us, its windows were partly covered by strips of wood and barbed wire. The train was empty, the doors open. Through what remained of our windows and some gaps elsewhere we could watch that train. We wondered why it was there. By midday we had the answer. A fleet of vans began to arrive; in their cabs there were French gendarmes and German soldiers who got down and unloaded the vans' contents. We looked on as a lengthy flow of prisoners emerged, both men and women, and were made to line up on the platform below us. There were at least seventy women of varying ages, and a hundred or so men, nearly all of them young. Among them were a black-bearded priest and two French gendarmes still in their uniforms. We quickly found out that they'd been brought from the Hâ fortress. Like us, they were herded into their wagons, which were immediately closed and sealed.

In the evening we set off. We tried our best to catch the name of each station we passed through, in the hope we'd discover the direction we were heading. We were soon past Agen, then Montauban. The train was travelling fast, shooting through all the little stations. At 2 a.m., we passed through Toulouse without stopping. On we went all of the 10th without stopping: Carcassonne, Béziers, Montpellier. On the 11th at around 3 p.m., we came to a halt in a little station outside Nîmes. The guards opened all the wagon doors. We were given a few lumps of bread and a spoonful of jam each. We asked for water. A few young civilians happened to be on the station platform; our guards ordered them to fetch us some. The heat was intolerable. The sun was beating down out of a clear blue sky, turning our wooden boxes into furnaces. We could scarcely breathe. We were packed so tightly that our bodily odours and the sweat that streamed from us all day and all night mingled with everyone else's. Sleep was impossible. The contorted positions we were obliged to adopt half-paralysed our limbs.

I'd found myself this time in the same wagon as a few of my old friends from Vernet, including de Pablo, Juan Mossolin, and Pedrini. De Pablo was our interpreter, the person who most frequently went to the window slit to petition our *meister* for water, and too often was ignored. Mossolin was the model of patience and serenity. He'd compare the terrible things happening to us with events in the Bible, although, being a lawyer by profession, he'd challenge any detail he considered unreliable.

Many of the prisoners in our wagon were ill. Four or five had tuberculosis; one was constantly bringing up blood, and seemed close to death. He moaned and groaned all through the night. He couldn't force air into his lungs, and frequently he passed out. Despite the near-total darkness inside the wagon, I saw the excellent Mossolin hold him up to the window to get a few gulps of fresh air. Dostoevsky's *House of the Dead* couldn't compare with this! There were also a number of elderly men with the usual complaints of old age. Nearly all had heart problems. Some were barely alive; they were just waiting for the merciful release of death.

On 12 August, the train reached Remoulins, 25 kilometres beyond Nîmes and a further 25 short of Avignon. It was in Remoulins that we saw the body of a comrade being removed from the adjacent wagon. He'd died of asphyxiation and lack of food. He was a bank manager from Arcachon. The Germans had arrested, stripped and beaten him, ultimately causing his death. We watched as two of the station staff wheeled his corpse away in a barrow.

We remained in Remoulins until 17 August. During those five days we lived under the constant threat of being blown up by Allied aircraft. English planes flew over us day and night. They arrived in formations of twenty-five, thirty, often fifty. On neighbouring tracks, vast trains packed with war materiel stretched as far as we were able to see. Our situation was grave.

The Germans no longer lived on board the train. Apart from a few sentries who posted themselves none too close to our track, they'd taken shelter in houses at a safe distance from the station several fields away. We caught sight of the officials in charge of our train only at certain moments of the day, when they came to monitor the change-over of guards or the distribution of bread and water. They looked tense and terrified. In their panic, they scanned the heavens nonstop. I even saw some of them make a dash for it at the sound of a lorry's engine on the adjacent road.

On 15 August we heard that the Allies had landed on France's Mediterranean coast. Early on the 16th our wagons were opened and we were permitted to go in groups to have a wash at some nearby taps. I'd scarcely had time to improvise some sort of shower arrangement beneath the spurting water before the planes arrived. We were all hustled back onto the train and locked in once more. We were petrified, trapped inside our wooden boxes, and listening to the planes overhead, perhaps about to unleash their bombs on the station.

That's when Mossolin wrote a note to the official in charge of the convoy, asking to meet him. Mossolin intended to remind him that, according to an international convention, it was required that prisoners of war, whether military or civilian, be removed with all haste from combat zones. Mossolin gave the note to a sentry, who came back a few minutes later to collect Mossolin. We were concerned, watching him go. We knew all too well how our captors might respond. Half an hour after, Mossolin returned and gave an account of his meeting with the chief, who'd claimed that he wasn't aware of any such international convention, and if it did exist, the English and the Americans wouldn't respect it anyway. Mossolin had pressed him, nevertheless, and finally he obtained the promise that the matter would be looked into. Guidance would be sought from higher-ups. Thereupon the meeting was closed and Mossolin was assured that if any of our wagons caught fire or was badly damaged during a raid, the guards would be told to open the doors.

So, thanks to this fine and honourable German military man we were reassured that just as soon as we were dead or on fire, we'd be removed from the wagons.

On 17 August at 11 p.m., our train set off once more, heading in the direction of Lyon. A few hours later, once again it ground to a halt, this time at a little station which I think was called Pont-St-Esprit.

Chapter 7

The Allied forces which had landed on the coast of Provence were advancing rapidly. It seemed that their main push northwards was to be up the valley of the Rhône, precisely where we were at this critical phase of the war.

The Germans in charge of our train knew just how difficult it would be to move a train filled with prisoners up such a strategically vital line when they didn't even dare risk convoys of their own men and supplies beneath the Allies' fearsome and relentless bombardment. On top of which, the activities of the *maquis* everywhere were getting more and more dangerous for the Germans. While the planes were destroying bridges, stations, locomotive depots and huge amounts of rolling stock, the *maquis* was causing panic among the enemy by relentlessly attacking their trains and dynamiting the track.

For our German escort it was no longer a question of letting us stew for a few days at a time in some station or other, waiting for the track to be repaired. It was now urgent that we be removed from the battle zone; maximum distance had to be put between us and the Allies' remorseless push northwards. The result: at 8 a.m. on 18 August, we abandoned our train for good and transferred to another.

We had to clamber down the embankment where we were stranded under the Midi sun, which in August is already on fire by 9 in the morning.

Then our straggling procession set out through the vineyards, headed by the women, struggling with their cases and packages.

Our crocodile was guarded on either side by a line of gendarmes prodding us and shouting their usual menaces.

The railway bridge across the Rhône had been blown up. So instead, we had to negotiate our way over what was left of a bombed wooden bridge while it was still usable. We trudged through Châteauneuf-du-Pape, then headed along a back road to Sorgues. There, another rake of cattle wagons was awaiting us. We'd endured a forced march of some 17 kilometres, too much for several of our men and women who were already sick and weak from forty-eight hours without food or water. Several times, Allied planes buzzed us. Amid much swearing and cursing, the Germans made us lie flat, and they kept their guns trained on us until the planes had disappeared. Since they didn't open fire, I think the pilots must have realised that what they were seeing below were prisoners. They were saving their bullets for different targets, close enough for us to witness the start of their attack.

During the trek, especially at the beginning, several comrades took advantage of the general mayhem to make their escape, including two marvellous Spanish comrades: Vicente Muzas and Isaac Díaz. Among the women who got away was Madame Caubet, who came from the little village of Cazères-sur-Garonne.

It was about 5 p.m. when we arrived in Sorgues. We were exhausted, parched with thirst, and panting for breath. We couldn't have gone a step further. During the march we'd seen several of our number collapse to the ground. Either they'd fainted or had sunstroke.

At Sorgues, we were bundled into the waiting train. Then there were a number of air raid alerts. Several railway employees and local inhabitants arrived with offers of food and drink. The Germans relented. It was a very emotional experience to see the dozens of women at the station entrance come over to us bearing bread, fruit, tomatoes, eggs, and – most precious of all – water. No amount of it could quench our thirst. Everyone drank at least two or three litres each. The women and the railway staff had to keep bringing us more.

A few of our number managed to escape at Sorgues, among them police commissioner Heim, who simply walked past the guards, carrying a water churn. Philippe Hecht, a very brave comrade from the Vernet camp, also got away.

I must also record one little episode which did a lot to boost our morale. Four or five of us had been given the task of fetching more water from one of the fountains in the station. As we were making our way there, a distinguished-looking and rather dapper man began to follow us. Our guards shouted at him to scarper, to which he replied, 'I am the Mayor of Sorgues, and I have every right to know what is happening in my town.' With that, he joined us to express his support and solidarity.

In the middle of the night our train left in the direction of Lyon. At around 10 a.m., we stopped at Pierrelatte, a small station some 20 kilometres south of Montélimar. We were waiting for the doors of the wagons to be opened to let in some fresh air when we heard the familiar sound of aircraft engines. In their fright, some of our gendarmes dived beneath the string of wagons parked opposite us. Others leapt across a ditch and ran off into the fields. For several seconds – which felt like hours – we remained frozen with fear. We heard the burst of machine-gun fire, then cries, then more firing. We'd lain down on the floor as we had the previous time, huddled against one another. This time, however, there was a difference. At the window slit of every wagon, red-white-and-blue tricolour flags started to appear, poked out on sticks. They'd been prepared beforehand. In our wagon, the blue part was an old cardigan, the white a shirt, and the red a scarf. All these flags were waved frantically and must have caught the eye of the pilots because their machine-guns immediately fell silent. The comrades waving the flag from our wagon reported, 'They've stopped firing but they're still buzzing around flying low. They must be checking who we really are.'

Then, 'That's it, they're off.'

A few minutes later, we heard the voices of Dr Parra and Dr Van Dick, who were going along the train asking each wagon in turn if there were any wounded inside. For the second time, the one I was in was able to answer no. Dr Parra, who had been in effective charge of medical services at Vernet, was a well-respected Spanish surgeon. After three years in captivity, he was being deported like the rest of us.

But sadly, that day in Pierrelatte, Parra and Van Dick did have a lot of work. One of the leading wagons, which had been hit several times, was in a terrible state. The initial count there was nine dead and twelve wounded. A German soldier had also been killed; his body was lying on the ballast. Among the other dead were two Swiss. One of them, named Barrès, was a charming young man, an architect. He and I had become good friends in the Vernet camp. He was married and had two children. His family lived near Annecy in Haute-Savoie. He'd been accused of being in contact with the *maquis*, which is what had landed him in Vernet. He was a cultured and thoughtful person. The other Swiss was very young, a lad of no more than 20, who'd been working on a farm in France.

Once first aid had been administered to the wounded, the train set off again at a crawl. That said, it wasn't too long before we reached Montélimar. From my wagon, which had come to a stop directly opposite the station's entrance hall, I watched as the victims were taken away, first the dead, then the wounded. An ambulance drove onto the platform to collect them. It was a grizzly sight, those lifeless bodies stretchered off, comrades who up to a few moments before had been with us sharing the pain and suffering.

A number of railway staff had gathered at the door of the waiting room and were watching the sorry spectacle. But the German guards had instructions to clear them out, using force if necessary. We looked at one another, uttering words of tribute to honour and remember the comrades we'd just lost. We lamented their terrible fate, knowing full well, of course, that exactly the same could soon befall us.

At that point, a few of us decided we had to take matters into our own hands. We didn't propose to simply go on waiting to die without doing anything about it. The memory of the comrades who'd already escaped was playing in our heads like a mirage which nothing could make vanish. Before we were transferred to the train at Sorgues, a handful of prisoners in another wagon had escaped by prising up some floorboards and lowering themselves between the rails while the train was speeding along. The Germans hadn't spotted what was going on until it was too late. The reprisal was a savage roughing up for everyone else in that wagon.

We had to act very soon. Because, despite whatever the planes and the *maquis* might be doing to hinder our progress, our train was still rumbling on, even if agonisingly slowly. An episode such as the one that morning was one more gory moment in our continuing tragic odyssey.

We remained in Montélimar until nightfall. There was quite a commotion around the station. The men from the *Bahnhof* were pacing up and down outside the train, arguing with our guards, showing them various documents and bits of paper. A little while later we watched as a substantial group of gendarmes set off northwards up the track, armed to the teeth. The snippets of conversation we managed to overhear revealed that a large *maquisard* cell was thought to be planning an attack on the train to liberate us. Later, after my own escape, I was able to confirm the rumour. I also learnt that Monsieur Caubet, from Cazères, the husband of the prisoner who'd escaped near Sorgues, had arrived in Montélimar with a group of *maquisards*, intending to take part in the operation.

All the while, the Americans were advancing rapidly up the Rhône valley. Leading the charge, their armoured trains were closing in on us. Once again it was a race between the Germans and the Allied forces.

Chapter 8

We left Montélimar on 20 August and got as far as Valence. The station was silent and deserted. There were only a few soldiers plus some French and German workmen here and there. We came to a stand beneath the station roof. The doors of the wagons were opened, and under guard we went to find water to drink and water to wash in. My wagon found itself directly opposite the station master's office. At a window on the upper floor we spotted a friendly-looking woman who was flanked by two fair-haired little girls. The woman, who we assumed must be the station master's wife, was watching us attentively, and whenever the gendarmes' backs were turned, she gestured her support and encouragement. At one point, she held up a piece of cardboard on which she'd scrawled 'Paris is surrounded. Stay strong.'

In the afternoon the Red Cross arrived, bringing us provisions. The train set off again that evening. Several comrades had managed to put the delay in Valence to good use. Very daringly, about twenty-five of them, almost all from the same wagon, had donned their outer garments and taken advantage of the open doors to get down to the platform and slip out of the station one by one whenever there was a lapse in surveillance.

As the bridge over the Drôme had been badly damaged, we had to change trains yet again. We were hauled off our wagons, and our furious German escort even made us carry their helmets and knapsacks. We made our way over the bridge on foot, sometimes balancing on makeshift planks in places where there was virtually nothing left of the bridge. Directly below was the swirling river. On the far bank, we were bundled into another waiting train. This time I found myself in a wagon of seventy men, packed like sardines. There were a few I knew from Vernet: De Pablo, Mauri, Ruiz, Gatell, Estève, Miron, Serrano, Cerbera, Hyla, Nicolas. Hyla was a Polish parliamentarian who'd been interned for several years. Now aged over 50, this good and honourable man had fallen ill, but he bore his suffering with the greatest fortitude.

We passed through Lyon on the 21st in the dead of night. By the 22nd we'd gone through Mâcon and then Chalon-sur-Saône, where the station lay in ruins. In Beaune, the Red Cross brought us soup, bread, and tomatoes. I can't stress enough how welcome that was! For the previous thirty-six hours not a single drop of water had passed our lips. The heat was intolerable. Many comrades had slumped to the floor barely conscious, so stifling were the conditions. In the foul, stinking air they gasped for breath through gaping mouths. We passed Dijon in the middle of the night of the 23rd. The little map I had with me showed that we'd now taken the line from Dijon to Is-sur-Tille and Jussey.

The entry in my log for 24 August reads: 'Heat. No water. No hope of escape.' We'd reached the lowest point of our wretchedness. The conditions we'd endured for so long had left us weak beyond imagination. We were barely recognisable as human beings. Such supplies of food as we'd started out with had run out. What with the heat, the starvation rations, and the days and weeks we'd been cooped up together in a few square metres, our bodies were dissolving into ghosts. Our faces were death masks drained of all colour, our eyes dark hollows. Our beards were long and bedraggled, our clothes a collection of filthy tatters. From 23 July onwards, we'd watched our physical state rapidly decline.

Some of us were broken mentally, existing silently in a private world of madness or transformed into gibbering wrecks.

From the very start, the thought of escape had been haunting me. Like other comrades, I realised that we could be saved only by escaping from this train. Quite a few times, especially when we were being transferred from one train to another, I'd come close, but each time there'd been some hitch or other and I'd had to abandon the idea. But now I had to act, come what may. The train was fast approaching the German border. Shortly, maybe in as little as two days, we'd be in enemy country on the other side of the Rhine, by which time any hope of escape would almost certainly have vanished.

On the morning of the 24th, the train halted in a wayside station. The guards distributed a few morsels of cake and a spoonful of jam to each of us. But they refused to bring us water. When we protested, they replied that it was the fault of our friends in the *maquis*, who yet again had forced the train to stop. A few hundred metres of the track ahead had been blown up. Under German surveillance, the repair gangs were already at work. For as long as the train was held up, we'd have no water.

It's then that the group of us who'd decided to find a way out of this hell got down to business. That morning we worked out who should do what. We identified the best place to breech our prison on wheels. We had to wait to be moving again before we could start. That didn't happen until the afternoon, when the train set off at barely a walking pace, feeling its way over the hastily mended track. But the moment the train picked up speed, we got down to it.

In 1878 Dostoevsky began his preparatory notes for *The Brothers Karamazov* thus: 'See if it's possible to lie flat between the rails while a train passes over you at speed.' [*NITTI'S FOOTNOTE: Henri Troyat,* Dostoïewski, *p. 542. Editions Fayard, 1940.*] Our answer to the great Russian writer would have been,

'Yes, Monsieur Dostoevsky, not only is it possible to lie between the rails while the train passes over you, but you can also lower yourself from it through a hole in the floor and lay yourself on the track while the train is moving.'

We had some makeshift tools: old scissors, a few knives, a long nail file, items we'd managed somehow to conceal whenever there'd been a search. We also had a short iron bar which a quick-witted comrade had picked up on one of the occasions we'd been let out. Once we'd decided where to start, we began to dig away at each end of a plank which ran width-wise across the wagon. At the same time we started to remove the hardened earth which was gluing it to the adjacent plank so as to widen the gap. It took us several hours.

We worked in relays, changing every half-hour and handing over the tools to the next group. We posted lookouts at the window slit to warn us if the train was about to slow down, in which case all activity had to cease. Because, every time we stopped, even if only for a few minutes, the guards would jump down from their carriages and run along the length of the train, checking that every wagon was still locked. If we halted in the middle of the night, they would crouch down to look under the train, flooding the track with torchlight. These men were hardened professionals who knew all the tricks in the book, including that one way of exiting a cattle wagon was to remove floorboards. So we ceased all activity whenever the train was stationary, and started again the moment it resumed its journey.

By nightfall, we'd removed two planks. But when we put things to the test and had a go at easing ourselves some of the way down between the wheels, we realised that the space was too narrow for the largest among us. One of those two planks had been a poor choice; the one next to it would have been much the better option.

Among the group preparing to escape was a French gendarme who'd been held prisoner in the Hâ fortress. His name was Barrière. He was one of the brigade at Ustaritz in the Basses-Pyrénées *département*. Then there was an engine driver from Bordeaux who showed us in minute detail the procedure for lowering ourselves safely to the track. With the floorboards lifted, he was able to explain the bits and pieces of tackle visible below. There was an iron triangle, part of the brake system, which we'd have to negotiate as we eased ourselves down, our heads towards the front of the train, feet towards the rear. We'd have to feel for the ground with our feet and then in one go drop our bodies onto the track. Once fully down, we'd need to lie absolutely flat and motionless, keeping our arms pressed tight to our sides. The whole manoeuvre would have to be executed in a single continuous movement. Our engine driver also warned us not to position ourselves too close either to the right-hand-side or to the left-hand-side wheels – but neither should we be dead centre! He added that the last wagon of a train always had a large heavy iron hook hanging down which if we got careless could easily smash our skulls.

We paid the closest attention to what he said. Our lives depended on getting everything absolutely right. But as we'd hear later, the sad fact is that though most of us did make it to safety, the bodies of five or six comrades, including Hyla, were found on the track, their heads and legs crushed.

After our engine driver from Bordeaux had finished giving us instructions, we did nothing further. We waited until dawn to go on with our preparations and to remove that extra plank to accommodate everyone who wanted to make their bid for freedom. I shan't ever forget the night of 23-24 August. Through the gap in the floor we contemplated freedom; the ribbon of gravelly ground speeding by between two rails was the symbol of our impending liberty.

Every time we stopped – which was often – we replaced the planks, covered them with blankets, and sat or lay on them, looking as unconcerned as we could to allay any suspicions should there be an inspection. Several times already, in some station or other, prisoners had been ordered out of their wagons so that a thorough examination of the walls, floor and roof could be made.

At dawn I fell asleep and slept like a log until two in the afternoon of the next day, Friday, 25 August. My body was contorted in the awkward position I'd had to adopt. And I was dying of thirst. Once fully awake, I saw that all along the train the doors had been opened, and prisoners were getting down and making their way in groups to relieve themselves against the wall behind the platform. We were in the station of Is-sur-Tille. At the far end of the platform gendarmes were watching us, looking particularly menacing. I, too, got down and managed to exchange a few words with some comrades from another wagon. One was a young Hungarian called Herz, who'd acted as an interpreter all through our odyssey. He told me that in his wagon the same 'exit strategy' as ours was planned for the next night. We wished each other good luck.

At Is-sur-Tille we were given no water or food, and soon the train was off again. By 5 p.m., the work to lift the final plank was almost finished. We were ready. Out of the seventy occupants of our wagon, around thirty had decided to escape. We did our best to persuade the others to join us, but most were simply too exhausted, physically and mentally. Such an adventure was beyond them; they were resigned to whatever fate awaited them. Some were hardly even capable of responding to our invitation; their only answer was to bow their heads and murmur their good wishes.

Evening arrived. To avoid any confusion at the critical moment, everyone was given a number. Sitting on my suitcase, which contained the few miserable bits and pieces I'd managed to hold onto through these chaotic weeks, I waited. I was fully dressed, including tie, beret and shoes, items we'd removed with our outer garments after we'd started the journey at Toulouse.

To make sure none of our clothing got snagged as we were making our descent, we tucked the flaps of our jackets into our belts, and our trouser turn-ups into our socks. At around 9 p.m., I exchanged a few words one last time with Hyla, who'd been sitting opposite me during this phase of the operation. He offered me a sugar lump, which I accepted eagerly, not having eaten a thing for the previous forty-eight hours.

We'd all agreed that once we were safely on terra firma, we should head off in the opposite direction to the train; we'd rendezvous approximately 1 kilometre from where we'd escaped. We were in the *département* of Haute-Marne, which was crawling with Germans. We'd also resolved to link up with the nearest unit of the *maquis* as soon as we could.

At about 9:30, I saw that we were passing through Lecourt station, on the Neufchâteau line. In the darkness I could just about make out the shadowy silhouettes of my comrades. The train was labouring up an incline. Our operation had begun. I moved close to my fellow escapers and saw that a faint light was coming in where the floorboards had been removed. My turn came. Held steady by two comrades, I started down between the wheels. The noise was deafening. I went through all the procedures I'd rehearsed so often in my head. I felt my knees jolt, and suddenly I was lying flat on the track between the rails, face down, arms tight into my sides.

The train was thundering by just a few centimetres above me. Though I knew that there were seventeen more wagons to go by, I wasn't counting. The train seemed endless. Somehow, I managed to get a glimpse back along its length and guessed that only a few more vehicles still had to pass. They did, and a few moments later, it was fresh country air I was feeling on my face.

For a while, I just lay there, not moving a muscle. I could make out the red tail-lamp on the rear wagon of the train receding at what seemed a frantic pace. I continued to remain motionless, my eyes fixed on the train. Then I felt my body for cuts and bruises. There weren't any.

At that point, I simply could not register that the night in all its immensity was welcoming me back to freedom. The red tail-lamp continued to get smaller and smaller until, finally, once and for all, it was gone. But the sombre rumble of the Phantom Train continued to sound across the sleeping land.

Timeline

This timeline is by no means exhaustive, but it aims to help the reader situate Nitti's life, and his deportation journey more specifically, in the context of historical events in France and beyond.

Date	Relating to Nitti's Life	Global developments
1899	Francesco Fausto Nitti is born in Pisa.	
1914		The First World War begins.
March 1916	Nitti, aged 17, volunteers to fight in the IWW (13th Reggimento artiglieria da campagna).	
1917		Russian Revolution and the rise to power of Lenin.
1918		End of the First World War.
June 1919	His uncle Francesco Saviero Nitti becomes Italian prime minister.	
June 1920	Saviero steps down from power and is replaced.	

Date	Relating to Nitti's Life	Global developments
October 1922		March on Rome, Benito Mussolini comes to power and Italy becomes ruled by fascism.
1923	Mussolini's *squadristi* target Saviero and his family and they go into exile in France.	
	Nitti joins 'Giovane Italia', a clandestine student group against fascism.	
10 June 1924		Kidnapping and assassination of Giacomo Matteotti by fascists.
Dec 1926	Nitti is arrested and condemned to five years on Lampedusa and Lipari without trial.	Italian antifascist Silvio Trentin leaves Italy for France.
Late 1927	Emilio Lussu and Carlo Rosselli arrive on Lipari.	
Jan 1928	Lussu meets Rosselli and hatches an escape plan. Asks Nitti to join.	
27 July 1929	Lussu, Rosselli, and Nitti escape and head to France.	

Date	Relating to Nitti's Life	Global developments
	Rosselli , Luzzu, and Nitti found *Giustizia e Libertà* in Paris	
	Marries Ada Ameriga D'Angelo.	
1930	*Escape*, his memoir about his escape from Lipari, is published by G.P. Putnam's Sons.	
Nov 1931	Birth of first son, Vincenzo.	
July 1934	Birth of second son, Josef.	Trentin sets up his library in Toulouse.
1936		Start of the Spanish Civil War.
1936		Popular Front comes to power in France under Léon Blum.
Mar 1937	Nitti leaves his family to fight for the Republican cause in Spain.	
June 1937		Rosselli and his brother are murdered by *Cagoule* members.
April 1938		Édouard Daladier replaces Léon Blum at head of government.
September 1938		Munich accords are signed.

Date	Relating to Nitti's Life	Global developments
Jan 1939		Barcelona falls to Franco's army.
	Interned in Argelès, then Collioure camp. Meets Trentin and Bertaux.	La Retirada, where half a million refugees from Spain arrive in south-west France.
August 1939	Released from Collioure.	
23 August 1939		Nazi–Soviet pact.
1 September		Hitler invades Poland.
3 September		Great Britain and France declare war against Germany. The Second World War begins.
22 March 1940		Paul Reynaud replaces Daladier at head of French government.
9 April 1940		Denmark and Norway invaded by Germany.
10 May 1940		German invasion of the Low Countries and France.
13 May 1940		Panzer divisions cross over the Meuse into Sedan.
19 May 1940		General Weygand is made commander in chief to replace Gamelin.

Date	Relating to Nitti's Life	Global developments
10 June 1940		French government leaves Paris.
16 June 1940		Paul Reynaud resigns and is replaced by Marshal Pétain.
17 June 1940		Pétain calls for arms to be laid down. Forms a cabinet to discuss an armistice with Germans.
18 June 1940		General Charles de Gaulle makes a speech in London to invite those who want to continue the fight to join him.
22 June 1940		A Franco-German armistice is signed.
25 June 1940		The armistice officially begins.
October 1940		Pétain and Hitler shake hands in Montoire.
Spring 1941	Pierre Bertaux founds first resistance movement in Toulouse, the *Réseau Bertaux*. Nitti joins and is in charge of resistance actions.	
		Germans invade the Soviet Union and Stalin joins the Allies in a fight against the Nazis.

Date	Relating to Nitti's Life	Global developments
December 1941	Nitti is arrested along with Jean Cassou, Pierre Bertaux, and almost all members of the *Réseau Bertaux*. Initially spend time in the military prison of Furgole.	
		The first mass convoy of 'racial deportees', or Jews, leaves France as part of reprisal policies.
April 1942		Pierre Laval comes back to power and begins the *Relève* scheme to send French workers to Germany in exchange for prisoners of war.
July 1942	Cassou and Nitti are both tried and condemned to one year's imprisonment. They are held in Lodève and then Mauzac.	
16 July 1942		13,000 Jews are arrested in the Vel d'Hiv round-up in Paris.
		The mass deportation of Jews as part of the Final Solution begins. 42,000 Jews deported from France to extermination camps that summer.

Date	Relating to Nitti's Life	Global developments
September 1942		Laval tightens laws on forced labour to impose departure for Germany on certain groups of young French workers.
November 1942		Allies land in North Africa and Germans cross the demarcation line to the 'Free' zone. All of French territory now occupied.
February 1943		Laval imposes the Forced Labour Service (STO) on all French youth, who now risk deportation to work for the German war effort.
May 1943		National Resistance Council (CNR) is founded.
June 1943		French Committee for National Liberation (CFLN) is created.
10 July 1943		Allies land in Sicily.
July 1943	Nitti and Cassou are released but arrested immediately and sent to Saint-Sulpice-la-Pointe.	
July 1943	Cassou is freed but Nitti, as a foreigner, is transferred to Le Vernet.	

Date	Relating to Nitti's Life	Global developments
8 September 1943		Capitulation of Italy.
2 April 1944		Germans massacre civilians in Ascq.
April 1944		Intense Allied bombing campaign in Paris region.
June 1944		Jean Cassou named Commissioner of the Liberation by the CFLN.
6 June 1944	Nitti hears of the Allied landings.	Allied landings in Normandy, Operation Overlord begins.
10 June 1944		Massacre of Oradour-sur-Glane
14 June 1944		De Gaulle makes a speech in Bayeux, one of the very few liberated towns at this stage.
15 June	Germans take over Le Vernet (Nitti dates this to 9 June).	
26 June		Allies take Cherbourg.
28 June		Collaborationist Philippe Henriot assassinated by the Resistance.

Date	Relating to Nitti's Life	Global developments
29 June	Nitti sees his family again in camp visiting room, his wife and two children.	
30 June 1944	The last internees evacuate Le Vernet from dawn. Leave the camp and spend sleepless night in Caffarelli police barracks in Toulouse.	

The Timeline of the Phantom Train

2 July 1944	Nitti boards the train.	
3 July 1944	Train leaves Toulouse in direction of Bordeaux. Ange Alvarez is the first to escape.	
4 July 1944	Train is bombed in Percoul-Médillac. Three more escape the train.	
7 July 1944		Massive Allied bombing campaign on Caen in final effort to take the city.
9 July 1944	Train arrives in Bordeaux and will park there for three days.	Part of Caen is liberated.

12 July 1944	The deportees are marched in the night to the Grand Synagogue in Bordeaux.	
19 July 1944		Caen is fully liberated.
21–23 July 1944		Massacre of *maquisards* and civilians on Vercors plateau.
31 July 1944	Around 4 p.m., the German guards select ten hostages who are escorted from the synagogue, including Albert Lautmann.	
1 August 1944		The Phantom Train hostages are executed in Souge camp.
7 August 1944	Deportees told to pack bags.	General Von Choltitz arrives in Paris to take over command from Otto Abetz.
8 August 1944	Marched from Grand Synagogue back to train, which departs once more.	
10 August 1944	A group of nineteen prisoners from Fort du Hâ make their escape. More and more escape over the following days.	Railway workers begin strike in Paris region.

13 August 1944	The train stops at Remoulins. The body of Léon Cigarroa, from Arcachon, is removed. He died of asphyxiation. Maria Damiani, local resister, manages to organise Red Cross relief for the deportees in the train. One prisoner escapes.	
15 August 1944		French and American troops land in Provence. Police strikes begin in Paris.
16 August 1944		Allies announce they will circumvent Paris. Debates immediately start among resisters who are torn between immediate insurrection or waiting for the Allies.
18 August 1944	Long march from Roquemaure to Sorgues in unbearable heat. Over thirty manage to escape.	
19 August 1944	Bombing on Pierrelatte station leaves many dead. Twelve escape.	Paris insurrection begins with occupation of the Police Prefecture. In Toulouse, Cassou is wounded and Pierre Bertaux becomes Commissioner of the Liberation in Toulouse.

20 August	Cross the Drôme river and receive some water from Red Cross outside Valence. Seventeen escape.	The Germans force Pétain to leave Vichy. Swedish Ambassador Raoul Nordling proposes truce and Von Cholititz accepts.
21 August 1944	Ten escape in another crossing by foot before boarding another train.	
22 August 1944	Train arrives in Lyon-Perrache and heads towards Chalon-sur-Saône the next morning. Only four escape over next few days.	Barricades are being built around the city by resisters and Parisians.
23 August		Grenoble and Aix-en-Provence are liberated. General Leclerc receives order from Eisenhower to enter Paris.
24 August 1944	Arrive in Dijon in the evening, where there is great confusion and some Germans are starting to flee.	
25 August	Nitti escapes from the train and spends several days in hiding. He is one of fifty-six who escape on the night of 25-26 August.	LeClerc enters Paris with 2nd D.B. De Gaulle arrives and walks from Montparnasse to Hôtel de Ville.

26 August	Final four escape from the train. Train crosses Rhine river and speeds deeper into Germany.	Crowds welcome de Gaulle in Paris.
28 August	The Phantom Train arrives in Dachau.	
Late August-early September	Nitti joins a *maquis* and is involved in their operations as the fight to liberate France continues.	
13 October 1944	Commemoration ceremony in Toulouse for the Phantom Train hostages executed in Souge camp.	
23 November 1944		Liberation of Strasbourg.
Winter 1944-45	Nitti's memoir is published by Éditions Chantal.	
1945		End of war in Europe

Bibliography

Archival Sources

Archives Nationales

19880016/4/2 Corrèze. Crimes de guerre commis par les Allemands en Corrèze. Prisonniers dans la Synagogue de Bordeaux.

1988016/8/2. Haute-Garonne. Crimes de guerre commis par les Allemands en Haute Garonne. Dossier 15205/4839. Transfèrement en Allemagne de prisonniers politiques. (affaire du train fantôme) (1946-47).

F/7/14747. Nitti (Francesco Fausto) Journaliste et écrivain; 1936–1938.

Mémorial de la Shoah, Centre de Documentation Juive Contemporaine (CDJC)

DLXI-1, testimony of César Chamay.

DCCXCIII-64 Tracts contre l'oubli des horreurs de la guerre. Claude Urman. '*Jeunesse Héroïque. Il y avait un camarade. Biographie de François Lafforgue*', ed. Association des Amis des F.T.P.F. (Strasbourg).

CCXXXVI-62 Déposition non datée de Raymond Lévy sur les circonstances de sa déportation de la prison Saint-Michel de Toulouse et de son évasion du 02/07/1944 au 25/08/1944.

Archives Départementales du Calvados (ADC)

726W/16909/2. Exécution des prisonniers politiques de la prison de Caen.

Service Historique de la Défense, Vincennes (SHC)

GR 28 P 4 220 / 10 – Nitti.

Institut National de l'Audiovisuel (INA)

Interview with Pierre Bertaux, 21 August 1974, <https://www.ina.fr/ina-eclaire-actu/video/i07344814/pierre-bertaux-resistant-a-toulouse>

Patrimonio dell'Archivio Storico, Senato della Repubblica, Fondazione Nenni

'Unità 671, Nitti Ada', <https://patrimonio.archivio.senato.it/inventario/scheda/pietro-nenni/IT-AFS-051-000675/nitti-ada>

La Contemporaine

F/DELTA/RES/0797/IV/11/dossier 77/8 (1987) – Témoignage de Ginette Vincent (née Baudry) 1987.

Foundation Mémorial de la Déportation (FMD)

Livre-Mémorial, <http://www.bddm.org/liv/index_liv.php>

Joseph Onfray, *Tragédie de la Déportation* (1954).

Jacques Adam, 'Impressions et souvenirs de 23 mois de déportation chez les nazis'.

Memorial Associations

Amicale du Train Fantôme, <http://www.lesdeportesdutrainfantome.org/>

Mémorial du camp d'Argelès-sur-Mer, <https://www.memorial-argeles.eu/fr/>

Mémorial François Verdier Forain, <http://francoisverdier-liberationsud.fr/>

L'Association du Souvenir de Fusillés de Souge, <https://www.fusilles-souge.asso.fr/>

Personal Archives

Personal Archives Rosemarie Oster-Grellety.

Personal Archives Family de Roquemaurel: Récit Christian de Roquemaurel de l'Isle, *Voyage au centre de ma vie* (1986).

Personal Archives Family Nardone: Récit de Damien Nardone.

Published Primary Sources

Memoirs

ÉGO 1939-1945, Écrits de guerre et d'occupation, Centre de Recherche d'Histoire Quantitative (CRHQ) and the University of Caen, <http://www.ego.1939-1945.crhq.cnrs.fr/>

Charles d'Aragon, *La Résistance sans héroisme* (Geneva: Tricorne, 2001).

Jean Claude Barbas, ed., *Philippe Pétain: Discours aux Français (17 juin 1940–août 1944)* (Paris: Albin Michel, 1989).

Marie Bartette, 'Les étapes d'une déportée', *Le journal d'Arcachon,* 45 (juin 1945).

Hélène Berr, *The Journal of Hélène Berr* (London: MacLehose, 2008).

Pierre Bertaux, *Mémoires Interrompues* (Asnières: PIA, 2000).

Pierre Bourdan, *Carnet de Retour avec la Division Leclerc* (Paris: Payot & Rivages, 2014).

Bernard Le Chatelier, *Matricule 51306: mémoires de déportation* (Paris: La Bruyère, 1984).

Winston S. Churchill, *The Second World War, Vol. II Their Finest Hour* (London: Penguin Books, 2005).

Daniel Cordier, *Alias Caracalla* (Paris: Gallimard, 2009).

Charlotte Delbo, *Auschwitz and After* (New Haven and London: Yale University Press, 1995).

Jean Dutourd, *Au Bon Beurre* (Paris: Gallimard, 1972).

Henri Frenay, *The Night Will End: Memoirs of the Resistance* (London: Abelard-Schuman, 1973).

Jean Guéhenno, *Journal des années noires, 1940–1944* (Paris: Gallimard, 2002).

Annie Guéhenno, *L'Épreuve* (Paris: Bernard Grasset, 1968).
Agnès Humbert, *Résistance, Memoirs of Occupied France* (London: Bloomsbury, 2009).
Raymond-Raoul Lambert, *Diary of a Witness, 1940–1943* (Chicago, IL: Ivan R. Dee, 2007).
Primo Levi, *If This Is a Man/The Truce* (Little, Brown Book Group, 1988).
Simone Martin-Chauffier, *A bientôt quand même ...* (Paris: Calmann-Lévy, 1976).
Francesco Fausto Nitti, *Escape: The Personal Narrative of a Political Prisoner Who Was Rescued from Lipari, the Fascist Devil's Island* (New York: G.P. Putnam's Sons, 1930).
Francesco F. Nitti, *Chevaux Huit, Hommes Soixante-Dix* (Toulouse: Éditions Chantal, 1944). Quotes from the English translation in this edition are referenced as Nitti (2025).
Francesco Fausto Nitti, *Il Maggiore è un rosso* (Edizioni Avanti, 1953).
Raoul Nordling, *Sauver Paris:* mémoires du consul de Suède (1905–*1944)* (Brussels: Complex, 2002).
Marcel Picard, *J'étais un correspondant de guerre* (Lille: Janicot, 1946).
Charles Rist, *Season of Infamy: A Diary of War and Occupation, 1939–1945* (Bloomington, IN: Indiana University Press, 2016).
Jorge Semprún, *The Cattle Truck* (London: Serif, 2005).
Léon Werth, *Deposition 1940–1944: A Secret Diary of Life in Vichy France* (Oxford: Oxford University Press, 2018).

Newspapers

'Putnam tells police of threat on life; letters seeking to prevent publication of Nitti book given to officials', *The New York Times*, 18 January 1930.
Bulletin d'information édité par la concentration antifasciste italienne, Paris, 20 March 1930.
Emilio Lussu, 'The Flight From Lipari', *The Atlantic*, July 1930.
Giustizia e Libertà, year IV, no. 25, 18 June, 1937.
Frédéric Vergès, 'Une journée à l'enfer de Collioure', *L'Humanité*, 14 May 1939.
'Le train fantôme', *Le Messin*, 1 February, 1947, 4.

Oral History Interviews

Corinne Brillié, Paris, 14 November 2023.
Norbert Nardone, Toulouse, 17 December 2023.
Rosemarie Oster-Grellety, Toulouse, 16 December 2023.
Hugues de Roquemorel, Paris, 14 November 2023.
Edith Silve, Sorgues, 18 August 2024.
Jean-Daniel Simonet, Paris, 14 November 2023.
Jeannine Teissier, Sorgues, 18 August 2024.

Secondary Sources

Le Maitron: Dictionnaire Biographique Mouvement Ouvrier Mouvement Social <https://maitron.fr/>

Le Train Fantôme: Toulouse, Bordeaux, Sorgues, Dachau (Études Sorguaises, 1991).

Henri Amouroux, *La grande histoire des Français sous l'occupation: quarante millions de pétainistes, Juin 1940–Juin 1941*, Vol. 2 (Paris: Robert Laffont, 1977).

Claire Andrieu, *When Men Fell from the Sky: Civilians and Downed Airmen in Second World War Europe* (Cambridge: Cambridge University Press, 2023).

Paul Arrighi, 'Silvio Trentin et le mouvement de résistance libérer et fédérer: de la résistance vers la révolution', *Guerres mondiales et conflits contemporains*, 226(2) (2007) 121–30.

Jean-Pierre Azéma, *From Munich to the Liberation (1938–1944)* (Cambridge and New York: Cambridge University Press, 1984).

Raphaële Balu, 'The French *maquis* and the Allies during the Second World War', in Ludivine Broch and Alison Carrol, eds, *France in an Era of Global War, 1914–1945* (London: Palgrave Macmillan, 2014) 192–210.

Olivier Bataillé, 'Fascistes et antifascistes à Toulouse: l'Italie déchirée dans le Sud-Ouest (1925–1945)', in *Le Midi dans la nation française. Actes du 126 Congrès national des sociétés historiques et scientifiques*, Terres et hommes du Sud, Toulouse, 2001 (Paris: Editions du CTHS, 2002) 207–221.

Arnd Bauerkämper and Grzegorz Rossoliński-Liebe, eds, *Fascism Without Borders: Transnational Connections and Cooperation between Movements and Regimes in Europe from 1918 to 1945* (New York: Berghahn Books, 2017).

Marc Bergère, *L'Épuration en France* (Presses Universitaires de France, 2018).

Jean-Pierre Besse and Thomas Pouty, *Les fusillés. Répression et exécutions pendant l'Occupation (1940–1944)* (Atelier, 2006).

Ludivine Broch, 'Professionalism in the Final Solution: French Railway Workers and the Jewish Deportations 1942–1944', *Contemporary European History* 23(3) (2014) 359–81.

Ludivine Broch, 'Martyred towns at the liberation: the case of the Massacre d'Ascq' in Broch and Carrol, eds, *France in the Era Global Wars, 1914–45: Occupation, Politics, Empire and Entanglements* (London: Palgrave Macmillan, 2014) 50–72.

Ludivine Broch, 'Colonial subjects and citizens in the French internal resistance, 1940–1944', *French Politics, Culture and Society*, 37(1) (2019) 6–31.

Gemma Caballer, '"Pour la renaissance des villages abandonnés": Quaker Humanitarian Aid in a France at War', *Quaker Studies*, 24(1) (2019) 109–39.

Nicola Cacciatore, 'Missed connection: relations between Italian anti-fascist emigration and British forces in Egypt (1940–1944)', *Modern Italy*, 24(3) (2019) 265–79.

Constance Classen, *Worlds of Sense: Exploring the Senses in History and Across Cultures* (New York: Routledge, 1993).

Peter A. Coates, 'The strange stillness of the past: toward an environmental history of sound and noise', *Environmental History*, 10 (2005) 636–65.

Matthew Cobb, *The Resistance: The French Fight against the Nazis* (London: Simon & Schuster, 2009).

Monique-Lise Cohen and Éric Malo, eds, *Les camps du Sud-Ouest de la France, 1939–1940* (Toulouse: Privat, 1994).

Alain Corbin, *Village Bells: Sound and Meaning in the Nineteenth-Century French Countryside* (New York and Chichester: Columbia University Press, 1998).

Alain Corbin, *The Foul and the Fragrant: Odor and the French Social Imagination* (Cambridge, MA: Harvard University Press, 1986).

Stéphane Courtois, Denis Peschanski, and Adam Rayski, *Le Sang de l'Étranger: Les immigrés de la M.O.I. dans la Résistance* (Paris: Fayard, 1989).

Hanna Diamond, *Fleeing Hitler: France 1940* (New York and Oxford: Oxford University Press, 2007).

Laurent Douzou, *La Résistance française: une histoire périlleuse: essai d'historiographie* (Paris: Seuil, 2005).

Laurent Douzou, *Le Moment Daniel Cordier: Comment écrire l'histoire de la Résistance?* (Paris: CNRS éditions, 2021).

Lucien Febvre, 'La Sensibilité et l'histoire : Comment reconstituer la vie affective d'autrefois ?', *Annales d'histoire sociale (1939–1941)*, 3(1–2) (Jan.–Jun., 1941) 5–20.

Sarah Fishman, *We Will Wait: Wives of French Prisoners of War, 1940–1945* (New Haven, CT, and London: Yale University Press, 1991).

Shannon Fogg, *The Politics of Everyday Life in Vichy France: Foreigners, Undesirables, and Strangers* (Cambridge: Cambridge University Press, 2009).

Thomas Fontaine, 'Chronologie: Répression et persécution en France occupée 1940–1944', *Mass Violence & Résistance, Sciences-Po* [online], published 7 December 2009.

Thomas Fontaine, 'Déporter: Politiques de déportations et répression en France occupée, 1940–1944', doctoral thesis from Université Paris I, Panthéon-Sorbonne (2013).

Tanja von Fransecky, *Escapees. The History of Jews Who Fled Nazi Deportation Trains in France, Belgium and the Netherlands*, translated by Benjamin Liebelt (New York: Berghahn Books, 2019).

Hugo García, Mercedes Yusta, Xavier Tabet, and Cristina Clímaco, eds, *Rethinking Antifascism: History, Memory and Politics, 1922 to the Present* (New York: Berghahn Books, 2016).

Simone Gigliotti, *The Train Journey: Transit, Captivity and Witnessing in the Holocaust* (New York: Berghahn Books, 2009).

Robert Gildea, *Marianne in Chains: In Search of the German Occupation of France 1940–45* (London: Pan Macmillan, 2011).

Robert Gildea, *Fighters in the Shadows: A New History of the French Resistance* (London: Faber & Faber, 2015).

Bruno Groppo, 'Entre immigration et exil: les réfugiés politiques italiens dans la France de l'entre-deux-guerres', *Matériaux pour l'histoire de notre temps*, 44 (1996) 27–35.

Anne Grynberg, *Les Camps de la Honte* (Paris: La Découverte, 1991).

W.D. Halls, *The Youth of Vichy France* (Oxford: Oxford University Press, 1981).

Ulrich Herbert, 'Forced Laborers in the Third Reich: An Overview', *International Labor and Working-Class History*, 58 (2000) 192–218.

Julian Jackson, *France: The Dark Years, 1940–1944* (Oxford: Oxford University Press, 2003).

Julian Jackson, *De Gaulle* (Cambridge, MA: Belknap Press of Harvard University Press, 2018).

Eric Jennings, *Vichy in the Tropics: Pétain's National Revolution in Madagascar, Guadeloupe and Indochina* (Stanford, CA; Great Britain: Stanford University Press, 2001).

Eric Jennings, *Free French Africa in World War II: The African Resistance* (New York: Cambridge University Press, 2015).

Philippe Joutard and François Marcot, *Les étrangers dans la résistance* (Besançon: Le musée, 1992).

H.R. Kedward, *Occupied France: Collaboration and Resistance, 1940–1944* (Oxford: Blackwell, 1985).

H.R. Kedward, *In Search of the Maquis: Rural Resistance in Southern France, 1942–44* (Oxford: Oxford University Press, 2003).

John Larner and Giuseppe Nangeroni, 'Justice and liberty, an alliance of republicans, democrats, and reformist Socialists founded by Carlo Rosselli and others in 1929', *Britannica*, <https://www.britannica.com/place/Italy/Anti-Fascist-movements>

Pieter Lagrou, *The Legacy of Nazi Occupation: Patriotic Memory and National Recovery in Western Europe, 1945–1965* (Cambridge: Cambridge University Press, 2000).

Laurent Lutaud and Patricia Di Scala, *Les naufragés et rescapés du 'train fantôme'* (Paris: L'Harmattan, 2003).

Henri Michel, *1944: La Libération de Paris* (Brussels: Complexe, 1990).

Chris Millington, *France in the Second World War* (London: Bloomsbury, 2020).

Pierre Milza et Denis Peschanski, eds, *Exils et migration: Italiens et Espagnols en France, 1938–1946* (Paris: L'Harmattan, 1994).

Bob Moore, *Survivors: Jewish Self-Help and Rescue in Nazi Occupied Western Europe* (Oxford: Oxford University Press, 2009).

Philip Nord, *After the Deportation: Memory Battles in Postwar France* (Cambridge: Cambridge University Press, 2020).

Jean Odin, *Les Quatre-vingts* (Conseil Général de la Gironde, La Presqu'île, 1997).

Richard Overy, *The Bombing War: Europe 1939–1945* (London: Penguin, 2014).

Robert Paxton, *Vichy France, Old Guard and New Order, 1940–1944* (New York; Toronto: Norton Library, 1975).

Denis Peschanski, *La France des Camps* (Paris: Gallimard, 2002).

Guillaume Piketty, 'Economie morale de la reconnaissance. L'Ordre de la Libération au péril de la sortie de Seconde guerre mondiale', *Histoire@Politique*, 3(3) (2007).

Miranda Pollard, *Reign of Virtue: Mobilizing Gender in Vichy France* (Chicago, IL, and London: University of Chicago Press, 1998).

Stanislao G. Pugliese, *Carlo Rosselli: Socialist Heretic and Antifascist Exile* (Cambridge, MA: Harvard University Press, 1999).

Pietro Ramella, *Francesco Fausto Nitti: L'uomo che beffo Hitler e Mussolini* (Rome: Aracine, 2007).

Fabio Fernando Rizi. *Benedetto Croce and Italian Fascism* (Toronto: University of Toronto Press, 2003).

Mary Louise Roberts, *D-Day Through French Eyes, Normandy 1944* (Chicago, IL, and London: Chicago University Press, 2014).

Henry Rousso, *The Vichy Syndrome, History and Memory in France since 1944* (Cambridge, MA: Harvard University Press, 1991, 1987).

Guy Scarpetta, *Guido* (Paris: Gallimard, 2014).

Raffael Scheck, *Hitler's African Victims: The German Army Massacres of Black French Soldiers in 1940* (Cambridge: Cambridge University Press, 2010).

Leigh Eric Schmidt, *Hearing Things: Religion, Illusions, and the American Enlightenment* (Cambridge, MA: Harvard University Press, 2000).

Mark M. Smith, *Sensory History* (Oxford: Berg, 2007).

John Sweets, 'Mouvements Unis de la Résistance', in François Marcot, ed., *Dictionnaire historique de la Résistance* (Paris: Robert Laffont, 2006).

Martin Thomas, *The French Empire at War 1940–1945* (Manchester: Manchester University Press, 2007).

Grégory Tuban, *Les séquestrés de Collioure: Un camp disciplinaire au Château royal en 1939* (Perpignan: Mare nostrum, 2003).

Grégory Tuban, *Camps d'étrangers: Le contrôle des réfugiés venus d'Espagne (1939–1944)* (Paris: Nouveau Monde, 2018).

Grégory Tuban, 'Collioure Un "bagne fasciste" en France', *Retronews*, 28 May 2018.

Karine Varley, *Vichy's Double Bind: French Collaboration between Hitler and Mussolini during the Second World War* (Cambridge: Cambridge University Press, 2023).

Nicolas Violle, 'La reception de l'assassinat des frères Rosselli dans la presse populaire parisienne', *Matériaux pour l'histoire de notre temps* (2000) 42–49.

Fabrice Virgili, *Shorn Women: Gender and Punishment in Liberation France* (Oxford: Berg, 2002).

Nikolaus Wachsmann, *KL: A History of the Nazi Concentration Camps* (London: Little Brown, 2015).

Nikolaus Wachsmann, 'Lived experience and the Holocaust: spaces, senses and emotions in Auschwitz', *Journal of British Academy*, 9 (2021) 27–58.

Nicolas Wade, 'The search for a sixth sense: the cases for vestibular, muscle, and temperature senses', *Journal of the History of the Neurosciences*, 12(2) (2003) 175–202.

Gerald Wiest, 'The origins of vestibular science', *New York Academy of Sciences* (2015) 1–9.

Olivier Wieviorka, *Normandy: The Landings to the Liberation of Paris* (Cambridge, MA, and London: Belknap Press of Harvard University Press, 2008).

Olivier Wieviorka, Julie Le Gac, Anne-Laure Ollivier, and Raphaël Spina, *La France en chiffres – De 1870 à nos jours* (Paris: Perrin, 2015).

Olivier Wieviorka, *The Resistance in Western Europe, 1940–1945* (New York: Columbia University Press, 2019).

Claire Zalc, *Denaturalized: How Thousands Lost Their Citizenship and Lives in Vichy France* (Cambridge, MA: Belknap Press of Harvard University Press, 2020).